DEMON HUNTER

EMBOSEWYN TAZKUVEL

BOOKS BY EMBROSEWYN

AURAS
How to See, Feel and Know

SOUL MATE AURAS
How Find Your Soul Mate & "Happily Ever After"

UNLEASH YOUR PSYCHIC POWERS

PSYCHIC SELF DEFENSE

LOVE YOURSELF
Secret Key To Transforming Your Life

22 STEPS TO THE LIGHT OF YOUR SOUL

ORACLES OF CELESTINE LIGHT
Complete Trilogy of Genesis, Nexus & Vivus

CELESTINE LIGHT MAGICK SERIES
ANGELS OF MIRACLES AND MANIFESTATION
144 Names, Sigils and Stewardships to Call the
Magickal Angels of Celestine Light

WORDS OF POWER AND TRANSFORMATION
101+ Magickal Words and Sigils of Celestine Light
to Manifest Your Desires

CELESTINE LIGHT MAGICKAL SIGILS OF
HEAVEN & EARTH

SECRET EARTH SERIES
INCEPTION (BOOK 1)
DESTINY (BOOK 2)

PSYCHIC AWAKENING SERIES
CLAIRVOYANCE
TELEKINESIS
DREAMS

Published by Kaleidoscope Productions
PO Box 3411; Ashland, OR 97520
www.kaleidoscope-publications.com

ISBN 978-0-938001-03-4 Ingram Paperback
ISBN 978-0-938001-34-8 Amazon Paperback

Book layout and design by Sumara Elan Love
www.3wizardz.com

DEMON HUNTER

Embrosewyn Tazkuvel

"That which has been lost is given again in fullness, for my teachings bring joy and that which I ask does not burden but enlightens, for it is the Gospel of love, of life, and of light.

"Verily, I say unto you: This generation shall not pass away until all that has been hidden is brought again into the light, for it is the epoch for the fulfillment of promise.

Oracles of Celestine Light
Nexus 1:20-21

TABLE OF CONTENTS

PROLOGUE

Though this book is written in the form of a novel for your reading pleasure, the account you are about to read is *not fiction*. These are real events that took place in my life describing a vast and very tangible unseen world.

Before I pass from this Earth, I thought some of you might be interested in knowing the reality and magnitude of the invisible world that exists all around us, and in the multidimensional universe beyond Earth. What you do not see is vaster than you can imagine and filled with a myriad of exotic people, fascinating cultures, and astounding creatures you probably thought were only myths.

My discovery of the invisible world surrounding us and its unseen and sometimes menacing occupants, my knowledge of it, and my ability to interface with it, developed gradually over a period of years at first, and then was suddenly thrust upon me almost fully formed. For the most part, I present it to you in the order that I learned about it myself.

Some parts at the beginning may have some mystery, only to come together like a jigsaw puzzle in later chapters. Thus it was for me, as I first learned about the structure and denizens in the mysterious dimensions we cannot usually see, and how to understand and interact with them.

Whether in the lives of the people on our Earth, or those of mystical civilizations in other dimensions of space and time, the destroyers of lives and relationships on many worlds are demons. They are a diabolical scourge and the hidden source of more hardships, pain, schisms, and sorrow than most people can fathom. The only force demons fear are the Taz, the Demon Hunters: ordinary men and women of every race and culture, awakened to their greater gifts of power and their calling to unleash it upon demons.

I have wanted to write this book for many years. However, it needed to wait until several of the key people I wrote about had passed from this life, as they cherished secrecy and never would have allowed me to put their story in a book while they were still alive. A couple of the individuals mentioned are still living, and I changed their names in the manuscript to protect their identity and privacy.

My fondest hope is that Demon Hunter will also give solace and closure to many people who have lost or been alienated from loved ones for inexplicable reasons, particularly sons and daughters under the age of thirty when people tend to be very impressionable, less cautious, and more influenceable by demons. If you or someone you know committed suicide, or ruined their life with reckless behavior that was completely out of character for them, and you have always asked yourself: *"Why! Why did they do it?"* You may find the answer in this book and finally be able to have peace in your heart.

On another note, most demons swear profusely, with at least one cuss word in almost every sentence. They use swear words both to put down and humiliate others and as adjectives to add emphasis to the point they are trying to make. As a wise man once told me, "swearing is the effort of a feeble mind to exert itself forcibly." That seems to be exceptionally true with demons, as there are many dimwitted among them. However, you will find no swear words in this book or even *$@#! symbolic substitutions. I find the essence of the words spoken is much clearer without the distraction of swear words and hope you do too.

All in all, the unseen worlds and the remarkable creatures and characters, both good and evil that dwell within them, are more fascinating, complex, and diverse than any of the depictions of popular media. I invite you to come with me now on a journey into a beautiful, marvelous, and sometimes formidably dangerous dimension of reality that some of you may learn to visit as well.

Embrosewyn Tazkuvel
2021

CHAPTER
One

A dragon came that day, one of the fire-breathers that had been his friend. It gently flapped its expansive wings a few times and alighted upon the verdant green meadow with the softness of a butterfly, belying its great size and brushing aside the lesser beings that had gathered together from all parts of the realm to pay our last respects. Normally, dragons were creatures of solitude and would never deign to allow any other denizens of this world to be in their presence. But this was not a normal day.

One after another the leaders from the various clans came forward and stood on the dais wreathed in a profusion of colorful flowers, to extol the virtues of the man whose bravery and fidelity to the light had touched all of their lives, and saved a great number of them from an untimely death as well.

As a last parting, after everyone had said their final words of tribute and farewell, a coming together in unity occurred unheard of in the annals of history. In unspoken unison, motivated solely by the inexorable pull of the resonance in their own hearts, every person and creature present stepped forward forming a great circle around the raised wooden platform on which the body of this incomparable warrior lay.

Those of us that had fought by his side in so many battles extended our arms and raised the tips of our swords to the sky. The leialli lifted their spiral horns and began to blow the melodious, magickal musical notes unique to each. The many davos and akara present raised their hands above their heads clapping to a cadence as they shouted his name over and over, and soon we all joined in. The glash spoke not a word, but stomped on the ground and made it shake.

Then the golden dragon inhaled a big breath and all was quiet as we waited in exquisite silence for what we knew was coming next. With a mighty exhale a wide stream of fire shot out of the dragon's mouth, enveloping the platform upon which my dearest friend and mentor lay, igniting the cord of dry wood beneath it into a blazing funeral pyre.

As I watched the flames consume him I knew how happy he would be to know his ashes would now always be a part of his beloved Corsalain. I reflected back upon the first time I had met him and the astounding journey that had brought me to where I was now, to who I was now. The crest of the waves of life often lift those who least expect it to places and opportunities they had never even imagined. Thus it was with me. It actually all began with a lucid dream.

Chapter 1

Although I didn't know it at the time, I first encountered demons face to face, during the 1980's, in my early thirties, during one of my vivid lucid dreams. As a teenager and into the first decades of adulthood, I couldn't wait to go to sleep every night because the distant worlds I traveled to with the speed of thought in dreams were where the greatest adventures of my life took place. Oftentimes my dreams were so vivid and detailed it was a challenge for me to distinguish whether I was awake or asleep, even after I woke up!

The giveaway that I was experiencing a vivid, lucid dream and not my *real life*, was the precious perk that in my lucid night travels I could consciously alter the flow of the dream. If things weren't going the way I liked, I just mentally commanded them to alter in ways to my preference. For instance, if bad guys were shooting at me with machine guns and all I had to protect myself with was a tiny pistol, I could instantly transform it into a bazooka and blow the bad guys away.

Feeling completely invulnerable, a superman with unlimited powers within the worlds of my sleep time creation, I was shocked one night while exploring a newly visited world, to encounter a most despicable man that refused to conform to my wishes.

He was sitting on a rock and appeared to be stark naked! There was a white goose struggling to escape from the man who held him upside down on his lap and tightly against his body with one arm. The scoundrel's long, disheveled black beard flowed over parts of the bird creating a sharp color contrast. His equally long and scraggly dark hair clumped together in twisted strands, looking like it had not been washed in a very long time, if ever.

This foul man was plucking the soft down feathers out from the goose and dropping them into a woven reed basket to his right. With each heartless pull of a feather the obviously fatigued goose would squawk in pain and protest. The man's response was always the same. Without uttering a word, when the goose cried out in pain he would knock the bird hard on the side of its head with the backside of his hand causing the poor goose's long neck to snap over to the side. As the gooses cries faded into a whimper, the man would crack a slight smile and let out a quiet chuckle of warped satisfaction after every blow to the helpless bird.

This was a situation I absolutely could not tolerate or allow to continue. I thought quickly about what would be a just punishment and decided to make the goose become enormous, a hundred times its normal size and then turn around in vengeful fury and eat the man. And thus I imagined it, and commanded it to be so. But for some inexplicable reason that left me utterly baffled, nothing happened.

However, the man must have felt the righteous energy of my thoughts and desired action. He stopped plucking the goose for a moment and looked up at me with an intimidating scowl.

"Go away Izbo," he growled.

I wasn't sure why he was calling me Izbo as that wasn't even close to my name, but I was determined that though my lucid dream skill had failed me once, it would not fail me again. I envisioned the goose suddenly flying up out of the man's arms, with the hapless scoundrel flailing helplessly trying to catch it. As the goose ascended higher than his grasping hands could reach, it dumped a big, slimy glob of poop right on his face.

It was a just and fitting conclusion to a cruel and heartless scene. Unfortunately, it didn't happen. Once again nothing changed! Nothing at all! Nothing except a glaring look and a smug chuckle from the tormentor of the goose.

He looked at me and cracked an evil smile

"Your silly mental games have no power over me Izbo and you are irritating me. Go away now or I'll track you down, the real you, and pluck your hairs out next!" "

He stood up holding the poor goose by its neck as it helplessly flailed its wings and took a menacing step toward me.

I am ashamed to say, that I was so shocked by his truly ominous threat, and being completely unable to affect his cruel actions, or anything at all in my lucid dream, that I suddenly awoke in my bed with a deep, foreboding feeling. My heart was beating quite rapidly and I was sweating, even though the night was cool.

CHAPTER

Two

The day following my strange dream, I went about my daily activities in ways that would have seemed perfectly normal and routine to any friends or family observing me. However, inside my mind, I was beset by questions, doubts, and yes, a little fear.

I had learned to have complete control in my lucid dreams many years ago, and had never experienced even one in recent years that would make me doubt my ability. I still did not comprehend how I could imagine impossible things, such as the goose in my dream instantly growing to one hundred times its normal size. Nevertheless, despite improbable scenarios, I had come to believe that some of the places in my dreams were not merely flights of dream fantasy, but were in some way real worlds, with unknown creatures and alien inhabitants that I was somehow visiting.

However, whether real or imagined, I was utterly perplexed as to who the malicious goose down plucking man was, or was supposed to represent from the lucid dream that I had been unable to control. I thought about it a lot for several days thereafter and was unable to come to any conclusions. I also tried to find that evil tormentor again in my lucid dream travels every night for the next week, but was unsuccessful.

Being unable to find the malevolent long black bearded man in any subsequent dreams, or come to any conclusion about the events I had witnessed and was unable to control, I just let the matter slip from my mind as an unsolvable mystery. There were plenty of other fun and exhilarating places to discover in my lucid dream night travels that I wanted to explore. No sense getting bogged down pondering the one inexplicable experience. However, I had to revisit that thought about a year later when I had another odd dream, and it wasn't with the same villain.

During this lucid dream I found myself walking into an old row house, like the type I had seen in some of the northeastern cities I had visited as a kid. It was daytime on a bright warm summer day.

I opened the squeaking, slightly sagging front door as if I had permission to enter the house without knocking. The interior of the home had the dank musty smell of a house that had been around for many years with multiple generations of families having lived in it. I found it odd that though it was a brilliant sunny day outside, it was dark and foreboding in the house. All of the blinds were drawn down over the windows and only a couple of dim lamps illuminated the rooms.

I heard what seemed to be a loud argument between

a man and a woman coming from the second floor, interspaced with long bouts of laughter. It was a very strange juxtaposition.

I stealthily climbed up the stairs to investigate, ruing the creaky old boards that betrayed my approach. However, either the two people yelling and laughing didn't hear the creaks or they didn't care, because their shouting quickly followed by laughter never stopped.

Passing through the narrow, dimly lit hallway I entered a room at the end of the hall where I had determined the sounds were coming from. The scene that met my eyes was extremely incomprehensible.

The room was a cozy, femininely decorated bedroom. A slim woman I guessed to be in her early thirties was curled up tightly in a fetal position with the covers all askew, sobbing quietly and rocking slightly back and forth.

A middle aged man and a younger woman stood on either side of the bed looking down at the hapless lady in distress while laughing hysterically. Both were strangely dressed, or I should say barely dressed. I wondered to myself if I was in a horror nightmare or some type of deviant sexual dream.

The short, swarthy, barefoot man yelled out at the woman curled up on the bed. His hairy chest was barely covered by a ridiculous pair of red suspenders pulling up what looked like a lime green Speedo swimsuit.

"You are worthless! Nobody wants you, not even your own parents. You are so ugly, nobody will ever be your friend." "**EVER!**" He repeated very loudly for emphasis.

He was extremely animated as he spewed his vicious

words. He flailed his arms back and forth, and his long dark dreadlocks flopped around with his movements.

Both he and the bare-chested voluptuous woman standing on the other side of the bed broke into uncontrolled fits of laughter after he spoke, as if he had just told the funniest joke they had ever heard.

Once they regained some composure, the woman took a turn throwing word daggers at the poor woman on the bed. The antagonist had long flowing red hair and about as perfectly curvaceous of a body as a woman could have, but her beautiful face was contorted by the vile words she hurled at the lady on the bed.

"Just kill yourself! There's nothing in this world for you! There's no one in this world who wants to see you, or hear you. Just kill yourself. Do it now. Slice your wrists. Do it! Do it! It will be over quick. Your misery will end. Your pain will be no more. Do it! Do it! Do it!"

Both of the peculiar people standing next to the bed once again began laughing with demented craziness. The woman pinched her own nipples and reached down beneath her g-string, which was the only piece of clothing she was wearing, and began to stimulate herself.

"By Lucifer, this just gets me so hot!" she exclaimed with passion.

The man lifted his right arm and laughed even harder as he pointed at her.

"Yeah, you're real hot in your mind Varina. Too bad you can't feel physical sexual pleasure to go along with your mental masturbation."

Suddenly, the woman on the bed let out a muted, soul-wrenching scream that shook me to my core. It was only then that I noticed she was holding a razor blade in her left hand and was moving it slowly toward her exposed right wrist.

Since I had entered the room I had been dumbstruck by the incomprehensible scene unfolding and had not moved or spoken as I tried to make sense of it. But seeing the lady on the bed about to slit her wrists jolted me out of my mental stupor. With a few quick steps I was at the right side of her bed, which was the direction she was facing, curled up on her bed.

As I passed in front of the nearly naked lady standing next to the bed, I slammed my upraised palm strongly into her chest to clear my path. My blow caused her to take several steps backwards. My right hand just continued down in a fluid movement and quickly slapped the razor blade out of the hand of the woman lying on the bed and it went flying across the room.

I turned and backed against the wall by the head of the bed so I could clearly see the two antagonists in the room and have the wall behind me if I needed to defend myself.

However, it was a needless worry. Both the man and the woman were standing motionless staring at me. Their hands hung limply and motionless at their sides with their mouths widely agape in astonishment.

"Did you see that?" the woman stammered disbelievingly. "The Izbo touched me."

"Don't be ridiculous Varina," the man berated. "He just ran past you and startled you into backing up. It is impossible for him to have touched you."

Varina was miffed. "He didn't just touch me. He

pushed me backwards! I had nothing to do with it!"

The man looked at me intently with a deep scowl on his face while he continued speaking to Varina.

"Either you are lying to me, and I would expect nothing less of you, or this is not a normal Izbo," he said pointing his finger at me.

"This must be a Taz, the boogey man of demons. They are supposed to be formidable foes, but this guy looks too wimpy. Nevertheless, if what you said is true he cannot just be your average psychic Izbo lost in a dream."

"I am telling you the truth," a miffed Varina verified. "He physically pushed me away from the bed with forceful strength. His body has substance."

I looked at them in a superior way knowing my body in reality did not have substance in the dream state of my night travels. I had supreme confidence that in this form I was not only invulnerable, but I could lucid dream any scenario I desired.

For the time being I decided to let the scene just play out as it was occurring. It made my dreams more interesting if I let the characters play their parts however they wished. But I couldn't help bursting their bubble at least a little bit.

"I can see you and hear you, and what I have seen and heard is despicable."

The man smiled broadly, "Thank you for the compliment. We do our best."

He pursed his lips and nodded his head. "So you are a Taz."

"If that is what you want to call me," I affirmed, even though I had no idea what he was talking about.

Suddenly Varina threw a temper tantrum, thrashing her arms up and down and stomping her feet on the ground.

"Why are we wasting time with this creature Gilgore!" she protested. Just ignore him! We almost had the girl."

She held up her thumb and forefinger about an inch apart. "The girl was this close to committing suicide. Can we please get back to the task at hand?"

"Bah!" Gilgore exclaimed. "We can induce suicides every day. However, the chance to kill a Taz only comes along every century or so, and then only to lucky demons."

Gilgore pointed at me with his left hand and I couldn't help but notice his dirty, pointy fingernails. He held up his right hand and snapped his fingers. Immediately a short sword similar to what the Roman soldiers used to carry materialized in his hand. Without further ado he charged at me aiming the sword for my heart.

Smugly, I commanded a shield to appear as a defense before his lunge struck home. But the shield never materialized and he stabbed me mercilessly through my heart. I was shocked to feel the blade pierce my body and hear it stick into the wall behind me. As I quickly began to lose consciousness the last thing I remember was looking into his fiery, evil eyes and seeing the triumphant grin on Gilgore's face.

The next thing I remember was becoming conscious lying on my back. My eyes were still closed as I vividly relived my last moment of being stabbed through the heart with a sword. Somehow I was still alive though I didn't know how, or for how long. I feebly reached up and felt my chest that I knew would be awash with blood, but it didn't feel wet.

I reached up with my other hand searching for the hole in my chest, but it wasn't there. Slowly I opened my eyes. The moon was shining through a small double hung window with enough light that I could make out some of my surroundings. The bookcase on the far wall looked familiar as did the window the moonbeams were shining through.

I propped myself up on an elbow so I could see everything through the dim lighting. My mind was still back in the room with Gilgore, Varina and the helpless girl on the bed. It took some mental effort to focus and get some clarity and accept that I was no longer there, but somewhere else.

As I looked around the room, it took a few minutes for me to realize that I was back in my own bed, awake and alive, with no blood on my body and no hole in my heart.

Wow! What a dream! It had felt and seemed more real than any dream I had ever experienced! Yet it was just a dream and I was still alive and well. I thought about that for a moment and realized that I couldn't wait to go have another one of those wonderfully vivid adventure dreams!

CHAPTER
Three

Once again I spent some days pondering my latest dream with the demented antagonists that were torturing others in some way. However, this time I was determined not to leave the matter unresolved. It was obvious that these were not normal lucid dreams by any stretch of the imagination. For one thing, I had always been a happy, optimistic person and my dreams reflected that mindset. I was accustomed to having vibrant adventure dreams that were fun and exhilarating, not dark and foreboding.

Then a possible solution popped into my mind. Perhaps it would not be the answer to all my questions, but it would lead me in the right direction.

One of the advantages of lucid dreaming is I could decide just before I fell asleep where I wanted to travel to with my Night Self during my dream state. My last dream had revealed the names of the two people that were trying to convince the girl on the bed to commit suicide. Whether they were real or imagined people I didn't know at that point. Nevertheless, I was confident that if I pictured them in my mind and said their names aloud, I would find them again that night in my dreams. And so I did.

I didn't recognize them at first. As I entered my dream, I found myself standing hidden behind a large conifer tree in a forest looking into a small clearing where about a dozen men and women were gathered, sitting on logs around a campfire talking in low voices.

It was daytime and I could see everything clearly. There appeared to be no other people or dwellings nearby. I spotted Gilgore in his red suspenders and green Speedo swimsuit and Varina with her luscious long red hair sitting on the opposite side of the fire. I assumed she was still wearing her tiny G-string, but from my semi obscured vantage point I could not see it and she simply looked ravishingly naked.

There were four other women in the group and they had quite a mixture of appearances. One middle aged lady was smartly dressed in a modern pants suit and looked like she belonged in a corporate board room.

Another, with her long blond hair in a pony-tail, just looked like a typical bored teenager in jeans and a tank top.

The third looked like Samantha from the old TV show *Bewitched*. The last lady appeared to be someone in her early twenties and was as bad of a dresser as Gilgore. Every article of clothing from her shorts, to her shoes, to her dressy blouse, was completely mismatched in color and style. She also had her hair dyed blue and spiked in at least six long points standing straight up right down the middle of her head from front to back.

The six men, other than Gilgore, were an equally diverse lot. One of them had a bushy black beard, flannel shirt, jeans and boots and he looked like a lumber jack. In fact, upon looking closer I saw that he even had a long-handled axe lying on the ground beside him.

One man was dressed in a similar professional style as one of the ladies. He was wearing a business suit and tie with his short-cropped hair carefully combed. He looked like a corporate man, or maybe an accountant.

One very large, immensely muscular fellow was completely naked, and I mean completely. Besides not wearing any clothes, he had a totally bald head and a clean shaven face. His dark eyes were quite sunken in his skull which gave him a truly odd almost inhuman appearance.

The other three men all appeared to be somewhere in their thirties. One clean shaven fellow was dressed rather preppy with a V-neck brown sweater over a button-down collar shirt and a pair of dark slacks and shoes.

Another had a goatee and wore a pair of faded jeans and a v-neck t-shirt and sandals.

The last guy appeared to be in his late twenties or early thirties. He looked like he had just stepped out of a surfing movie with shoulder length brown hair and a rugged, even handsome clean shaven face. His flowered, Hawaiian shirt, knee length khaki shorts, and bare feet added to the image. If Varina was the female embodiment of a desirable woman, this fellow would fill that position as a man.

Considering my next move I was unsure how to proceed. When I went to sleep and contemplated my lucid dream travels of the night, I envisioned confronting Gilgore and Varina. That had ended badly for me in our last confrontation and I had no plan on how to have a different outcome this time. Whatever I chose to do, I knew success would be a great deal more difficult having to face ten of their friends as well. Not to mention they were probably like Gilgore and could manifest weapons out of thin air with a snap of their fingers.

I lay on my stomach and stealthily crawled up to the very end of the low vegetation at the edge of the clearing hoping to hear what the group was discussing. Their voices were audible, but they were conversing in some foreign language I did not recognize at all. Luckily language was one aspect of my lucid dreams I was sure I could control. Though they might continue to spout foreign gibberish I would hear clear English.

After I made that small adjustment to the scene, I was able to tune in just as Gilgore was speaking, and lo and behold he was speaking about me!

"It was so glorious when I killed the Taz. You should have seen the look on his face as my sword pierced his heart. It was the most surprised, astonished and disbelieving look anyone could ever have. It was my greatest triumph!"

"Stop telling us this stupid story," the man dressed like an accountant grumbled. "You did not kill a Taz. Even if you did, I am tired of hearing the story."

"I agree!" the teenager with the pony tail exclaimed. "Once was interesting. Now we have lost track of how many times you have told this story and we are going to have to kill you if you don't shut up about it!"

Gilgore looked at the teenager with a wide grin on his face. "Bring it on!" Gilgore said happily. "I like being killed. It feels so good. Now that you have made that delicious threat, I will be sure to tell this story over and over until you follow through with the execution."

"Or we could just depart and leave you to tell your story to the trees," the corporate lady interjected.

Surf boy shook his head and laughed. "Anyway, I am sure whatever you did and to whomever you did it to, it was not to a Taz."

"It was," Varina defended. "I was there and saw the whole thing. That man pushed me with his hand. Only a Taz could do that."

"Yes, yes, we all like to exaggerate our adventures to make ourselves feel big and important," the lumberjack said. "But have any of us ever encountered a real Taz in all of our long existence? So what is the chance that Gilgore and Varina really encountered a Taz? Nil to nothing."

"I agree," Baldy said slamming his fist into the palm of his other hand. "I would love to truly meet one and squash him, but it is only a dream."

Corporate lady held up her index finger and wagged it at Gilgore. "The very fact that you think you so easily killed this form, whatever it was, is a testimony that it could not have been a Taz. One of them would not have gone down so easily without defending themselves. I was among a group of over fifty of us that fought with a single Taz several hundred years ago. Of that group, only me and one other survived and that was merely because

31

the Taz departed and let us live. A true Taz would not just stand there and let you run them through with a sword. And if it was a real Taz you encountered, you and Varina would not be here to tell the story."

The lumberjack picked up a fist size rock and threw it at Gilgore hitting him smartly in the head, though he seemed to suffer no ill effect. "So just shut up about it Gilgore! Nobody here believes you and nobody here wants to hear your ridiculous story again."

My mind was aswirl with thoughts and questions from everything I had heard from this group of twelve very strange mismatched people. I decided not to confront Gilgore and Varina that night, but willed myself back out of the dream and awoke in my bed. It was still night time, but I could not get back to sleep. My thoughts were racing, pondering and considering all that I had just heard and what it might mean.

CHAPTER
Four

The next day, I decided I needed to quickly gain more knowledge as nothing I was experiencing or hearing in these recent dreams made any sense.

The largest library in the area was in Seattle. It was my first visit to that large of a book depository and I was a little lost, but found the librarians to be very helpful. This was, of course, before the days of the internet, where information is at your fingertips.

I spent the rest of the day combing through many dozens of books on dreams, lucid dreams, astral travel, the paranormal, demons, ghosts, aliens and anything abnormal I could find that might help me understand what I was envisioning or experiencing in my lucid dreams. After over six hours at the library I had not found anything that even remotely sounded like the events from my dreams.

Driving home I mentally reviewed some of the clues from the dreams I had experienced with these strange characters to see if they would add up to any type of coherent understanding.

I remembered that in my first dream, the long black bearded naked man plucking the live goose called me an Izbo and was unafraid of me. He knew I was in a dream and even threatened to come harm me during my daytime awake state, which at the time seemed like an empty threat as characters from my dreams didn't come to life when I was awake.

During my dream with Gilgore and Varina, Gilgore called me a Taz and tried to kill me on the spot and thought he had succeeded, and I at first thought he had stabbed me through the heart with a sword.

In my last dream it seemed nobody knew exactly what Gilgore had encountered when he met me, but they were sure I wasn't a Taz.

Whatever these Taz were, they were obviously quite formidable, because the corporate lady said one had killed about fifty of them in a fight or battle.

The more interesting part of her remembrance was that she said this event had occurred hundreds of years earlier. That was the key point that stuck out in my mind over everything else that I was thinking about from these dreams.

None of the people sitting around the fire in that last dream took any exception to the corporate lady who was talking about being alive for hundreds of years. I had never encountered a single person in any of my lucid dreams over all the years I had been lucid dreaming that had ever claimed to have lived longer than a normal human lifespan. Now I was confronted by a group of twelve who accepted that incredibly long time span nonchalantly, as if it was an inconsequential comment.

I decided to try spying on Gilgore and Varina once more to gain additional insight into who these people were and what they represented. Once my head lay upon my soft pillow, I spoke aloud my last thoughts before I fell asleep. This assured they would be firmly imprinted into my conscious mind so they would easily slide over into my subconscious mind when I was asleep.

"Go to Gilgore and Varina," I commanded my Night Self. "Go in secret, hidden from their awareness, but close enough to hear everything they say and witness everything they do."

As I became aware of my dream, I realized I was standing in some type of closet. It was full of books on layers of shelves behind me that started near the floor and continued up above my head.

Peeking through the crack at the center of the accordion doors, I spotted Gilgore sitting at a small desk two rows back in what appeared to be a windowless classroom. The room was dimly lit and I could see no source for the pale yellow luminosity that was present, but it was still sufficient illumination to clearly see all around the room. Varina was nowhere to be seen, but there was at least thirty other students in the class, all sitting at individual desks like you would find in a High School.

A slightly rotund man with a full white beard that tapered to a point, and a long, pointy nose with spectacles perched upon it, was standing at the head of the class speaking to what seemed to be the students.

Like every other group of these odd dream people I had encountered, they were all dressed in such a mismatch of clothes and personal appearance styles that it would be fruitless to try to describe them all individually. Just know that from a middle-aged boardroom executive to a young, naked nymph, you could scarcely imagine a room full of a more diverse group of people that would seem to have nothing in common to draw them together.

I should also add that in this group I noticed multiple races, including some that I would say were not even human. The aliens all had two legs, two arms, two eyes and other human anatomical parts, but green or blue skin, strange ears, and in one case a pair of curved spiral horns, made classifying them as nonhuman an easy call.

I listened in silence as the man at the head of the class, whom I took to be the instructor, began to speak.

"Let me congratulate each of you in finally succeeding, after what for many of you has been many millenniums of failed attempts, to make it through a Nexus to a 1st Dimension world.

"While a few of you have recently arrived on this Earth in just the last couple of hundred years, most of you have been here for at least several hundred years. All of you are disgraced as having never been able to inhabit an Izbo.

"To help end that tragedy, in today's class we will be covering, *How To Take Over The Body Of An Izbo In The Quickest Manner*. The secret isn't in the takeover technique, but rather in wisely choosing your victim as one that will be easy to inhabit.

"Of course one of the greatest perks of inhabiting an

Izbo body is you get to physically feel everything they feel, including sexual pleasure. Be mindful that physically experiencing sexual orgasm is addicting. Pause in your lust and make an effort to use your poor excuse for a brain. Though you may think that you might like to inhabit a prostitute who has sex many times a day, you will find that is not the wisest or most fulfilling choice.

"Sadly, most Izbo bodies cannot last more than several years when you inhabit them before they die, commit suicide, or go insane. Due to their fragility it is important to have sex often with many people before the body is useless to you. However, you will have more fulfillment if you learn to pace yourself so you do not lose your Izbo body too quickly. I recommend limiting yourself to having sex three times a day.

"Realize that if you are using an Izbo that you are inhabiting wisely, you will be able to simultaneously maximize their degradation, and hence your own pleasure, while also coaxing them to have overall healthy habits. By prompting them to take actions to extend their life, your opportunities for pleasure through their physical body will be extended for more of their years.

"Though there is also a great deal of physical pleasure from smoking, taking drugs, and eating like a glutton, you should try to rein in those habits if your Izbo has them, or at least not encourage over indulgence, so you will be able to experience more time in their body.

"Once your Izbo's body begins to rapidly wear out because of your presence, you should also set a goal to have them contract multiple venereal diseases so you can spread those plagues to as many other Izbos as possible.

"Remember, beyond your own physical pleasures derived from inhabiting an Izbo body, the destruction you can do to other Izbos is monumentally greater than what you can do just whispering into their ears as invisible beings. So inhabiting an Izbo cannot just be about sexual pleasure.

"You can inhabit a politician and destroy the lives of all of their constituents and maybe even start a war that will kill tens of thousands of Izbos! You can inhabit a husband or wife and cheat on your spouse and abandon your children. You can inhabit an employee that embezzles money from their company. If you do a really good job, you can wipe out the company and put all of the employees out of work. You can inhabit a member of the military and sell secrets to the enemy, or work for a company and sell their secrets to rival companies or countries. You can poison public water supplies, instigate race riots in the cities, spread false rumors about influential people and do countless wonderful acts to hurt many Izbos!"

The instructor rubbed his hands together with apparent glee. "Let's return now to the point of this class and that is, how to most quickly and easily inhabit an Izbo.

"Believe it or not there are actually Izbos that call out to Lord Lucifer for help. Of course they are the easiest to inhabit because they are requesting it, even if they do not realize that is what they are doing.

"However, because they called upon Lord Lucifer, he chooses the demon he will reward with the opportunity to inhabit the Izbo. Out of the billions of demons existing

Chapter 4

on the multitude of planets in the 1st Dimension, it is unlikely that any of you will ever get that privilege."

Wow! Finally, I knew with certainty who these people were supposed to be. Despite their appearance mimicking humans, they were demons! And according to the instructor there were billions of them! I had begun to suspect my dreams might be showing demons and was relieved and settled upon receiving that confirmation.

My only previous experience with a demon was in 1975, when I was 20 years old and attending Coast Guard Gunner's Mate School on Governor's Island; a small 172 acre island just off the tip of cosmopolitan Manhattan, and the nearby Statue of Liberty on nearby Liberty Island. All of Governor's Island at the time was a US Coast Guard base.

The only way to get to Governor's Island was a ten minute ride on a small two-deck ferry. One day my roommate Dan called me and told me he was over on the Manhattan side waiting for the ferry. He asked if I would take the ferry over to meet him as he had just watched the movie, *The Exorcist*, at a theater in Manhattan and he was inexplicably terrified to the very core of his being.

I hurried down to the terminal and caught the next ferry over to Manhattan. All the way over I couldn't even imagine how a movie could frighten Dan. He was 6'4" tall, 240 pounds, and a virile man in every sense of the word. Nobody messed with Dan, or if they were that foolish to try, they rued the day.

Arriving on the Manhattan side, I disembarked into the ferry terminal and saw Dan sitting alone in a corner. I walked over to him and was astounded to see him visibly shaking.

"What's up brother?" I asked.

Dan just shook his head and looking down muttered, "I can't talk about it."

"Let's get on the ferry before it leaves," I said motioning to him.

Dan followed me silently. We were the only passengers on the ferry and we went up to the top deck. I was hoping the expansive view of the harbor and the fresh air would clear his head and heart.

We were leaning on the railing looking out over the harbor. I asked Dan if he wanted to talk about it now and he mumbled almost incoherently about the movie and demons and being possessed.

As the ferry began to pull away from the dock it let out a loud blast from its air horn. Because Dan and I were on the top deck, we were very close to the horn and it was incredibly loud.

Dan's reaction was immediate and horrifying. He put his right leg over the railing and attempted to leap off the ferry into the dark, churning waters below.

I was standing to his left and quickly grabbed him by his waist and with all the strength I could muster pulled him off the railing. We tumbled together to the deck and he was cursing and thrashing about incoherently.

Although it was something I had never experienced or even read about, I innately knew Dan actually had been possessed by a demon. I felt if I did not do something right then to rectify the situation, he would probably find a way to kill himself before the ferry completed its short ten minute trip to Governor's Island.

Instinctively, I laid my two hands on his forehead. He opened his eyes and stared at me with fierce intensity, but he stopped thrashing violently. His body was still spasming all over, but he made no effort to stop me.

In a loud voice, the words to say just flowed out of my mouth without thought. I commanded, "In the name of Jesus Christ I banish you, demon, from this person!"

No sooner did I utter those simple words than Dan closed his eyes, took a deep breath and seemed to go to sleep in a calm and still repose. After a couple of minutes he opened his eyes, sat up, and then stood up. He was still a little weak and unstable on his feet, but obviously his normal mental self again.

"Thank you brother. I think you just saved my life," he said humbly looking into my eyes with his hand on my shoulder.

"I guess you really did have a demon," I smiled consolingly. "And I must have just done my first exorcism."

I snapped my focus back to the present class as the instructor began speaking again.

"The second easiest type of Izbo to inhabit is either one that is very depressed, drunk, or high on drugs, or one that is suffering from mental illness.

"I encourage you not to inhabit Izbos with severe mental illnesses. However, it is fine to inhabit a normal Izbo, or one with slight mental illness, and drive them into serious mental illness and insanity.

"But if you start at that spot, you are left with an Izbo body you cannot do much damage with or to. You probably will not find many people that want to have sex with you, and your Izbo will likely already be unemployed and unmarried or divorced.

"You will be unable to influence your Izbo's mind very much because it is no longer there. And your Izbo's body will likely die much sooner than one that begins mentally healthy when you inhabit it, so your fun in an Izbo body will end earlier than if you had made a better choice of who to inhabit in the first place.

"Depressed Izbos on the other hand, are easy targets. As demons you can bring sunshine as well as darkness. You have great powers to influence the minds of Izbos, especially those whose minds are confused and depressed for the moment.

"When you first attempt to inhabit a depressed Izbo, do not make the mistake of trying to make them more depressed. There will be time enough for that in the days to come. Your only objective should be to fully inhabit their body. Do that by bringing a little sunshine into their life.

"They will always have some food, beverage or drug that is their comfort crutch: the item they turn to that makes them feel a little better. Whenever you see them turn to their comfort crutch, just attach a bit of your auric essence to the item before they consume it. By doing so they will also be unknowingly swallowing a little of your essence. In a period of just a few days they should be completely open to being fully inhabited.

"Izbos that get drunk or high frequently on drugs are other good targets. They are more challenging than the depressed Izbos because their negative state often lasts only for hours rather than days. But if you persist for some months, usually about six to eight months, depending upon the frequency of the drunk or high state, you will eventually be able to merge your auric essence with theirs.

"The drunks and drug crazed will often recognize your presence, but most will also comprehend that there is no way for them to get rid of you, although a few misguided souls might try. Those feeble and fruitless attempts are always worth a few laughs.

"Now everyone take out the pad of paper and pencil from your desk," the teacher instructed.

"I want you to make a list of all the actions that you can think of that would be destructive to the lives and happiness of Izbos; particularly any that cause massive loss of life to other Izbos, or cause your Izbo to abuse their bodies such as frequent, unprotected promiscuous sex, or alcohol and drug abuse. But remember, you have to walk the edge of the knife. You want them to abuse their bodies, but not so much that they die too quickly and you have to depart."

It was at this point that Gilgore raised his hand. "Can I ask an off topic question?"

"You can ask," the teacher agreed, "but it is very unlikely that I will answer."

There was a lot of laughter in the class following his reply. Gilgore put down his head and seemed to be embarrassed.

"Go ahead and ask your question," the instructor prodded, as it seemed Gilgore had changed his mind after the laughter.

"I want to know about Taz," Gilgore said lifting up his

head.

"That would be a monumental waste of time," the professor said perfunctorily. First, it is unlikely that anyone in this class will ever encounter a Taz. Second, if you are unfortunate enough to do so, you will be banished to Oblivion for at least a few hundred years.

"That is all that you need to know about Taz. You will probably never encounter one, and if you do, it will not matter because you will soon be essentially dead for several centuries."

CHAPTER
Five

The instructor's last words caused quite a commotion in the class. Some of the students were laughing uncontrollably, while others seemed angry, standing up waving their fists and shouting at him.

One extremely thin fellow with sunken cheeks, hollowed eyes and scraggy clothes clinging to an emaciated frame yelled loudly, "Taz are overrated, if they are even real! There is no creature from the physical world that has such power over a demon!" His sentiments were boisterously echoed by several others in the class.

The instructor lifted his arms and waved his hands downward. "Calm down, calm down; I find this a useless subject. As I said, it is highly unlikely that any of you will ever encounter a Taz unless you are inducted into a battle at the behest of Lord Lucifer. In which case very few of you will survive. Now I have a torment to get to and I do not want to waste any more time on this meaningless topic."

Looking intently at the instructor, Gilgore spoke up loudly and caused everyone in the class to immediately quiet down by his boast. "Thalgin, I HAVE encountered a Taz and I killed him!"

The instructor, whose name was apparently Thalgin, looked down his bespeckled nose at Gilgore with disdain while laughing hysterically.

"Alright Gilgore, I will indulge you for a tiny moment because the class seems interested," he stuttered out through laughter. "Tell us about your amazing encounter with a Taz."

Accepting Thalgin's invitation, Gilgore stood up in all seriousness with his head held high and walked to the front of the class. He proceeded to relate our encounter in perfect detail. When he was done, he walked quietly back and sat down at his desk.

Thalgin brushed the palms of his hands together a few times and then addressed the class while looking directly at Gilgore with dismissive disdain.

"This was NOT a Taz. Gilgore, the ignorant excuse for a demon that he is, obviously encountered an Izbo with strong enough psychic abilities, that in this state, he could see and speak with demons.

"I'm sure most of you have encountered those special types of Izbos in the past, probably on multiple occasions. Though you can converse with them, they can't hurt you and you cannot hurt them because in their dream form they have no real substance.

"However, you can hurt them and even kill them, if you can scare them enough in their dream state to cause their physical sleeping body to have a stroke or heart attack."

Thalgin looked down his nose again at Gilgore. "The fact that the Izbo just stood there and let you stab his ethereal dream body with a sword, then immediately vanished to return to his sleeping body, is absolute proof that you merely encountered an Izbo with strong psychic abilities.

"If that had been a Taz he would not have allowed you to stab him and you would not be here to tell the story. So that is that," Thalgin said smugly rubbing his palms together again.

Gilgore exploded in anger at Thalgin's put down of his experience. He leaped up from his desk, grabbing and flipping it up in the air as he stood up. The desk rotated a couple of times in the air and then crashed down on the head of the lady demon that had been sitting behind him. She stood up, her face flush with anger, and rushed at Gilgore in rage.

For a few minutes, the two of them lit into one another with screeches, screams, the foulest of language, and a rain of fists, kicks, and bites. The demons nearby stood up and backed away to give them room to fight. Eventually the two combatants calmed down and despite the ferocity of their encounter, it seemed that neither had done any damage to the other.

When the class returned to some semblance of order and everyone was mulling about by their desks, Thalgin addressed them enthusiastically.

"Good to see the fighting demon spirit! We need more of that, so feel free to find reasons to quarrel with your fellow classmates; the more violently the better!

"But I really will be leaving to torment an Izbo very shortly, so if you wish to receive any further insight, SHUT UP AND SIT DOWN!" He exploded suddenly from his calm demeanor.

Obediently, all the demons sat down at their desks and looked up at Thalgin like a model class of well-behaved students. It was actually both odd and humorous to see such a rapid transformation from anger and violence to peace and calm.

"Let us now conclude this class with its original subject of how to inhabit an Izbo," Thalgin began.

"Just like some idiotic Izbos will call upon Lord Lucifer for help and then be easily inhabited by the demon of the Lord's choice, more often the stupid, ignorant Izbos will just call upon demons and demonic forces for help without the knowledge of how to do it safely.

"When this happens, the first demon to respond will find an Izbo completely exposed and able to be immediately inhabited at that very moment. It is really my all-time favorite opportunity for inhabiting Izbos.

"Simply stop thinking evil thoughts for a moment and match your aura to theirs. Will it to merge into their aura. If you are successful, it will be done that instant because of the momentary opening the Izbo created by their request. Most often you will get a high-quality Izbo from which you can enjoy years of pleasure with their body, and be able to use them to cause delightful misery to other Izbos.

Gilgore raised his hand. "Yes, what is it?" Thalgin asked in a perturbed tone.

"I still have questions about the Taz," Gilgore said matter-of-factly.

There was a chorus of groans of protest from the class and Thalgin threw his hands up in anger.

"Stop with this ridiculous subject! We will not waste another moment talking about it!"

"But the Taz I killed did not have an ethereal dream body. His body had substance. He used his hand to push Varina back away from the bed. He also took the razor blade out of the girl's hand just before she was going to slit her wrist.

"That was a real razor blade and a physical girl. How could he have done those things if he was only an ethereal Izbo?

"Even we demons have very limited ability to physically move or affect items in the physical world, and certainly no Izbo in a dream-state can do it."

Thalgin drooped his head deeply for a moment, his patience obviously running thin. Lifting his eyes, he looked squarely at Gilgore. "Please remember, by your own recounting of the events, you also thought Varina had just been pushed back by an auric force, not a physical force."

Gilgore objected. "She assured me the physical palm of his hand hit her forcefully on her chest."

"Yes, yes," Thalgin said patronizingly. "An auric force psychically projected can feel perfectly physical, but it is not.

"She may have thought he physically pushed her, but you said it was with his right hand. If he was going to send out an auric force to affect a demon, it would be most powerful coming out of his right hand.

"But an auric push would be all that he could muster, as even a strongly psychic Izbo cannot hurt a demon. If he had been a Taz, he would not have just pushed her."

"What about taking the razor blade from the girl?" Gilgore interjected.

Thalgin shrugged. "You didn't say he physically grabbed it and held it in his hand. Even a Taz could not do something that tangible in the 1st Dimension.

"You said he knocked the blade out of her hand and it flew across the room. He also did that with his right hand. This would be an easy action for an Izbo with powerful psychic powers and the ability to project auric energy."

Thalgin crossed his arms and looked at Gilgore with impatience. "I am not going to talk about this anymore. All the evidence points to the fact that you merely encountered a strongly psychic Izbo with the ability to project auric force. You were able to have some fun and the encounter gave you a fulfilling outcome that may have even caused harm to the Izbo back in the physical world.

"However, as I said earlier, the greatest evidence of what it was NOT is your presence here today. If that had been a Taz, nobody would be seeing you again for several centuries."

CHAPTER
Six

Gilgore nodded his head a little and seemed to grudgingly accept that what Thalgin said must be true. Thalgin's explanation was a relief for me too. It gave some closure as to who and what exactly I was in all of these strange lucid dreams. It was obvious to me at that moment that I must be one of those humans with strong psychic and auric abilities that Thalgin spoke of, as both abilities had been with me from my earliest childhood.

"Alright then!" Thalgin said exuberantly. "Let's finish today's class and because there is some interest, we will further explore the strange creature called a Taz in another lesson sometime in the future when we do not have anything important to discuss.

"Now comes the best part of today's class," Thalgin said with relish.

He held up a small black bag and shook it a bit.

"Inside I have thirteen pieces of dried Izbo skin that

have been spelled so you can hold them. Each piece is about the size of your hand and represents one of the Thirteen Sacred Blessings.

"These are very rare artifacts in and of themselves, but it is the message written on each of them in dried Izbo blood that is the real treasure. Each note of Izbo skin has the soul location of an Izbo in their prime that has called out for demonic help, along with inhabitation instructions specific to that Izbo. The note is enchanted for invisibility and will only be revealed to the successful demon when we meet again tomorrow.

"I have also put a spell of invisibility over each of the Izbos for the moment, so no other demon can find them.

"Each Izbo is focused on attaining or using primarily one of the Thirteen Sacred Blessings for their personal advantage. It will be extremely easy for any of you to inhabit one of them.

"I am going to take these skins out of the sack one at a time and hold them up with the writing facing away from you. You need to use your psychic abilities to determine which of the Thirteen Sacred Blessings I am holding up.

"The first demon to ascertain the correct answer with a single call, will receive the Izbo skin with the Izbos soul location.

"Anyone that makes an incorrect call will be disqualified from making a call on the next turn. No demon that has obtained a skin can make a call for another.

"Are we clear on the rules?" Thalgin asked. All the demons nodded and grunted their assent.

"Very good." Thalgin reached into the bag and held

up one of the dried human skins. "What Sacred Blessing is this?" he asked.

For a moment nobody said a word. I assume they did not want to make an error and lose their next turn. Finally, a demon in the back spoke up, but he was not correct. Two others followed him and they also guessed incorrectly.

Then a demoness in the front row said, "greed."

With a wide smile Thalgin handed her the skin. "That is correct!"

The psychic deduction game progressed fairly quickly. I have to confess I was impressed with how psychically capable the demons were. The first few skins found the first couple of demons deducing an incorrect answer. But by the third or fourth demon the correct answer was stated.

As Thalgin went through his stash of human skins and the choices were whittled down from thirteen, the demon deducing correctly was usually the first or second one to state their psychic insight.

In a matter of minutes the skins for greed, wrath, deceit, gluttony, hate, pride, selfishness, indolence, and chaos were gone. Only four more skins remained in the bag. Standing unseen in the closet I was trying to psychically deduce the answers myself. I patted myself on the back for getting three of the four correct. I never would have guessed the last, which ended up being the only one Thalgin really cared about.

Thalgin held up the black bag and shook it again. "These last ones are three of the Sacred Blessings with the greatest potential for destruction of Izbos and the

Izbo world.

"The fourth skin remaining is for the most powerful Sacred Blessing of all. But it is unique because it is the only one of the blessings that Izbos also value. This most wonderful of all demon blessings is knowledge.

"It is a great prize my demented fiends, for the demon that inhabits the Izbo who has great knowledge. Because that Izbo's knowledge then becomes yours, and in both the demon and Izbo worlds, knowledge is power!

"Because of the value of the skin of knowledge, I have spelled it to give me the same access to the knowledge in the Izbo's mind as the demon that inhabits him. Otherwise, I could never give up this skin to another demon; it is too precious and I just would have kept it for myself."

"Now everyone in the class may make a play for these last four. No one is disqualified if they already have won a skin. I don't grant this out of a sense of fairness, which I abhor, but out of a fervent desire to see the greatest possible torment among Izbos. I want the most powerful demons to win because that will ensure the greatest Izbo misery.

"If you have already won a skin and you win one of these four you may trade the skin you previously won to another demon for a future favor."

Thalgin hesitated. "There is a catch to these last four. I have already said they are the best ones, and all of you know all the ones that have already been allotted. I am sure it is easy, even for you dimwits, to deduce the three that remain in the sack in addition to knowledge.

"Therefore, I declare a Scadonz for the prizes. After I

say *go,* you may begin to attack each other any way you wish. The last four demons remaining in the room will be blessed with one of the four premium skins.

"All thirteen of the victors must appear again in this classroom tomorrow at the same time. I will then reveal to each of you who your victim is, and give you some tips on how to use them for the maximum destruction to other Izbos."

"Go!"

What happened next is indescribable. One moment everyone was calm and still, silently listening intently to Thalgin explain how the last four skins would be distributed. The very next breath after Thalgin said 'go' all hell broke loose, literally. All thirty demons started ferociously fighting with one another, but not in any semblance of the way humans would fight.

There was an ear-splitting crescendo of noise from the screams, screeches and curses being yelled in voices louder than any human could muster. Few demons were standing on the floor. Most had levitated and were in blurs of tumult as they furiously fought with other demons and flew around the room bouncing off the walls, ceiling and floor like pinballs in an arcade machine.

Sometimes two would gang up on one and seem to exterminate him or her, only to see the expunged demon rise back up a few seconds later and attack someone completely different.

Every demon manifested deadly weapons out of thin air, from broad-bladed double axes, to spiked mace balls on chains, and lots and lots of swords, and they made deadly use of their weapons.

Demon heads, arms, and legs were lopped off right and left. One demon with a really big scimitar sword swung it down on the head of another demon and split the guy in half all the way down his body. The sword exited out the demon's groin, and the two halves of the vanquished demon's body fell away in opposite directions.

One decapitated head with a pink Mohawk haircut rolled right up to the door I was secretly standing behind. Looking down at the head with its closed eyes I couldn't tell if it was a demon or demoness.

With all the demon bodies flying around I was surprised none had yet crashed into the door I was hiding behind; although they were all so focused on killing each other that they probably wouldn't have even noticed me.

I looked back up for a couple of seconds at the chaos whirling like a tornado from hell in the room. When I glanced down again at the dismembered head, it had vanished!

Nor was it the only demon to disappear. In the short time it took to take a deep breath, all the demons that had been vanquished and their various dismembered body parts, began to rapidly vanish. In a few blinks of my eyes only the four victorious demons remained, or at least partially remained, as all of them were missing one body part or another.

The skinny emaciated demon I had noticed earlier was there, minus one of his feet and an ear. Plus he had a wicked deep gash across his neck where another demon had not quite succeeded in beheading him. He looked so weak and muscleless I was surprised he had been able to beat anyone in a fight, let alone emerge as one of the four formidable victors.

A tall, muscular demoness with short-cropped black hair, dressed in roman-like armor of flat iron plates pieced together with leather was also a victor. She was gently cradling her lopped off forearm in the crook of her other intact arm.

A shapely blue skin demoness with tightly braided long blonde hair, wearing a pink harem outfit was also a victor but one of her red eyeballs had been gouged out and she was holding it in her hand.

The last victor was the demon with two spiral horns coming out of his head, only now he just had one and a half. The horns slanted back at a steep angle from their roots near his forehead and protruded a little past his head in the back. I imagine they had proven useful in the fight.

I was also fascinated to notice that despite their severe wounds, none of the demons were bleeding! Scanning the room where over a dozen demons had been killed, and most others severely dismembered, there was not a drop of red blood anywhere, or any other color! Maybe demons didn't have blood I speculated.

Through all of the fighting swirling around the room Thalgin had been sitting almost with disinterest in a wooden chair in the corner of the room. After the battles were over, he stood up and walked toward the four victors shaking his head negatively.

"You are a sorry lot. I am surprised that any of you won. I suppose that is a sad testimony of how inept all of the others were that, despite your own obvious deficiencies, you were able to best them.

"And it was all too quickly. If even a few of you had some modicum of skill, the Scadonz would have lasted much longer and been far more enjoyable for me and all the other demons watching from afar."

With apparent reluctance he reached into the black sack, and one by one gave a skin to each of the four victors.

"Lust for you," he said to the demoness handing her a skin.

"Doubt" for you," he said handing the skin to the emaciated demon.

Moving to the next demon, Thalgin stopped and held his gaze for a moment, "and for you my horny miscreant, I give Despair, one of the truly great, great blessings. Make sure you use it well and are worthy of it."

Thalgin stepped up in front of the blue-skin demoness. "Kalizia, why are you still holding your eyeball, dimwit? The sooner you put it back, the sooner it will heal."

The demoness nodded her head and quickly popped the eyeball she had been holding back into her eye socket and her eyelid closed over it, I assumed to begin the healing process.

Thalgin held up the last skin without giving it to her.

"Remember this skin of knowledge is especially spelled. I want to know everything in the mind of the human you inhabit. To ensure that is the case, this skin also has another spell on it. If you try to deceive me and counterspell the skin, it will erase all the knowledge in your brain as pitiful and small as it might be."

The one good red eye of the demoness opened wide in surprise when she learned about the second spell that could obliterate her knowledge and memories.

"Are we clear? Thalgin asked the demoness. Kalizia nodded her head in a confusing way, a little up and down showing agreement and a little side to side showing disagreement.

"I do not think you can do a spell that will erase my brain," Kalizia said doubtfully.

"Oh you don't," Thalgin said haughtily, as if he was speaking to a little child.

"I am a Level 7," Thalgin asserted with a piercing stare at Kalizia. "And you are what?

"A Level 4," Kalizia admitted hesitatingly.

"I have three levels of knowledge and experience greater than you," Thalgin pointed out with a superior air. "Three levels more skill; three levels more magick.

"I am to you like you are to a Level 1. Do you remember how little you knew as a Level 1? Do you realize how much more powerful you are now as a Level 4?"

Kalizia nodded her head in silent agreement.

Thalgin bored into Kaliza with a piercing ice pick tone of despite. "So does your half-wit mind finally comprehend that the power I wield as a Level 7 is beyond your comprehension, and sucking out your memories and knowledge with a spell is something you best not doubt?"

Kalizia bit her lower lip and answered tentatively. "Maybe."

Her refusal to acquiesce to him infuriated Thalgin. In the blink of an eye he held a curved scimitar in each hand and he swung them with deadly intent at Kalizia. But she instantly materialized a curved metal shield and blocked both of the swords and then used the shield to knock Thalgin hard on top of his head.

Thalgin lowered his scimitars and they disappeared. He glared at Kalizia, then spoke angrily and abruptly to all of them. "Return tomorrow, same time, same place.

"If I am in a better mood I will be here to give you some tips and activate the enchantments in the skins, which will impart the knowledge you need to locate and inhabit your Izbo.

"If I don't show up, you can torture Kalizia for taking away your rewards with her insolent actions!"

With those parting words Thalgin just vanished. If I had blinked I would have missed it. One second he was there and the next he was not. He was quickly followed by the remaining four demons that all suddenly just disappeared as fast as a snap of fingers.

Cautiously I opened the doors to the closet and peeked about in the room. I assumed all the demons had left the vicinity, but I didn't really know. Perhaps they had just become invisible and were still present.

The room appeared to be a classroom, so it was possible that it was attached to a larger educational institution. Maybe none of the demons that had been in this class were still around, but any number of others might come into the room at any time.

With those cautious thoughts in mind, rather than stick around and possibly be attacked by an invisible foe that might still be hanging around, I willed myself back home and out of my dream.

I immediately awoke lying on my back in my bed. Unable to fall back asleep, a nagging doubt kept running through my mind. Were my recent sleep time experiences with demons really anything more than very long, very detailed, multi-night lucid dreams? They all seemed too fanciful to be real.

There were times in the past where I had continued a dream from the previous night to the next night, and sometimes for three or four nights, picking up right where I left off. Those dreams were my most vivid and lucid. Maybe I was just taking that ability to the next level.

I determined to look for a way that I could know with certainty, one way or the other, whether I was just dreaming or somehow experiencing bizarre real events.

If these were merely very creative lucid dreams, I was fine with just being able to experience imaginative entertainment while I slept. But if I was truly seeing and interacting with the unseen world of demons, I needed to be far more prepared in knowledge and ability to defend myself than I was at the moment; because at the moment I felt pretty ignorant and helpless.

CHAPTER
Seven

To my surprise, I ended up falling into a deep and restful sleep sometime after I returned from my clandestine visit to Thalgin's class. Tending to my mundane chores and responsibilities during the day, my mind was completely distracted from the tasks at hand. I had so much to think about from all the unworldly things I had seen and heard during my Night Self travels that I felt a need to ponder it for at least a week.

However, the luxury of that time was not available. I knew I had to return that night to hear what Thalgin would tell the demons about the message on their precious human skins.

Nevertheless, I had already learned a great deal from my visit to Thalgin's class and my earlier dreams. I was surprised to see that demons came in a myriad of human shapes. Some would seem harmless and innocuous like an introverted accountant. You certainly would not pick them out of a crowd or feel threatened by them.

Others looked the part of what people imagined demons looking like, such as the fellow with the scary visage and two horns protruding out of his head. Many, like the blue skinned Kalizia in a harem outfit, would be assumed to be aliens or someone on their way to a Halloween party.

Demons certainly did have a wide range of clothing and personal appearance styles that seemed to include every human race, plus a few like Kalizia that we certainly didn't see in the physical world.

In my lucid dream world they could levitate; they didn't bleed, and they could appear and disappear in the blink of an eye.

Thalgin had also referred to other demons who were not present watching the fighting taking place during the Scadonz. That sounded like being able to see what was occurring in a distant location, as another one of their abilities. Or perhaps they used a technology such as simple surveillance cameras. Cloistered in my closet peeking out through the narrow crack, I hadn't seen anything like a camera, but they could have been there.

The demon bodies seemed to have some kind of physical substance, which was evidenced by all the dismembered body parts in the Scadonz. However, as none of them seemed too concerned about losing an arm, leg, or even a head, they obviously must have the ability to reconstitute their bodies. And remembering Gilgore's comment about how he enjoyed being killed, it was evident that even when chopped up they were not actually dead.

They also must live an unimaginably long time as Thalgin mentioned that any demon banished by a Taz would be gone for centuries.

Coupled with the demons well-talked about ability to "inhabit" a human, and remembering the girl on the bed that Gilgore and Varina had been tormenting, and whom Gilgore referred to as being a "physical girl," it would seem as if my experiences were somehow anchored in reality and not just dreams, but I was still uncertain if that was true or how it could be true.

I reminded myself that I knew from the experience with my friend Dan that demons were real and could exist in our physical world, completely unseen and undetected, with the nefarious ability to influence and even control vulnerable humans. Whether or not I could somehow actually see and converse with them on another plane of existence while my physical body slept, was still an open question.

Contemplating that what I had seen in my dreams might be a physical reality visible in my altered sleep state gave me a queasy feeling in the pit of my stomach as I wondered how Thalgin had obtained his dried human skins. Did he take them off of a live human or a dead one? And if it was a dead one, was it someone he had just killed? And how would something like that even work? If demons were without corporeal substance or visibility in our world, how could they go about acquiring the physical skins of humans?

Demons could also do magick beyond their personal powers and abilities. Thalgin spoke about placing enchantments and spells of invisibility on both the skins and the potential human victims he had lined up to be inhabited. As he spoke about it casually without questioning or response from any of the demons in the class, magick obviously was fairly common in their world.

Demons being able to use magick was not surprising to me. I had been interested in magick since my teenage years and had read many of the famous and rare books on the subject. Though the books were quite convoluted and convincing in their descriptions and rituals, I found the methods they outlined to be either impotently ineffective, or effective only if dark forces were called upon.

I considered that as demons have undeniable magickal knowledge and abilities, they are probably quite happy to share it with any human that uses black magick rituals and calls for the help of dark forces. However, demons would charge a very high price for their assistance, and I doubted whether they would tell any of their victims ahead of time what the full, life-destroying price would be.

Most of the white magick knowledge that I had acquired that actually worked in tangible ways, were techniques, words of power, and simple rituals I had perfected on my own after much trial and experimentation calling in and coalescing magickal energies of light which I could sense.

Though I felt confident in a few powerful bits of magick I had mastered, despite nearly two decades of study and practice I knew I was still merely a novice, and wholly unprepared to face the magickal abilities of demons. For instance, the spell of invisibility that Thalgin spoke so casually about, was one I had no idea how to craft in a white magick way.

Immersed in my thoughts and analysis, the day seemed to fly by, and soon it was time to exchange my Day Self for my Night Self and return to the demon world at Thalgin's class.

I lay on my back on my bed with the covers pulled up to my chin as the night air coming through the open window was a bit chilly.

Closing my eyes I programmed my Night Self for where I wanted it to journey in my sleep. "Appear hidden inside the closet in Thalgin's class at the time when he first will be seeing his students again from the previous day."

In just a few minutes I was asleep, and some unknown time after that my Night Self materialized inside the same closet as the previous night, cautiously peering through the crack at the center meeting line of the double doors, at a room full of demons.

CHAPTER
Eight

Thalgin was once again at the head of the class looking at some papers on top of his small desk. His students were just taking their seats after apparently milling about waiting for the class to get started. There were fewer of them than yesterday's class. I speculated that perhaps some of them had been so badly injured that they had been unable to reconstitute their bodies sufficiently to attend today's class. I soon learned that was not the reason.

Unexpectedly, a vast blast of fire shot out and encompassed the room from the vicinity of Thalgin's desk. None of the demons seemed to be injured by the fire, but some were quickly patting out little flames that had taken hold on their clothing.

"Alright then," Thalgin began, "now that I have your attention, let's begin this most important class."

Thalgin walked in front of his desk bringing him closer to his students. "You will notice that only the victors from yesterday are present in today's class to learn the invaluable knowledge I will be imparting.

"This in itself is a lesson for both you the victors who are here, and for all the losers who are not. Let this lesson be pounded into your mentally challenged minds: rewards are for winners!

"Unlike Izbo's, who tend to want to foolishly reward everyone as if they were the winner simply because they participated, demons with their far greater understanding of motivational psychology, give punishments rather than rewards to the losers.

"When someone is punished for losing, they acquire an incentive to give more effort the next time so they will not receive a punishment. When they are rewarded for losing, they give no extra effort during the next challenge because they know there is no need, as they will receive a reward regardless of whether they win or lose.

"In this case, our lesson today will give you priceless insights into inhabiting Izbo's. Because of that superior knowledge, you will have far more opportunities in the future to cause destruction and devastation in the Izbo world and become famous demons.

"The worthless losers of the psychic insight challenge and the Scadonz will not be here to gain those insights. They will inhabit far fewer and less important Izbo's than you. They will cause far less destruction in the Izbo world than you will be capable of achieving. The losers will be demons nobody knows and nobody wants to know.

"On another subject, this meeting is closed to all eyes and ears of most demons. Other than those demons higher than me, nobody will receive the knowledge imparted here except the thirteen winners in this room! See that it stays that way!

"Remember knowledge is power. The more knowledge you have that other demons do not, the more advantage you have over them and over Izbos, and the greater possibility that you will have to become a noteworthy demon wreaking havoc in the Izbo world."

Thalgin ran his hands down his chest a couple of times as if he was brushing off dirt.

"Alright then, let's get started. Even though each of you only have a skin targeting a single Izbo weakness, I am going to speak about all thirteen of the Sacred Blessings. And in every case, though the Izbo may be motivated primarily by one of the Sacred Blessings, they will in fact have several that they regularly embrace.

"The thirteen of you certainly are very fortunate to be able to gain this knowledge about all of the Sacred Blessings and how to use them against Izbos, rather than just the single one that is on the skin you possess.

"I am not revealing this knowledge to you out of any desire to help you in your miserable lives, even though that will be a beneficial consequence for you.

"In order to receive this knowledge you must swear an oath of allegiance to me, right here, right now. It is a very simple oath. You must covenant to immediately come to my aid if I call you and do anything I ask or require of you.

"The knowledge I will impart to you is something you will be able to benefit from for eternity. However, you will only be obligated by your oath to help me a single time in any way I demand.

"If there is anyone that does not wish to pledge fidelity to me on those terms, depart now."

None of the demons moved from their chairs or asked any questions, so Thalgin proceeded. Between his thumb and forefinger he held up what appeared to be a large, golden-colored capsule. He walked up to the nearest student, a tall, muscular blonde with tightly braided hair, and placed the capsule in the palm of her hand. She pulled her fingers in around the capsule.

"Repeat these words," Thalgin demanded. "I swear an oath with Lord Lucifer as my witness that I will on one occasion only, immediately come to the aid of Thalgin when he calls, and do anything he commands."

The demoness repeated the words of the oath Thalgin dictated. He moved on to the next student, placed the golden capsule in the palm of his hand and he repeated the oath of allegiance to Thalgin.

One by one Thalgin went to each demon in the room and the oath ritual was repeated. When the last demon had sworn his oath, Thalgin took the golden pill from him, popped it in his mouth and swallowed it. A wide smile of evil satisfaction crossed his face.

"Very good. All of you have more potential for demon greatness than I had originally assessed. Now I will keep my part of the bargain. Let's look at how to receive joy and fulfillment by using the Sacred Blessings against Izbos.

"The Sacred Blessings were chosen by Lord Lucifer as they are root motivations in both demons and Izbos. Every demon worthy of the name aspires to embody all of the best ones like greed, wrath, gluttony and deceit, while also being skilled at inducing Izbos to crave one or more and travel down the demonic path.

"It is important to note that many of the Sacred Blessings are closely related and it is to your advantage to encourage as many as possible to manifest when you are working on the degradation and downfall of Izbos in preparation of inhabiting them.

"For instance, you may have the skin for Greed, which is the base root of much evil, or so it would seem, but maybe it is not. Greed is most often associated with greed for more money. But why does the Izbo want more money? What deliciously illicit thoughts have you dropped into their simple mind, which is so ridiculously pliable and influenceable?

"Perhaps you encouraged the Izbo to have sexual or possessive Lust for another Izbo and they are motivated by greed to have more money to capture the favor of the Izbo they lust after.

"Or perhaps the greed is motivated by Pride. Perhaps the Izbo wants to have power over other Izbos, or be looked up to and admired by them. Great wealth is one of the most effective ways that Izbos use to induce other Izbos to admire them.

"However, if you are doing your job, the true Izbo, the one no one else sees, will be perverted in a short time to be rotten to the core, and not at all admirable except to demons.

"Clearly understanding and cultivating the interconnectedness of the Sacred Blessings with the Izbo you are working with, is the secret to being able to rapidly merge your aura with theirs and merge into their body so you can experience physical pleasures.

"And then the true fun begins! Once you have inhabited an Izbo you can convince them to literally do anything! Izbos are so pliable and easily led down the paths of the Sacred Blessings.

"There are so many joyous physical pleasures you can induce Izbos to partake of; with uninhibited sex, unlimited food, and crushing power over other Izbos being three of the most fulfilling.

"However, it is important that you pace yourself. Give your Izbo some self-restraint. Don't allow them to wallow in the Sacred Blessings too deeply, too rapidly. Their frail Izbo bodies and minds cannot handle that much pleasure and they will die too soon.

"After you have used up the life of the Izbo targeted on your skin, you will want to choose and cultivate another one on your own. Keep these thoughts in mind as you select your next victim.

"Though I make it sound easy, you all know that inhabiting an Izbo is difficult. It is not something where you just hop into another Izbo when your current host dies.

"The majority of demons have never inhabited an Izbo in the many thousands of years they have been demons! Many others have only had the opportunity once or twice in a millennium or two.

"I suspect most, if not all of you, are in the former group. You have never been able to go beyond leading Izbos into immorality by appearing in their dreams and sending wicked thoughts into their minds when they are drunk or stoned. Am I right? Raise your hand if you have ever inhabited an Izbo and you can come up here and tell us all about it."

Not one demon raised their hand.

"As I suspected," Thalgin said dismissively.

"All the more reason you better listen attentively to what I say. Your skins are guaranteed. No matter how inept and stupid you might be, the Izbo on your skin is so morally compromised that you will inhabit them quickly and easily.

"Once you get a taste of your first inhabitation you will be ravenous for another after your first dies. Because of my lessons, you might actually become successful at inhabiting another in another few hundred years or so.

"When choosing your next victim, remember that the younger and healthier the better, if you want to enjoy their body for the longest time.

"If you begin with an Izbo in their teens or early twenties, as Izbos count time, you can expect to have their body last at least into their early fifties, as long as you pace their indulgences.

"If you start with one in their early fifties they will likely die from overindulgence in five to ten Izbo years, unless you are very judicious and pace them at a much lesser rate than a younger one.

"Regardless of their age, as you lead your Izbo down the path of debauchery, dishonesty, and despair, pacing the descent of destruction is vital to be able to use your Izbo for the longest period of time and to cause the greatest amount of damage to other Izbos and the Izbo world.

"Let's take sex for an example. No matter which of the

Sacred Blessings you have focused on cultivating in your Izbo, sex will of course be a major part of all of them. Physical sex is a most divine pleasure and understandably you will want to experience it often, but not too often!

"As I said earlier, inciting sexual release in one way or another is good on a restrained pace of not more than three times a day.

"If you do more than that, it will give you more pleasure; that is undeniable, but it will also take too much of your Izbo's time in the short day that they are awake and active. That will give you less time during their limited lifespan to use their body and life to help debase and destroy the Izbo world.

"Never forget the greater goal of Lord Lucifer to bring the Izbo world into an immoral, debauched embrace of the Thirteen Sacred Blessings. Inhabiting an Izbo must be for far more than just your own personal pleasure.

"Much to my disgust as to how any demon could be so stupid, as you know there are overly gluttonous demons that inhabit an Izbo, usually females, but sometimes males, and then cause them to have dozens to more than a hundred spontaneous orgasms each day, without any relief or sexual stimulation.

"Make sure you are never that stupid! That type of misguided indulgence of demonic sexual satisfaction is so short-sighted I would personally banish a demon who did it to Oblivion if I had that power.

"Of what use in the grander scheme of Lord Lucifer to degrade and demoralize the Izbo world, is causing one single Izbo to have endless orgasms? Selfishness is a wonderful quality, but not if it is so extreme that it fails to be supportive of the goals of Lord Lucifer.

When a demon is so overly selfish that they focus only on deriving endless sexual orgasms from the Izbo body they inhabit, that Izbo will end up hiding from the world in their house until they die.

"They will avoid interactions with other Izbos to avoid the embarrassment they know would occur when they started having uncontrolled orgasms in public.

"Their death will likely happen within a couple of years rather than decades, either from simply wearing out their body or suicide because of their hopeless plight. They may have given the demon inhabitor endless physical pleasure, but the Izbo will have been useless to the larger goals of Lord Lucifer.

"I certainly hope I do not have to remind you that Lord Lucifer also banishes demons that displease him. But unlike a Taz banishment, which only involves enduring cold, dark and utter boredom for a few centuries, when Lord Lucifer banishes a demon, they experience non-stop torture and death over and over again without pause, for the entire time of their banishment.

"Enough said. Let's continue the discussion about the age of the Izbo to be inhabited because there is something else important to consider. Though this is usually a skill only mastered by upper-level demons you should all try to achieve it as each attempt will bring you closer to your goal the next time.

"Though it is often the most rewarding choice and long-lasting fulfillment to inhabit a younger Izbo, sometimes it is far more satisfying and rewarding to inhabit an older one, even though you will have fewer years in their body.

"You may not be able to coerce them into having as much sex as the younger ones, but they will have other demonic virtues that will give you another kind of fulfillment, and maybe even demon fame.

"If you are wise in your selection, you can find Izbos in their fifties and sixties and sometimes even seventies that have already achieved a high position in life.

"Some will be successful business people, other ones that have already made a profitable profession of influencing other Izbos, such as ministers or movie stars.

"The best of these inhabited puppets are often politicians. Most are already more deceitful and two-faced than many demons. And many, even without demonic influence, have embraced one or more of the Sacred Blessings to attain and keep political power.

"Though you may inhabit one of these elder Izbos for less years than a younger one, because of the position of power, wealth, and influence that they have already attained, you can do much more damage in the Izbo world by corrupting the minds and morals of the weak even further."

Suddenly Thalgin stopped speaking and held the tip of his fingertips of his left hand to his forehead. "Wait a moment, I am receiving a message of importance.

"Oh, that is wonderful," he said, apparently talking to himself. Then he looked up and addressed the class. He seemed to be having difficulty speaking as he was very excited, scared, or frustrated, I wasn't sure which. He was lifting his feet up and down and jiggling his arms around as if he was dancing a happy jig, but his face was contorted in what looked like rage.

"You miscreants are about to be honored beyond your worth!" he spat out. I have just been told that Ugar, a Level 13 demon, is coming to speak about what I was going to speak about.

"Apparently, even though I am a Level 7, some among the higher levels felt I have been less than coherent in my explanations. I am being removed and punished. Ugar will take my place."

Thalgin waved feebly. "Hope to see you in hell."

No sooner had Thalgin spoken his last word than he soundlessly vanished. Exactly at the same moment, another demon appeared in the same spot Thalgin had been standing, and my oh my, he looked the part!

CHAPTER
Nine

As Ugar appeared, every single demon in the room sat up straighter. Their eyes were wide open looking intently and perhaps with some awe and fear at the large ferocious demon standing before them.

There was no doubt he was a demon. Besides his frightening visage, his aura exuded malevolence.

From my vantage point in the closet near the front of the right side wall, I was as close as the nearest demon to Ugar and could see him clearly. He was beyond frightening. He was the epitome of what many people think of when they picture a demon.

He peered out at the quaking demons in the class through black abyssal eyes and a deeply furrowed scowl. He was massively muscular and his physique was easily seen as the only clothing he had on was a ragged pair of pants terminating just below his knees in shredded material and braided sandals on his bare feet.

His chest was absent of clothing but heavily adorned with intricate tattoos and numerous piercings with what appeared to be pieces and carvings of bone.

His skin was dark red and covered with many small wart-like bumps, particularly on his face. Some were oozing little yellow drops of pus. His head was bare of hair but had multiple scarred gashes running across it.

I silently thought to myself, I'm so glad that he can't see me hiding back here.

No sooner did I think that thought, than before he had spoken a word to the waiting demons, Ugar turned his head and stared intently right at the closet doors as if he was sensing me!

I shrank back into the dark corner of the small shelved room while sending out a mental thought, hoping it would be picked up out in the classroom: *nothing but books in there*. I even pictured myself as a big book leaning against the corner of the closet.

My thought must have had an effect because Ugar soon turned his attention back to the demon students." How many of you are Original Demons?" he asked curtly.

Well that was a curious question I thought. Eight of the thirteen demons raised their hands in reply.

"How many are Metastasis Demons?" Ugar asked gruffly. Three other demons raised their hands in response.

"Of those that have metastasized, who has been a demon for the shortest period of time?"

The three that had acknowledged being Metastasis Demons quickly conferred with a few words and a demoness very politely addressed Ugar. "Your horribleness, I metastasized in 1482 as Izbos count years."

Ugar just grunted unintelligently in reply. He scanned the room with an intimidating scowl, shaking his head in silent disapproval.

He looked keenly at two of the demons sitting next to each other in the center of the group. One was a pleasant-looking man and the other a nice-looking woman. They appeared like people who would be easy to have as friends, and not demon-like in any way by their appearance.

Ugar spit onto the floor, then bared his teeth and fangs, snarling at the remaining unaccounted demons.

"What of you two vermin? What are you?" he jeered. "If you are not Originals and are not Metastasis, that must mean you are Purgatories." He spat out his last word with utter disgust.

"You look like you should be sitting in an Izbo church rather than a demon class room. In the space of my taking thirteenth breaths, tell me your story. Do not attempt to lie or deceive me and finish before I breathe my thirteenth breath or it will be your last breath for a very long time."

The man stood up quivering and holding onto his desk for support. "Forgive our Izbo-like appearance your horribleness. It is all that we can muster at the moment. I am Calanstio and this is my wife Belozina. We are as you surmised, Purgatory Demons.

"We first metastasized into demonhood together in 1565, but we were very ineffective and kept gaining

Energy of Light despite what we thought were our best efforts to be evil, and we degenerated into Purgatory Demons.

"Today we can barely maintain our demon powers except in short bursts, such as when we were fighting the other demons during the recent Scadonz.

"Even then, we only prevailed over the other more powerful demons because we fought together as one, protecting each other and always attacking others with our two to one advantage.

"We attended this class in a desperate attempt to become better demons and regain our status as Metastasis. We desperately want to learn how to cause more havoc in the Izbo world. They tortured and killed us when we were Izbos, simply because we loved one another and we want revenge."

Being sure to finish within thirteen of Ugar's breaths, Calanstio, stopped speaking and quickly sat down.

"Love is contrary to the Sacred Blessing of hate," Ugar spat out contemptuously. "I trust you no longer love each other."

"Oh, I hate him with my greatest passion!" Belozina proclaimed loudly. "Because we metastasized together, we are tied to one another for eternity. It is the most damning curse.

"Our inability to grow our demon powers individually is why we lost the capabilities of Metastasis Demons and now must manifest as weak Purgatory Demons, barely able to be demons at all."

Ugar smiled a wicked grin, his words hissing out of his mouth like a snake. "Perhaps your curse will end up being your blessing. As you both were victors in the Scadonz, you will have the opportunity to inhabit two separate Izbos. For this, your curse of always being united because of how you metastasized must be temporarily broken.

"If you each insure that the Izbo body you inhabit is thoroughly debauched, and in particular, has sex with many different partners, your mutual unfaithfulness and freedom from the chains of Izbo monogamy will be able to break the bond of your former love, which still binds you."

"Lord Lucifer the Great!" Calanstio cried out triumphantly.

Belozina seemed equally ecstatic. She pounded her fists up and down on her desktop in furious joy. "I will finally get to be the demoness I know I can be!"

"Do not get too excited," Ugar cautioned threateningly. "Being as inept demons as you are, you are much more likely to fail, which will just reunite you in purgatory hell; too much light to be demons and too much darkness to be Izbos.

"As you know, we have no devices to keep time as we have no need, for we are eternal. The exception of course is for Purgatory Demons. The clocks we do not have do tick for you, and I believe your time is almost up.

Ugar held his left hand against his cheek and stroked his pointy black goatee with his right. "Let me see, you metastasized in 1565, which was almost 500 years ago as they tell time on the Earth you were birthed upon. When you get to 500 your time as Purgatory Demons is over.

"If you have not yet once again fully become Metastasis

Demons, then Lord Lucifer will personally throw your bodies into the sacred lake of fire where you will forever burn but never be consumed."

Both Calanstio and Belozina looked down dejectedly while all the other demons in the room started laughing, clapping, and stomping their feet in excitement.

"Yes, yes, Ugar assured them. "Of course all of you will be invited to attend the beginning of their damnation torture and revel in their screams of agony as their naked bodies are first submerged in the fiery molten lake.

"However, lest we get too giddy at the prospect of being witnesses to their exquisite torment, we must remember that these two nobodies might surprise us and turn the time in their Izbo victims into a memorable habitation and become somebodies."

There were multiple grunts of disgust at the prospect of the Purgatory Demons succeeding with a noteworthy Izbo inhabitation and not getting thrown into the lake of fire.

Suddenly Ugar shouted out in fierce anger. "The rest of you demon scum are not much better than the Purgatories! There are eight Original Demons in this class. That means you were among those of us in the original horde that escaped the cursed realm of Elohim and were transformed into illustrious demons.

"You have been demons for countless Izbo millenniums. You are disgraces to the demon world! Thousands and thousands of years you have been demons, and yet you are so unsuccessful at harming Izbos that you have to take a class on how to inhabit them!

"If it were up to me, I would banish your souls after long and agonizingly painful torture. But Lord Lucifer has commanded all Level Thirteen Demons to make extra efforts to raise up the slackers among the horde. That's you!"

Ugar looked at the demons with disgust. "The lot of you are such a disgrace to the demon world!" he spat out with venomous anger.

"Most of you have been demons for many thousands of years and yet you have less knowledge in your tiny little brains than Izbos who seldom even live to one hundred years. How is such mammoth ignorance even possible?"

Ugar walked menacingly into the classroom between the demon students sitting at their desks. He held a long-bladed dagger in each hand, with blades that undulated like snakes and needle-pointed tips instead of heads.

"Here are some blades I'm sure you have never seen. They will not banish you, but they have been spelled by Lord Lucifer himself to cause any demon stabbed with one a wrenchingly terrible pain. So I am going to treat you today to a sensation you usually cannot feel as a demon to such a great extent. You can thank me later."

As he passed each student, some on his right and others on his left, he stabbed them violently in their heads sticking the blade into the hilt.

Some of the students he stabbed in the forehead and the tip of the snake blade punched all the way through their head and out the back of their skull.

Others he stabbed in from the top of their head. A couple of demons were stabbed through the back of their head with the tip of the dagger blade emerging on the other side of their skull a little above the spot between their eyes.

None of the doomed demons tried to flee or resist. As each demon was stabbed they cried out in screaming agony and pain and slumped face-first onto their desks, apparently dead!

When Ugar had completed his heartless task, he slipped his daggers into sheaths on either side of his waist, walked to the front of the class and sat on the desk facing the bodies of all the slumped over dead demons still sitting at their desks.

CHAPTER
Ten

After a few minutes some of the demons I had assumed to be dead begun to move slightly. Within another couple of minutes all of the demons were sluggishly rousing themselves. Most were holding their obviously aching head with one or both hands and had a dazed and contorted look on their face. Ugar smiled with heinous glee as he watched the recovering demons.

"Why did I just cause all of you the most painful pangs of death? I did it because I could; because I am a powerful demon and you are not. I did it as a lesson for you to never forget, at least once your tiny destroyed brains fully reconstitute; that a demon that does not employ every opportunity to use and demonstrate their power, may as well not have the power.

"You knew that resistance to a Level 13 demon would be futile and only bring about more anguish and greater punishment. So you sat unmoving in your chairs, waiting for your brains to be scrambled and the terrible pain you knew would be coming."

Ugar smiled a wicked haughty smile.

"I inflicted this excruciating pain upon you as a lesson to help you to remember to use your power when you are inhabiting Izbos. Use it all. Don't hold back.

"Once you merge your aura with theirs, the more aware among them will know you are present. Although most will be too ignorant of the unseen world to realize it is a demon inside them.

"To your delight, they will be horrified to realize they have been inhabited by something dark and dangerous. The strongest will even seek out priests or other Izbos with knowledge of the arcane to exorcize you out of their bodies. Of course, you must not allow this to happen.

"Once they are inhabited, your Izbo will still have conscious control of their words and actions. You cannot control them to the point that you can force them to say or do whatever you wish.

"Inhabiting them simply gives you unfettered, unrelenting access to their mind and the joys of experiencing any physical pleasures your Izbo experiences, from food to sex.

"However the physical pleasures will seldom come unless you are incessant in your assault on their thoughts. An Izbo has to sleep away a third of their life, but you do not. So your insidious warping of their mind can take place not just in their dreams, but also every moment that they are awake.

Be ceaseless in your attacks on their mind, placing lustful thoughts for those things that they should not be having such thoughts about. Give them images throughout their day and night of wallowing in great wealth, with servants rushing to submissively do their bidding, with many garages full of expensive cars, of reveling on their gigantic yacht, of gorging on gourmet foods and desserts, of being famous and going from one decadent party and sexual encounter to another.

"Once they have those desires strongly implanted in their minds to the point that they maintain them without any push from you, up your game to the next level. Now that they are ravenous to attain the unattainable, you must make them willing to do anything to get it.

"This is actually the key to the downfall of the Izbo world. When we can get enough of them to abandon good character and morality and faithfully live by mottos such as the *end justifies the means*, or *all's fair in love and war*, then we are on the path to victory.

"If you understand the progression of Izbo souls you have useful insights to help you inhabit their bodies and minds.

"The soul of Izbo babies originates in a mysterious and still unknown manner, in the cursed realm of Elohim, even as all of you did, before your awakening and ascent to the demon world. Their physical parents are merely the creators of the physical body that temporarily holds their eternal soul.

"The Twelve Profane Curses: Balance, Faith, Hope, Generosity, Love, Humility, Tranquility, Order, Benevolence, Temperance, Honesty and Energy, were encoded into Izbo souls from before they were born as impossible challenges; supposedly to help them strive to become more than they were while living the experiences of physical life.

"They are ideals that can never be sustainably attained as they are contrary to the base instinctual urges that are embodied in the first twelve of the Thirteen Sacred Blessings: Lust, Doubt, Despair, Greed, Hate, Pride, Wrath, Chaos, Selfishness, Gluttony, Deceit, and Indolence, which were also encoded into all souls when they were created.

"The interesting aspect is, both the curses and the blessings are encoded into every Izbo's soul. This allows them to innately recognize the traits when they see, hear, or experience them.

"However, there is a visceral attraction for the Blessings. For example, every Izbo instinctively wants to be lazy, to have more by doing less, and lusts after people or the possessions that they desire. They have to consciously suppress their natural attractions for the blessings to not indulge in them. Hence, it is easy for you to give them the push and assure them it is fine to indulge.

"On the other hand, the Curses are not the natural inclination of Izbos. Nobody would by their own uncoerced choice, weigh themselves down with such useless burdens. Izbos have to be brainwashed and indoctrinated by their parents and religious and other leaders to strive to live the Curses. Hence, it is easy for you to convince them to stop striving for the unattainable and unrewarding.

"Only the thirteenth of the Sacred Blessings is not a natural desire of either demons or Izbos and that is

Knowledge. Everyone would like to have more because it is obvious that knowledge is power, but few demons or Izbos are willing to make the sacrifice of time and treasure to attain it.

"As long as Izbos waste their limited lifespans during the two-thirds of it that they are awake, striving to embody the unattainable Twelve Curses, they are doomed to always be longing for personal qualities that they can never sustainably achieve.

"This demonically devious structure was put in place during the creation of souls to insure that Izbos would always feel humble, guilty of their shortcomings, and less than angels and other beings from the cursed realm of Elohim. Subsequently, they willingly worship the odious leaders of that realm as Gods and messengers of God, and willingly give up their natural instincts and acquiesce to be controlled in the actions of their lives.

"You can take advantage of this built-in Izbo weakness to follow the dictates of those in authority, especially religious leaders, by inhabiting and influencing those very leaders, and through them, all that follow and obey them. Priests and politicians are the very best types of Izbos to inhabit.

"As demons, you have successfully rid yourself of any attraction to the Twelve Curses. You realized how impossible it was to achieve those diabolical aspirations, versus how easy it was to embrace and be in harmony with the Thirteen Sacred Blessings.

"Now you must find ways, especially when you inhabit an Izbo, to get them to accept the same reality. Get them to also turn their back on the Twelve Curses and embrace the Thirteen Blessings.

"You must help them to understand that trying to live up to the Twelve Profane Curses will bring them misery, poverty, and rejection, while living with an anything goes gusto guided by the Thirteen Sacred Blessings, will reward them with happiness, wealth, fame and power.

"Ultimately, when you inhabit an Izbo, you must convince them that everything they believed about the good way to live life is exactly the opposite.

"You must convince them that what they had thought of as bad is really good and everything that they thought of as good is bad. This begins with the most important Sacred Blessing to pervert their mind with initially, which is selfishness.

"Izbos are taught by their religions and cultures that benevolence and sacrifice, and even being a martyr, are good aspirations."

"Yeck!" Ugar burst out in obvious disgust at his own words.

"You must turn that warped thinking around and make them realize the only good personal trait, goal or aspiration, is the one that helps satisfy their carnal lusts, and brings them more money, fame, sex, or power, or all of those wonderful blessings!

"Then you must convince them that to attain those rewards the quickest and surest way, it is only right, proper, good and natural, for them to be greedy and be willing to use deceit and dishonesty to gain them.

"At this point, some of the Izbos inhabited will be well on the path to becoming Metastasis Demons. However, only a very few, less than one in ten thousand, will become harmonized enough with the Thirteen Sacred Blessings, and lose enough of their Soul Essence of Light, to shed their Izbo skin and actually be elevated to demonhood.

"So do not waste your time trying to turn your Izbo into a demon! "Your biggest focus, beyond enjoying the physical pleasures of their body, must be to influence your Izbo to take actions that are destructive to the lives and happiness of other Izbos.

"If you inhabit a leader or any person of influence, or help them to become one, you can have a wonderfully destructive effect upon thousands, even millions of Izbos!

"Delightfully, some destructive acts of Izbos can become like a line of dominoes falling down. The first fall leads to another, then another and another, until the Izbo world is destroyed by their own actions!"

Ugar paused, stroking his goatee and looking up at the ceiling in thought.

"Let me give you a great example so it is clear in your minuscule brains the optimum way to get Izbos to be self-destructive on a large scale.

"This is a classic example of how to lead Izbo's to believe that good is bad and bad is good, and how causing them to fall into one pit leads to even more pitfalls.

"Several decades ago on the Earth where you soon will be inhabiting Izbos, urged on by demons, there were lingering race animosities among some of the white skins against those of black skin that had been freed from slavery in the not too distant past."

I was confused when I heard many groans of disapproval after Ugar's last words. Ugar moved his hands up and down to quiet the class.

"I know, I know, you all were greatly saddened to see the end of slavery. Certainly it was a pinnacle of demon joy to see all the misery it caused among the black skins and how thoroughly it perverted the white skins away from the principles of the Twelve Curses and led to an embrace of the Thirteen Sacred Blessings.

"Not to worry, even greater destruction was coming and in a marvelous, insidious, demonic way.

"After slavery ended, spurred on by relentless demon persuasion, many of the white skins were convinced that the black skins were getting too uppity and actually believed they should have the same equal rights and access to property and opportunities as the white skins.

"Even more alarming to the white skins was the realization that the black skins were having more babies than the white skins. In a few decades, they could be the majority population in some areas!

"To counter this perceived threat to white skin dominance, demonically influenced white skin leaders decided that the perfect tool to control the growth of the black skin population and any other off-color Izbo, was to remove the stigma of unmarried sex and eliminate the often unintended consequences with legalized abortion after the quickening.

"Abortion of course had been practiced since ancient Izbo times and was considered perfectly fine by most Izbos, including religious ones, as long as it was done before the quickening, when the soul of the Izbo first entered the fetus and began moving and responding to stimulus.

"Because pre-quickening abortions were so widely accepted, by itself that practice did little to instill demonic values in Izbos. However, it was just the beginning of Lord Lucifer's plan to make a lie become the truth.

"Under demonic guidance abortion leaders fought political battles to legalize removing Izbo fetuses in the months after the quickening. In true demonic misdirection, they did so under the guise of supporting women's health and well-being.

"Their success in achieving their goals was only possible because they convinced enough Izbos that life did not actually begin with the quickening, but only after a full-term birth. Therefore, abortion was merely a woman's right to do as she wished with her body.

"Abortion clinics in non-white skin neighborhoods soon achieved the desired goals: births of non-white-skin babies fell wherever abortion was legal.

"This demonic campaign of deception was so successful that it quickly spread beyond the original minority neighborhoods and was embraced by the white skins as well. Under the unassailable banner of women's rights, it was soon touted as an inalienable right of a woman in regards to her own body."

"Think about how insidiously wonderful this practice is! With unrelenting demonic influence, we succeeded in getting Izbos to torturously kill their own children while convincing them they were doing something good!

"We persuaded them that it was not selfish, but prudent and wise to not be burdened with raising a child, especially if they were already economically challenged or unmarried. They happily accepted the justification that they were not being selfish or taking a child's life, but were hurting no one and merely helping themselves.

"Over time as the tendrils of the faux liberation of post-quickening abortion crept further into their lives, Izbos moral values in many other areas declined.

"Once it was acceptable to take a life without consequences, anything else was far less of an offense. Acts that had previously been morally repugnant were no longer considered to be.

"Izbos were freed to have sex with whomever they wished as often as their carnal urges desired, without needing to worry about the consequences of an unplanned pregnancy or public shame and scorn."

Ugar rubbed his long-nailed fingers together in glee. His eyes bugged out with an insane look and his wide fang-baring smile was grotesque and frightening.

"As a notable side benefit, this marvelously divisive issue of abortion successfully put Izbos at each other's throats, with ardent supporters of a woman's right to decide what happens with their body, opposed by equally fervent defenders of the old paradigm of protecting life after the quickening."

Ugar suddenly began to laugh hysterically. He could barely stop even though he seemed to be trying. Finally he haltingly got out what he was trying to say.

"I was thinking about how absurd it is that I need to explain these simple tactics of demon domination to you morons. It is funny in a sad sort of way that for all your thousands of years of life, and all your opportunities to gain knowledge, which is the most important of all of the 13 Sacred Blessings, you and your ilk are still imbeciles!

"Why is that? Why are you cretins still just trying to inhabit your first Izbo?"

None of the demons answered Ugar's questions. They just sat immobile and silent at their desks.

Ugar showed his displeasure by tapping his fingers impatiently on his desk waiting for someone to answer, but none obliged.

I was expecting Ugar to explode in anger, but he spoke calmly yet sternly to the unresponsive demons.

"When I ask a question, I expect an immediate answer, even if you do not know the answer. Otherwise, I may need to kill you again to wake you up!

"Or even better, use magick to turn you into stones as you are no more responsive than a big rock sitting at your desk, so you might as well be rocks!"

Wow! Ugar's last threat got an immediate reaction. All the demons started shouting out answers at once. It seemed they had a greater fear of being turned into a rock than they did of being killed with a dagger stab through their head.

Ugar smiled a wicked satisfied grin seeing their suddenly frenzied desire to answer his question. None of them accepted any of the blame, and instead found many excuses as to why their millennium of ignorance was not their fault.

After they settled down a bit, they forced Calanstio, the weakest among them, who was barely able to maintain his status as a demon, to stand alone and be their spokesperson. The reasoning apparently being that if he answered poorly and Ugar turned him into a rock, perhaps he would spare the rest of them.

Calanstio stood up quaking a little, knowing his fate might depend upon his answer.

"Your horribleness, although we do not all agree, the majority of us feel we have not been inclined to pursue greater knowledge, even though the demon world affords us many opportunities and institutes to gain more knowledge.

"According to most of my cohorts, the reason for this is, Knowledge is the 13th Sacred Blessing and they were constrained to first follow the 12th Blessing of Indolence, which prevented them from being interested in gaining more knowledge beyond that which required minimal effort."

Calanstio nervously sat down as he could see Ugar already fuming at his answer.

Ugar spoke his next words with measured cadence through gritted teeth obviously trying to hold back his anger.

"How did you halfwits ever conclude that the Sacred Blessings must be followed in numerical order? The proper way to use them is to focus on the ones you need most at any time and knowledge is needed at every time!"

Though he had obviously been trying to hold back his anger, when I saw his eyes light up like embers of a fire, I knew he had not been successful. Suddenly he raised his right hand and pointed his index finger at Calanstio. A beam of fire blasted out of his hand and hit Calanstio squarely in his head blasting it into flaming smithereens.

Several of the other demons began chuckling, obviously happy to see their ploy to focus Ugar's anger on the spokesperson worked and that Calanstio had suffered the brunt of his wrath, but that was not the case for long.

Without saying another word, Ugar once again lifted his right hand pointing his finger at one demon after another. In quick succession, he shot a fire bolt at each of their heads. In a matter of just a few seconds, the entire class remained sitting at their desks with tendrils of smoke rising from the smoldering stumps of their neck where their heads had been.

Ugar wiggled his fingers on both hands around as if exercising them from cramps, then disappeared from the room in the blink of an eye.

I guess class was over for the day. I waited around for some time for the demons to reconstitute and see what they would do next, but none of them came back to life. Perhaps they really were dead this time and would not be returning.

With nothing further happening in the class, I willed myself back home to my bed and a sound sleep. When I awoke refreshed in the morning, my first thoughts were recalling all I had seen and heard in my travels the previous night.

I chuckled and commended myself for my highly interesting vivid dreams, fairly certain now that because they were so bizarre they could be nothing else.

CHAPTER
Eleven

I returned the next two nights to the book closet in the demon classroom and was disappointed each time that none of the demons had reconstituted, neither Thalgin nor Ugar had returned, and nothing at all was happening, just thirteen, lifeless, headless demons sitting at their desks.

The one interesting thing I noted was, if I was having a Lucid Dream it was unlike any other. Though I had complete control of my thoughts and actions, nothing else I desired to occur changed.

I imagined the demons getting their heads back and returning to life, but nothing happened. I imagined Thalgin and Ugar returning and getting into a big fight, but they never appeared and the room remained eerily silent.

I walked into the windowless, wood-paneled classroom and tried to open the ornately carved wooden door with an iron lever handle to see what I would encounter on the other side. But despite my best efforts the door remained tightly shut.

I walked up to the blue-skinned demon and poked him on his back just below his shoulder. His cold, headless body seemed to have real substance and it slumped over on top of his desk from the force of my poke.

With absolutely nothing happening after two nights my strange dream world had actually become very boring. I returned home and decided that the next night would be my last visit to the demon classroom unless there was some new interesting activity. I definitely wanted to learn more about this variant type of Lucid Dream, but concluded I would need to find a new place to explore if there continued to be nothing interesting happening at the room of lifeless, headless demons.

I guess the saying that the *third time is a charm,* must be true, at least it was in this instance, because when I popped into the closet on the third night everything was back to normal. Ugar was ranting at the demons and all thirteen sat dutifully at their desks, with their fully restored heads, very much alive. Obviously, some types of demon deaths took longer to recover and reconstitute than others. I tucked that thought away into my mental file to remember.

I stayed quietly peeking out the crack for at least fifteen minutes listening to Ugar berating his students while extolling the virtues of the demon world and the weaknesses of Izbos. It was just the same old spiel. I wasn't learning anything new about demons or my variant Lucid Dream. Though all the demons were back, I was still bored. I found myself no longer paying close attention to Ugar's rantings and had just decided to go find a different world to visit in my night travels, when everything changed in an instant!

I heard Ugar tell the class, "today we have a visitor, one that will teach you many things with hands-on experience, which is the best way to learn. After this, I am done wasting my time with you miscreants. Go find your Izbo, inhabit them, degrade them, and use them to ruin the lives of as many other Izbos as possible."

I perked up at the announcement of a visitor arriving. Finally something out of the normal routine that might be interesting.

Ugar reached over to open the hinged top of a simple cube-shaped wooden box on his desk, and withdrew a small, peculiar device about the size of a basketball. It had a smooth outer metal ring that appeared to be made of gold, with two successively smaller inner rings; the middle one was the color of silver and the smallest looked like it was copper.

Ugar held the device by the outer ring with one hand before he set the base down on his desk. The strangest part about it was that the rings just seemed to be floating in space. At least from my vantage point, I couldn't determine how they were attached to one another or to the flat base.

Ugar looked up at the class and asked, "which of you poor excuses for a demon can tell me what this is?"

None of the demons replied. Ugar let out a sigh of exasperation.

"Of course it is a mystery to all of you. I should expect nothing less from a room full of clueless dunces!"

Ugar gently patted the top ring which was in a vertical position on the device. "This is a Yargon," Ugar said with apparent pride. "It is a very rare device from my personal collection, fashioned by the Davos of Farvely. I had to torture and kill six of them before I finally persuaded one of them to make it for me."

Along with every demon in the room, I was intently paying attention now as this was definitely new and interesting.

"What does it do?" one brave demoness ventured to ask. I expected to see Ugar blast her with a fire bolt for her impertinence.

But he just smiled baring his fangs again and replied, "It will help us get to know our visitor more completely."

Ugar pushed what I assumed to be a button on the base and the three rings began to rotate out of sync with each other, and the Yargon device begun to emit a quiet but high-pitched humming sound.

"Now let me introduce you to our visitor," Ugar continued.

He pointed directly at the book closet I was hiding in. "Behind those closed doors, peering through the crack, listening and observing us for all the days of this class is an Izbo, in a substantive state that you can grab and torture! Get him!"

Yikes! I had been discovered! I closed my eyes and quickly willed myself back home, but nothing happened! I tried again; still nothing. Hearing the clamor of desks being shoved out of the way and an angry group of demons racing to be the first to the closet door I was out of time!

As I had done once before, I faded back into the corner of the book closet and imagined and projected that I was just a book.

The closet doors were ripped open and I saw the heads of three frightful demons poking into my nebulous sanctuary. *Nothing here but books,* I projected. *Nothing here but books*, I kept repeating and projecting from my mind.

But the diversion didn't work this time. The ferocious, muscular blue-skinned demon reached in, grabbed me by the neck, and lifted me off the ground with one hand. I struggled with my legs flailing about while I tried to pry his death grip off my throat, but to no avail.

How can this be happening? I shouted with fear to myself in my mind. I was supposed to be immaterial, like a ghost without substance, able to blink away instantly or change what was occurring as I willed. No blue skin terror of a demon should be able to physically grab me! Even worse, it hurt! I physically felt the choking pressure as he squeezed my neck. I winced as the sharp points of his long nails embedded into my flesh.

The other demons moved all the desks to the edge of the room and blue skin slammed me hard on my back onto the wooden floor in the center of the room. All thirteen demons, plus Ugar, gathered around me in a circle.

As horrifying as that was, it became even more frightening when I realized I was naked! Lying on the floor with all the demons towering above me, I was more intimidated and worried than I had ever imagined I could be.

I tried numerous thought commands that would easily work in any of my Lucid dreams, beginning with having some clothes on, to having some weapons, to simply going back home. It was all futile. I still remained naked and defenseless, surrounded by what seemed from my low elevation prone position on the floor, to be gigantic demons!

Ugar came up and kicked me hard with the tip of his pointy black shoe causing me to involuntarily let out a yelp as I winced in pain. What happened to his surf-boy sandals I wondered as an aimless disconnected thought?

He looked at me with utter contempt like prey hardly worth the effort of the hunter.

"Foolish Izbo, you thought you could outfox a Level 13 demon? I have known you were hiding in the book closet from the moment I first appeared in this classroom. You can hide your body but not your aura; not from me. But I had to be patient. Because of your ability to untraceably vanish in an instant back to your home, I couldn't capture you until I could leave the class for some time and return with my Yargon.

"As long as it is running, that marvelous magickal device nullifies anyone's ability to vanish away, even demons, unless they know its' secret. Equally important in your case, it makes the normally incorporeal bodies of strongly psychic Izbo visitors like yourself have bodies of substance here in the 3rd Dimension that we can capture, torture and kill.

"I am happy to let you know that you have done your last transit back home. On this floor is where you shall die. And dying will not send you back home as it did with that hapless demon Gilgore who thought you were a Taz. When we kill you here, your body back in your pitiful world will also die.

"But not to worry, we will not be killing you yet. There is much wonderful torture we must enjoy first. And while you entertain us with your screams of agony, I will be able to tell the class more about your strange psychic abilities so they will be better prepared when they meet others like you.

"Secure him spread-eagled," Ugar ordered.

Immediately several demons dropped down and pinned me to the floor. My legs and arms were spread out and some other demons handed them thick leather straps that were wrapped around my ankles and wrists. Heavy nails were pounded with hammers through the excess length of the straps, securing my naked, spread eagled body tightly to the wooden floor.

Ugar opened the palm of his hand and picked up a tiny object that was the size and shape of a small gelatin capsule, except it was black and had a dull metallic look. He held the pill up and there were audible gasps from several of the demons.

Ugar looked around the circle. "Oh yes, this is what you think it is, a Zakcon," he said with ghoulish delight to the demons. "By the looks of fear I see, it would seem that some of you have had experience on the receiving end of these little wonders."

Ugar held out his palm. "Usually one Zakcon is sufficient to torture someone until they are driven insane from the pain, but I am going to show you an infinitely more painful and insidious method of torture using not one, but seven Zakcons!"

There was another gasp from the encircling group of demons. I was sure I was going to be a big disappointment to them. If demons were threatened and put in terrifying pain by a single Zakcon, there was no way I was going to last long if Ugar was going to use seven on me!

Ugar grabbed a Zakcon from his hand and gave it to a demoness. He gave a second to another demon. "Put one inside each ear," he directed.

He handed out two more and instructed the demons to, "put one up each nostril of his nose."

He put one more in the hand of one of the demonesses and instructed her to: "Put it in his mouth. Attach it with a fishhook to the inside of his cheek so he cannot spit it out."

The demoness squatted down over me and she stank horribly as if she had never taken a bath; ever! She pried open my mouth with her filthy fingers and jabbed the hook viciously into my inner cheek. The pain was intense and made me wonder again with some mental exhaustion, just what kind of dark, wayward dream I had gotten myself into.

Ugar handed out two more Zakcons to Calanstio and Belozina. "Put one of these inside his anus and the other inside his penis," he directed.

What? I think my eyes bulged out a bit hearing Ugar's last disgusting instruction. *Leave my butt and penis alone!* I yelled in my head, but I didn't want to give the demons the satisfaction of seeing my terror. I tried to remain calm and just looked up at the ceiling as I endured the indignity of the last two Zakcon insertions. Both were painful and terribly embarrassing, but at least the pain was less than the fish hook in the cheek.

Ugar was standing directly in front of me. He waved his hand in the air and said with a guttery growl, "Thomba!"

A glowing, translucent green dial about the size of a fist appeared floating in the air in front of him. He reached out and turned the dial. Immediately I felt terrible pain racing through every nerve in my body. I involuntarily screamed out in agony, which elicited fiendish smiles and murmurs of satisfaction from the demons surrounding me.

After a minute or so my body adjusted to the pain and I was able to grit my teeth together and prevent myself from letting the demons hear me scream again.

Ugar looked at me seeming to be quite satisfied with his handiwork. He pointed at me as he began talking to his demon students.

"Some of you may have encountered one or more of these strange Izbos during the times when you were tormenting other Izbos in their dreams.

"Though their physical body sleeps in places far away, because of their strong psychic abilities, they can come into our presence with ethereal substance and see and hear us. From the description Gilgore gave that I overheard before I deposed Thalgin, this is what he experienced with this Izbo," he said, pointing at me.

"This is an Izbo with very strong psychic abilities. There is a wide range of psychic talents and I don't know what his are. Shall we find out?" he asked with evil glee in his voice as he turned the glowing green dial up another notch.

I thought I had already experienced the worst possible pain with the first jolt, but this new level was unbearable. I couldn't stop myself from screaming in agony, not just once, but continually. Thankfully, after a minute or so, Ugar turned the dial back down to the lower setting.

Ugar kicked me in the testicles sending rockets of pain shooting out. Even so, it was somewhat masked by the pain I was feeling all over my body from the insidious torture device he was using.

"What are your psychic gifts?" Ugar demanded.

I shook my head and through my gritted teeth told him, "I see auras."

He kicked me viciously in the balls again. "Bah!" "Everybody can see auras. What else can you do?"

I was hoping to pass out from all the pain I was experiencing, but it wasn't happening. Once again through my tightly clenched teeth and an uneven rasping breath, I answered Ugar.

"You know I can consciously travel between worlds when my physical body is asleep. But until you started torturing me and I was physically feeling this pain, I thought all of this was just a very vivid, strange type of Lucid Dream. Now, this is all just pain and mystery."

Ugar turned up the Zakcon dial to a still higher setting. I was writhing in agony and screaming uncontrollably. After what seemed like forever he dialed it back to the lower setting. I am not ashamed to say that at this point I was sobbing as I tried to recover from the pain. I couldn't help myself.

Ugar grinned at me prominently displaying his fangs.

"You will be happy to know that though the pain you feel is real, the body you think is feeling it, is not. Your body here is just a magickal creation, like an animated Golem, to house your consciousness and allow us to physically touch and torture you, Now what else can you do?" he spat out venomously.

I took a big breath and let it out before answering. "I can see the future sometimes."

"You are trying to deceive me!" He stomped on the floor in anger. "The gifts you speak of are simple psychic gifts. You were not able to return night after night to the closet you hid in with just simple psychic abilities."

I didn't know what else to tell him. If I had known what he wanted to hear, I would have gladly said it just to appease him; but I was ignorant of what it was he wanted me to say.

"This is useless," Ugar spat out in disgust. "He is less than I had hoped he would be. I am going to leave the pain setting low. It will prolong his agony and slowly rob him of his vital essence.

"When it is low enough, one of the strong among you will be able to inhabit him and cause him to return to his home. With his psychic abilities, he will be a much better host than whomever you have a skin for, so just make a good trade for the skin with another demon.

"I have other pressing business but will return shortly." With those parting words, Ugar vanished in a blink, along with the dial to his insidious torture device. But the unrelenting pain in every fiber of my body remained.

A few of the demons squatted down so they could be closer to me. One bald oaf held a broad-bladed knife up.

"I am going to cut off some souvenirs; a couple of toes, a couple of fingers, an ear and his penis. Three gold warals if anyone else wants one, except the penis will be twenty gold warals because there is only one."

A demoness squatted down on the opposite side of my prone body and held up an even bigger knife. "We don't need to buy souvenirs from you, we can cut off our own."

Big knives appeared in the hands of one demon after another. Leering at me, they all began to squat down to cut off whatever part of my Golem body they wanted for a souvenir.

Suddenly a bright white light illuminated the room from behind the circle of demons. They all looked up in surprise and the circle of demons surrounding me parted as they turned to confront the newcomer in their midst.

I weakly lifted my head so I could see what was going on but thought I must be hallucinating in my pain. I blinked my eyes strongly trying to clarify the picture but still saw a slim, well-formed middle-aged woman with long black hair, in a flowing, floor-length white dress who didn't look anything at all like a demon.

Apparently, the demons didn't think she was one of them either as they all quickly charged at her screaming fiendishly, their hands full of a wide assortment of deadly weapons. I felt sorry for the poor woman; thirteen against one would not be much of a fight. Hopefully, she could blink out before they killed her.

Before the first demon could cut, stab, or pound her with one of their weapons, from out of nowhere she whipped out a long double-edged sword with an ornate hilt. Its size would seem to be too much for anyone other than a strong man to wield very long, but the lady in white swung her sword with amazing speed and accuracy.

She simultaneously defended herself and attacked. Her sword was a blur. It seemed as if it was everywhere at once as she wove an impenetrable net of protection against the simultaneous assault of thirteen crazed demons.

Nor did the lady stand in one place. She moved throughout the room with the fluid movements of a dancer as she fended off the demons and dispatched them one by one with her sword. She even stepped over my prone body a few times as she fought her battles.

One odd thing was, every time she killed a demon they blinked out. That was curious, as I remembered that Ugar had said not even demons would be able to blink out while his Yargon device was running.

To my utter astonishment, the lady in white had soon dispatched all the demons except blue skin and skinny guy. But a sword thrust forward into blue skin and then a thrust behind her into the skinny guy, without even looking, and all the demons were gone!

CHAPTER

Twelve

T he elegantly dressed lady warrior took a few deep
breaths recovering from her deadly exertion and
looked at me with her head cocked in curiosity.
Through everything, including up to that very moment,
I was still experiencing excruciating pain wracking my
body from Ugar's Zakcons.

The lady walked over and stood beside me. I was
embarrassed to be lying naked on the floor, but she
didn't seem to notice.

She held out her left arm horizontal from her body
with her palm facing down centered above my abdomen.

"Ookata!" she spoke loudly. No sooner had she said
the word than all of the Zakcons that had been placed
into my orifices popped out of my body and flew up to
her hand. She grasped them tightly in her hand and a
stream of black dust filtered out from the bottom of her
clenched fist.

Without a word spoken to me, she strode over to the

desk where the Yargon device was still spinning. Lifting her sword over her head she brought it crashing down, shattering the Yargon and splitting the desk completely in half.

She walked back and stood next to me again. Once more she held her hand out above my body.

"Caz Ookata," she said in a commanding voice. This time the nails binding me to the floor ripped out of the wood and flew across the room embedding themselves in the far wall.

With the nails gone I was able to easily slip off the thick leather cuffs. I sat up gingerly and very, very painfully. With pain still reverberating throughout my body, I slowly pulled one of the cuffs over to cover my privates.

The lady in white looked at me intently with vivid, sky-blue eyes. Once more she extended her arms, this time both of them, and laid her hands on top of my head. "Lajish," she spoke with firm quietness. As the last sound from that marvelous word escaped her lips, all of the pain in my body just vanished. I felt renewed, refreshed, and great!

"Thank you, thank you, thank you," I said in profuse gratitude. "Are you an angel?" I asked, certain that she had to be. But she surprised me with her answer.

She smiled and a pleasant little laugh escaped her lips. "No, I am not an angel and you are not a demon. I'm sorry I did not arrive sooner and that you had to endure this torture, but whatever are you doing here?" Her voice had an enchanting accent that I thought must be French.

I neglected to answer her question as I was too

consumed with questions of my own. "If you are not an angel, then what are you?" I asked in wonderment. "You just bested thirteen demons in only a few minutes, who themselves were the strongest victors in an earlier massive fight of thirty demons!

"What are you?" I repeated in awe, knowing I could not be looking at a normal mortal woman.

Once again she surprised me with her answer. "I am a mortal woman, just as you are a mortal man."

"I didn't say anything about your mortal state," I stammered. "Can you read my mind?"

She nodded her head in acknowledgment. "If your mind is open, we can connect telepathically."

I shook my head in negation. "That is not one of my abilities. I guess it is a one-way street."

She smiled her sweet smile again. "No, it is one of your abilities too. You just need to practice and it will come to you."

"How do you know? Do you know me?" I asked.

"I do not even know your name," she replied, "but telepathy is a latent psychic ability of all humans, especially you."

"Why especially me?" I wondered.

"I can feel it and see it in your aura," she told me. "You are strong. Your psychic energy center is very active. Telepathy and much more will come easily to you if you apply effort to manifest your gifts."

It dawned on me that I was being very rude throwing questions at my savior without even introducing myself or inquiring the same of her. "If I may ask, what is your name?"

She hesitated for a moment as if pondering whether she would reveal her name to me. Then looking me steadfastly in my eyes she said, "Genavieve."

"Your turn, Mr. Naked Man. What is your name, and how did you come to be in this place?"

Oops, I guess she did notice I was naked. Even though she had saved me from the demons, I hesitated for some reason to tell her my name, but relented and revealed my birth name. "I am Jesse. I thought I was coming here with my ethereal Night Self in a vivid, Lucid Dream, but now I realize this is some altered form of reality. It seems too outlandish to be real, but somehow it is."

Genavieve didn't respond. She cocked her head a bit and looked at me as if she was a little perplexed, so I continued with my explanation.

"I just recently began encountering demons in my Night Self travels. I found this to be some kind of demon school. I came here several nights to learn more about this world. Things just went bad when they discovered me hiding in the closet. Although I guess Ugar knew I was there all along."

Her face flashed alert wariness. "You saw Ugar?"

I nodded my head affirmatively. "I listened to his lectures to the demons for some hours before he pulled me out of the book closet, and turned me into a Golem so he could torture me. He actually left just a minute or so before you arrived."

"So close," Genavieve whispered in frustration.

I was incredulous. "You wanted to meet Ugar?" I shook my head doubtfully and immediately tried to dissuade Genevieve from confronting him.

"You are obviously very adept with your sword, but I watched Ugar in action. He can shoot beams of fire out of his hands. I watched him blast off the heads of thirteen demons in a matter of seconds. You would never even get close to him with your sword.

"You are lucky he wasn't here. Speaking of which, when he left, he told the demons he would be returning soon, so we need to be leaving before he comes back!"

Genavieve nodded her head in agreement, but with a different slant than I was planning.

"You are right, you should go home now Jesse. Perhaps we will meet again someday."

"Where will you be going?" I asked.

"I will be staying here awaiting the return of Ugar. I tracked him here to confront him and am most happy to hear he will be returning soon," she replied stoically.

"What? That's crazy!" I protested. "I just told you as good as you are, that you are no match for that monster. Why would you seek out a confrontation with him anyway? He has really big powers and he knows astounding magick."

She smiled at me with an all-knowing type of smile. "I have a few powers, and know a little magick myself," she replied almost mischievously. "I will be fine."

I started to protest what I perceived to be her foolishness again but she cut me off. "Go home Jesse. Do not return to the demon domains; it is not your time; you are not ready."

I started to reply to that cryptic comment but before the words came out of my mouth she waved her hand in front of her and said in a commanding tone, "barbaton."

As I was looking directly into her sky blue eyes I began to dematerialize and fade away. The last words I heard her say were the most confusing and enigmatic of all.

"By the way, your body is not a Golem."

Immediately I awoke wide-eyed and awestruck in my bed and I knew my life would never be the same.

CHAPTER
Thirteen

I was brimming with excitement and amazement at my recent experiences and looked forward with great anticipation to recounting everything to Skye, my adventure mate of recent years at the earliest opportunity. These would be the type of experiences she would love to hear about. Then I remembered three things that completely changed my mind.

I recalled my first encounter with the demon plucking the feathers out of the live goose who threatened to come after me in my physical awake state. If that was possible, demons could be a real danger to Skye if I spoke about my experiences and exposed her to that world.

Then I recalled the overwhelming power of Ugar and my torture at his hand. What little I knew of demons included that they were nothing to be trifled with. Besides warping your mind, they had plenty of physical powers, from brute strength to fire bolts that could hurt you as well. I wasn't sure which of their abilities could be active in the physical world, but didn't want to risk Skye being one to find out.

Lastly, I remembered the parting words of Genavieve that I should not return to the demon domains because I was not ready. If I was so ill-prepared and unaware myself to be around demons, it would be completely irresponsible to expose someone currently in blissful ignorance of the unseen world to possible danger.

Sadly, as much as I wanted to share my experiences with Skye, I accepted the reality that I really knew very little about demons and the ways they could hurt others. I couldn't risk my ignorance of the demon world possibly opening Skye up for any kind of mental or physical attack.

Perhaps I was just being overly cautious, but I choose to live by one of the mottos of the Wilderness Survival class I used to teach: *when in doubt, don't*. Over many years I had come to trust my doubts as psychic insights that should not be ignored.

I reflected for a week or so on Genavieve's admonition to not return to the demon domains, and I half-heartedly tried to follow her direction. During the next several nights I used my Lucid Dreaming Night Self to travel to some of my favorite places and activities in the past, such as volcano hopping on Xeador or walking amidst the thousands of vividly colored butterflies in the beautiful forests of Cobalis.

Though visits to these fascinating worlds were still breath-taking, my pleasure and appreciation for their wonder was not to the level it had been in the past.

A couple of nights I tried visiting worlds I had

never been to that I had overheard good things about on other travels. It was interesting seeing new creatures, fauna, people, clothing and architecture, but the truth was, I found myself longing to return to the demon domain to learn more about it. Everything there was so different and bizarre that I had to admit I was fascinated.

Until recently, all of my night travels had always been to places on my own planet Earth, or to other planets in our solar system or the Milky Way galaxy; places someone with an Earth-bound telescope could see in the distant sky.

Yet I realized that somehow, inexplicably to me at the moment, the dominions of the demons must be more unreachable than what we could normally see with our eyes. Whether that was in some other universe, or in an invisible realm that co-existed and interfaced with our physical world, I did not know.

And somehow when I was in the demon realms, my ethereal body had some type of physical substance. Genavieve's last words were that my body was not a Golem. Inexplicably my Night Self was no longer just like an invisible ghost, as I had been in all the previous night travels of my entire life. I could see the demons and they could see me. I could hear them and they could hear me. I could touch them and they could touch me, and hurt me very painfully, I cautiously reminded myself.

For better or worse, I decided to return to the demon domains that night. But where to go, that was the vexing question? My first thought was to go find Genavieve. I was a blank slate when it came to the demon world, but she obviously had the experience to fill in the blanks.

On the other hand, it was fairly certain that she would be angry that I had returned and she might refuse to help me further. Though she had saved my life, she never really told me who or what she was. Was she truly an ally? What was she doing in the demon world? She said she wasn't an angel. Was she some kind of variant demon? She seemed pretty intent on dispatching Ugar. Maybe she was part of a demon group that opposed him. All questions I would like to know the answers to, but for the present, I thought it best to not seek out Genavieve.

I assumed that could mean that only higher-level demons had that ability. If that was true, I should be able to find a way to safely spy at other locations in the demon world as I had done when I lay concealed by forest growth and listened in on the group of demons around the campfire.

Other than Ugar, none of the other demons were able to detect my presence by my aura when I was hidden in the book closet. I assumed that could mean that only higher level demons had that ability. If that was true, I should be able to find a way to safely spy at other locations in the demon world as I had done when I lay concealed by forest growth and listened in on the group of demons around the camp fire.

Contemplating my choices, I decided I needed to reconnoiter as much of the demon domain as possible so I could have a better understanding of its extent. I made a list of places I wanted to visit if they existed, as I was not really sure what would happen if I commanded my Night Self to go to a place that did not exist.

I planned to blink in and blink back home before anyone I might surprise with my appearance would have time to react. I was particularly worried that now it might be possible for my Night Self to be physically hurt, and fretted about what would happen to my sleeping body back home if that occurred.

In case my Night Self didn't remember, I wrote down all the places I wanted to visit on an open page of a spiral notebook that I had laid on the nightstand beside my bed. Whenever my Night Self blinked back home, the list could be checked for the next destination.

My prospective visiting list was pure speculation, as I wasn't sure any of the places even existed. Prior to my recent observations of demons, I just thought of them in a nebulous, undefined sort of way. I pictured them living primitively somewhere down below the surface in the underworld, as they are often depicted in books and movies.

My list for the first night included visiting:

- the largest congregation of demons

- the largest school, if one existed, as so far I had only seen a small classroom

- any non-demon race that existed in the demon domains

- any place I could see magick

- any place I could learn more about the demon hierarchy

I also wanted to test the abilities of my Night Self. In the past, I tended to take long journeys with my Night Self, simply by thinking of the location and then I was there. But once I arrived, my Night Self would move around, sometimes walking, sometimes floating and slowly flying to explore and move from one point to another.

However, I would not be very well hidden from demons if I was walking around or floating by over their heads. I wasn't even sure if the demon world variant of my Night Self could even float. As that variant in some inexplicable way had physical substance and was not just an ethereal form, it might be too heavy to get off the ground!

When I was in the demon demesne I wanted to test to see if I could blink within the realm and not just back home. Could I blink to the other side of a room? Could I blink from the inside to the outside of a building, or to the other side of a forest? I had never tried anything like that, but I was determined to do so that night. If I was successful, it could prove to be a very valuable defensive skill.

Once I fell asleep and my Night Self had cognizance, I willed myself to go to the realm of the demons, to a place I could be hidden and could observe the greatest number of demons in one location. I hoped this would allow me not only to get a better handle on the demon population and how they lived, but also to see a wide variety of characters so I could have a better understanding of how demons might look.

I wanted to see if they lived in small groups in caves underground or maybe in little hovels or villages, or small buildings like the windowless classroom.

Thus far the largest demon crowd I had seen was

the group of twelve that included Gilgore and Varina huddled around the campfire in the forest, and the thirty students, plus a teacher in the classroom. I had a lot of questions and this was the night to begin finding answers.

I closed my eyes and willed my Night Self to appear in a hidden location where I could secretly observe a very large group of demons.

When my Night Self materialized, I was in a small tower room made of stone blocks. I appeared standing next to one of four narrow horseshoe arched windows that were glassless and open to the air, overlooking a vast city on a bright sunny, cloudless day.

The altered version of my Night Self that I appeared to have when I was in the demon world could feel physical sensations and I noted that the air temperature was warm and pleasant, although there was a rank unpleasant odor permeating the air.

I moved across the room and peered out each of the other three windows that were evenly spaced around the circular room. The city extended as far as I could see in every direction! That was a shock to my expectations.

All of the buildings appeared to be made mostly of stone. Most were only one or two stories tall with an occasional structure of perhaps three to five floors. As far as I could ascertain, the tower I was in was the tallest structure in the city. My first thought after looking at all of the stone buildings was that they must not need to worry about earthquakes here.

Looking down from my raised vantage point, I saw a disorganized web of crooked dirt streets spreading out into the distance, crowded with a wide variety of what I assumed to be hundreds of demons walking to various destinations.

Like the demons in the classroom and the forest, those on the city streets came in many hues and physical appearances. They all seemed just as intent at dressing as outlandishly as the earlier demons I had observed.

One interesting aspect I observed was that walking seemed to be the only method of transportation. There were no wheeled vehicles, from hand carts to autos.

Other common features of human cities were conspicuously absent from the demon city as well. I could not see any animals whatsoever: no cats, dogs, birds or horses; nor were any trees visible. It was as if the city was dead to life except for the demons swarming about their barren stone city.

Before I could make any additional observations, I heard the shuffling of footsteps climbing the stairs of the tower. As there was no place to hide in the small empty room, I quickly blinked back home as soon as the tower door began to swing inward.

I awoke in my bed lying on my back and pondering with fascination and amazement all that I had observed in just the few minutes I had been in the demon demesne. There had certainly been a LOT more demons than I had expected to see!

And the city was so vast! Considering how many demons I saw just in the small area I was in, there must be hundreds of thousands or even millions of them in the city!

What did they all do? How did they spend their

time? What were all those buildings? Were they homes, businesses, or both? If they were businesses, what type of enterprises did demons engage in? Did they eat? Did they socialize? Did they have jobs? Who built their city? And where in the universe was this demon city in relation to my planet Earth? There were so many more new questions I needed answers to that I couldn't wait to go back to sleep so I could have my Night Self visit the next destination on my list.

When my Night Self was once again conscious, I willed myself to go to the largest demon institute of higher learning. I was completely unsure of what to expect. Would I just end up in another small classroom of around 30 students, or a large school complex?

As in my last travel to the demon city, I found myself in a small, open window tower overlooking a building complex. This tower was only about three floors up from the ground and no building in the group around me was more than two floors.

Once again almost everything was made of stone, but this place had a far different, more human-like ambiance. In many ways it looked similar to a small college campus. There were about a dozen large buildings sitting up on a hill surrounded by barren, desert-like open land. The cluster of red-tiled roofed buildings had a classiness and architectural style reminiscent of Southern California. And unlike the demon city, this campus had palm trees and even a large water fountain in the center of the campus, which all of the buildings were oriented around.

Several dozen demons were walking through the central plaza in various directions and everyone was distinguished as a student by the multiple books they carried crooked in their arms.

I decided this would be a perfect place to experiment with blinking to nearby locations. To limit the risk of instant recognition as a non-demon if I happened to blindly blink into a room full of demons, I imagined myself dressed as eccentrically as possible so I would blend in.

As I imagined myself so I became. I spiked my short hair with hair gel, put on a pair of Khaki safari shorts, and wore black sneakers with one calf-high pink sock with blue spots and another ankle-high striped yellow sock. I wore an open chest leather vest that had a swirl of black and white on the front and a putrid green color on the back with a large black circle with a dagger image in the center.

Wanting to look the part of a student, but oblivious to what books demon students read, I carried a hardbound Webster's Unabridged English dictionary under my arm. Disguised as incognito as I could be, I willed myself to test my short hop blinking ability by appearing at the walkway across the courtyard, as only a few demons were passing through it at the time.

I was elated to see my short-distance blink worked perfectly! I ended up several feet behind a group of three demons walking together exactly where I had pictured myself materializing.

Standing beside a bare stone wall with not even an alcove to hide behind, I had no choice but to begin walking in the direction of the demons, hoping anyone seeing me would just assume I was another demon student.

The demons I was walking behind entered a classroom. Not being brave or stupid enough to go in there, especially recalling my recent torture in a room full of demon students, I made a ninety-degree turn to the right down a narrow passageway just before the entrance to the classroom. It was dimly illuminated only by the daylight coming in from the far end, about fifty feet away.

I peered cautiously out of the far end, which opened up to another courtyard. It was much smaller than the main courtyard and was open on each side, with a single two-story building on the far side.

About half a dozen demons were milling about in the courtyard. I glanced back down the alley that I had come through, worried that other demons might take the same route to this courtyard, trapping me with demons behind me and in front of me.

Off to the right, through the open spot in the courtyard, I could see some gently rolling hills in the hazy distance. It seemed like a good time to test my blinking ability to a distant spot barely within my view.

It was an uneventful successful blink. The very second I willed myself to the hilltop on the far horizon that I focused upon, I was there. However, I soon found nothing else was.

As I scanned the horizon in every direction, it was just barren. Other than the oasis of the school I could still see as a spec on the horizon, everywhere around me was devoid of life. I might as well have been on the moon. There were no trees, grass, or any sign of any kind of life or habitation.

With absolutely nothing to hold my interest in the wasteland, I decided to blink back to the school. I wanted to learn more of what they taught there.

Without knowing if such a setup even existed, and unsure of where I would end up if it didn't, I willed myself to go to an empty classroom that adjoined one that was actively teaching a class. Immediately I materialized in a room dimly lit by a couple of narrow high windows and I could hear someone speaking on the other side of the wall that I stood next to.

Moving cautiously around the room, I walked over to a wooden plank door that connected to the room with the speaker. The door had no window and I dared not try to open it, but it did have a keyhole in the ornate iron handle plate, like the kind that fit the old long handle keys.

The hole was big enough that squatting down, I could see into the room pretty well, including the speaker at the head of the class, who was a very tall and skinny demon with a mass of short spiky hair on his head, and a long grey beard that came down to his waist. He was dressed in a black suit with a white shirt like a mortician.

Though the speaker's voice was somewhat muffled, I was able to make out his words.

"Now how you cast a spell to capture a basilisk is very important! At the least, if you do it wrong, you will be petrified if the basilisk looks you in the eyes. And worse, if this large, deadly beastie bites you, then you will quickly fall into an extended state of dormancy, similar to banishment, for several hundred years."

Chapter 13

I was overjoyed! This was fantastic! One of my greatest goals was to learn powerful real magick, and here I was listening in on a demon professor teaching it. I couldn't believe my good fortune, and I listened aptly for the professors' next words, hoping it would be about neutral magick and not black magick, as I wanted it to be something I could actually use.

I listened attentively as the professor continued his explanation. "The trick is to understand this is a two-part action. As we covered in yesterday's class on transmogrification, you must first spell yourself to have the appearance of a weasel, at least in the mind of the basilisk, as that is the only creature that a basilisk fears.

"The basilisk's ability to inject poison is nullified when it feels fear. It can still paralyze you by looking you in your eyes, but fear causes its poison glands to seal up. Even if it manages to bite you, no poison will be injected and you will be able to capture it as long as you are careful not to make eye contact and act quickly."

I was breathless with delight as I was listening. I wasn't sure what a basilisk was, but was eager to hear every word that was being said.

The professor continued his explanation. "As quickly as possible, after the basilisk shows initial fear, grab it tightly behind its neck with your hand. Because it still thinks you are a weasel, it will assume your hand is the weasel's mouth, and your fingers its teeth sinking into its neck. It will descend into an even deeper well of fear and go into shock and semi paralysis thinking it is about to be eaten."

The professor suddenly lifted his arm and zipped it

in a crossing motion with his finger pointing in front of him.

"Be warned! If you do not succeed at grasping the basilisk behind its neck within a few seconds of its initial fear of a weasel, it will sense that you are not its mortal enemy. Before you can blink it will move like lightning to bite you as you try to grasp it around its neck and you will be put into extended dormancy. It can also whip its tail around with frightening speed and power and knock you senseless and then bite you!"

The professor pointed to three life-size demon statues at the front of the class. "These are some of the demons that did not act quickly enough and are now good for nothing but storage racks."

He pointed to the demon statue on the far side of the room. "That fellow holding my coat has been gathering dust in this very room for over two hundred years. I have no idea when he or the other two will finally reawaken. Not to discourage you, as the reward is great, but this fate happens to probably nine out of ten demons that try to capture a basilisk.

"However, if you are among the one in ten that is successful, once the basilisk is stupefied by its fear, it will be a simple matter to roll it over onto its back. Cover its eyes with a cloth so you don't have to worry about making eye contact.

"The poison glands are located in little bulges on the neck just behind the head. Carefully insert a syringe needle into the gland and withdraw about a small thimbleful of the liquid, white poison. You can take a similar amount from the gland on the other side of the neck.

"Be exceptionally careful not to let the tiniest drop touch your bare skin as it will rapidly absorb through your skin and have the same effect as if you were bitten, except you will only be immobilized for a few weeks to a month and not completely petrified, depending upon how much poison you absorbed.

"Though greed is one of the Thirteen Sacred Blessings and normally a very wonderful trait, you must restrain your natural instincts and not take more poison than a thimbleful. The basilisk has a natural defense. If too much poison is withdrawn, it will cause it to immediately reawaken in a frenzied state of anger and you will surely be bitten before you can even think to blink away.

"If you manage to extract the basilisk's poison and escape its wrath, you will have gained an immeasurably valuable prize. You can trade even a single drop to other demons for countless gifts and favors. Even Lord Lucifer has been known to barter for basilisk poison from time to time.

"If you decide to keep it all for yourself, just knowing you possess it will immediately make you one of the most feared demons. You can place a drop on the end of your dagger or other weapon and cause the same prolonged state of dormancy to any demon you sink your blade into as if they had been bitten by a basilisk."

I was so intently listening to the demon professor that I did not hear the soft sounds of movement behind me. At the last moment I started to turn my head in reaction to a whisper of sound, but it was too late!

Before I could see an attacker, I felt a burning

sensation flash over my body, followed immediately by complete immobilization. I couldn't even move my lips or blink my eyes. My mind still worked and in a panic I was sure I had just been bitten by a basilisk or stabbed with a basilisk poisoned dagger like the demon professor had just been talking about!

CHAPTER
Fourteen

Unable to move a muscle, I could still think. With great urgency I willed myself back home. To my dismay that did not work either! I was utterly helpless!

Then my situation got even worse. By some unknown means I was blinked away and found myself still completely immobilized, standing in a room with a stone floor and stone walls. The dim illumination came solely from three narrow windows high above my head, at the top of a wall near where it met the angled roof.

I could hear what I thought was more than one demon shuffling behind me. I felt a sharp prod in my back and then a surprisingly angry voice I recognized.

"What are you doing here? Genavieve demanded.

She came around and stood in front of me. "I told you very explicitly not to return to the demon world," she said sternly.

Though still trepidatious about my situation, I felt a

139

wave of relief to see my captor was Genavieve and not some fiendish demon.

I tried to answer her, but of course my lips wouldn't move. Genavieve crossed her arms and looked at me fuming.

"You obviously did not follow my admonition to practice telepathy either, or you would have heard me screaming in your mind at your idiocy."

She looked past me and spoke to someone behind me. "Release him Qadir."

No sooner had she spoken than I felt the same brief full-body hot flash, and my body was once again able to move.

A slim elderly man that had apparently been my captor walked around me and stood beside Genavieve. He was of average height, with a short-cropped grey beard and a full head of grey hair that came down to his shoulders. His dark brown eyes had a twinkle of vitality and I had an immediate sense that this was a man of great experience and wisdom.

Though he had followed Genavieve's order to release me, it was easy to tell by his confident head held high, that he was her equal and not her servant.

"Well?" Genavieve said looking at me full of ire with her arms still crossed, "What have you to say about why you could possibly be so daft to return here? Was your previous near-death experience with demons insufficient? Are you so brave or foolish that you wanted to tempt fate once again by returning to their realm where they have the greatest power, without a clue as to how to defend yourself?"

Chapter 14

I shrugged my shoulders and lifted my eyebrows sheepishly. "I'm sorry to make you so angry. I don't think I really had a choice. Despite the very real possibility of death, I still felt compelled to return.

"After my earlier visits to the demon domains, something inside my heart and mind changed; my own world seemed so much smaller and mundane. I felt as if I had been living cloistered in a building my entire life, and for the first time, opened a door to a far bigger world than I had ever imagined existed. Despite the dangers of the unknown, I had to come to see more, to learn more of this still incomprehensible world."

My explanation did not mollify her and Genavieve was still very irate. "What would you have done if it had been demons that captured you instead of me and Qadir?"

I shrugged my shoulders and opened my palms apart in front of me contritely. "I don't know. Hope for your rescue again?"

Genavieve shook her head in obvious strong disagreement. "Very unlikely; I was happy to help you once, but now that I see you have a death wish, it would be a waste of my time to stand in your way by rescuing you from your foolishness once more."

"But you just did rescue me," I pointed out. "Why else would you have appeared behind me? You are my Guardian Angel, right?" I asked light-heartedly with a happy smile.

Genavieve did not return my warm smile. "We were not here because of you. Your presence was a very unpleasant surprise and interfered with our purpose."

"What was your purpose?" I asked lifting my eyebrows in curiosity.

"It is none of your business what our purpose was," she replied curtly.

"I am going to send you back to your home again right now. And you will NOT return here again! You will have a spell upon you. If you ever return to these domains, you will become violently ill. Every minute you remain, you will become sicker. Your only cure will be to return to your world. Am I being very clear now? Do you understand that you should not return here again?"

I nodded my head in dejected agreement, resigned to be banished back to the safety and boredom of my own world.

Qadir reached over and put a hand on Genavieve's arm. "Wait! Do not spell him or send him home."

Genavieve looked at Qadir with incredulity. "Why would you stop me old friend? He is like a babe. You know he will not last long if he keeps returning here. I am showing him mercy by sending him back and preventing his return."

Qadir shook his head in disagreement. "No, you might as well try to stop the tide from coming in. His destiny will continue to beckon him more every day, even as it did us. He will not be able to resist and he will find a way to return."

"But it is not his time," Genavieve objected. "He has not yet met his catalyst or his auric gold band would have enlarged. His abilities will be feeble until he is energized by his catalyst. At the moment, he is half in his world and half in ours. Without the amplification of his potential by his catalyst, he will surely be killed by the demons before he ever has a chance to fulfill his destiny."

Qadir nodded his head in agreement. "True, he would not survive on his own. That is why I am going to take him on as a protégé."

Genavieve looked at Qadir in wide-eyed shock. "Why would you want to do that, especially when the last time ended so badly?"

Qadir reached out and gently held Genavieve's hand. "We will all always feel the pain of that loss, but it cannot stop us from moving forward. There have always been Adepts and there have always been protégés, and so it must be if we are to continue the fight, as none of us have any longer lives than other mortals.

"With that in mind, I also want to retire."

I thought Genavieve had looked shocked a moment before when Qadir told her he wanted me to be his protégé, but her facial expression then was mild compared to her reaction at his latest statement.

"Retire! Since when?" she exclaimed in astounded disbelief.

"Since now," Qadir answered simply. "I have actually wanted to for a couple of years."

Qadir looked at Genavieve somewhat forlornly. "You know how ridding the world of malevolent demons takes a little of our life force with each banishment, not to mention the normal increasing frailties of simply getting older.

"Well, I want to be able to enjoy some of the splendors and pleasures of my adopted world of Sx while I still have a few years left. Demon hunting has sapped many of the years of my life, and now I do not have too many remaining. It would be so nice to live out the last of my days in tranquility and anonymity. This young man can take my place. I will mentor him. I know it is selfish, but you too will come to the same conclusion once you have been fighting demons as long as I have.

"I never said anything before, as there was no point. I was needed too greatly. But now a way to be replaced has miraculously materialized, and I am going to do everything that I can to make it so."

Genavieve looked at Qadir with sorrowful eyes. "Qadir, you are still greatly needed, now more than ever. Qadir…" her voice trailed off at a loss for further words.

Qadir patted her gently on her back. "It is ok, everything will be fine." He pointed at me. "This young man will be the new Qadir. I promise you he will be an improved version. I assure you nothing will be lost in my retirement. Have faith Genavieve."

Genavieve composed herself before speaking again. Her eyes had watered up and for a moment I thought she was going to shed a tear.

"I want to talk to you more about this soon, in another time and place. I am not fully accepting your choices to retire and making him your protégé."

Qadir smiled at her with a glint of mischievousness and happiness in his eyes. "As you wish, but you know I am unmoving like a rock once I have made a decision."

Genavieve nodded in understanding. "Yes, you are very stubborn Qadir, but even the largest rock can be moved with the proper leverage."

"Don't threaten me Genavieve," Qadir warned with a

disarming smile.

"Not a threat dear friend," she assured him, "just a promise to help you see all aspects of the situation that perhaps you are not yet aware of, or have not considered.

"Do you plan to tell the others?" she asked.

Qadir rubbed his chin in thought for a moment. "I suppose yes, when I see them next. They would find out eventually in any case. You are welcome to tell them if you see them before me."

"Very well," Genavieve said abruptly. "I am returning to Dinan. Our mission today has failed because of his interference," she said pointing at me.

"Good luck with that one. I hope you do not regret introducing him to our life prematurely."

With those final words Genavieve blinked out and I was left alone in an increasingly uncomfortable silence, as Qadir just stared intently at me while gently stroking his short grey beard with his fingers.

CHAPTER
Fifteen

W hat is your name?" Qadir finally asked.

I hesitated before answering. I had learned my real name during an angelic visit in the forest when I was sixteen. I wondered if I should give him that name, my birth name that I had given to Genavieve when we first met, or just make a name up, as there was still a nagging sense of caution in the back of my mind, warning me that everything may not be as it seemed with Genavieve and Qadir.

After all, Deceit was one of the 13 Sacred Blessings of demons. Perhaps everything I had experienced with Genavieve and Qadir was just an elaborate hoax to use me for some nefarious demon purpose. I decided to play it safe and choose the latter option and used a variation of a name I had always fancied from a book I had read many years prior.

"My name is Trevallion."

Qadir fished in a small pocket on the right side of the

satiny vest he was wearing and pulled out a small oblong object. It was perfectly clear and looked like a piece of quartz crystal that had been rounded and polished on both ends to be used as a massage tool. Qadir touched me on the top of my hand with the object and it immediately hazed over and turned completely black.

"It would be best if you did not begin our relationship with a lie," Qadir said solemnly. "Let's try again. What is your true name?"

Whoa! That was a surprise. A portable, magickal lie detector! I was still wary about telling him the name I was known by back home, even though Genavieve already knew it, so I told him the name the angel had called me years ago, "Embrosewyn."

"Embrosewyn what?" Qadir asked a bit impatiently.

"Just Embrosewyn," I answered.

Qadir touched my hand again with his crystal lie detector. This time the upper half turned white and the lower half turned purple. Qadir shook his head with disappointment.

"Well you are telling the truth, that is the white on the crystal, but it is a truth that you should not be telling just yet. The purple reveals that Embrosewyn is your Soul Name. I will keep that secret and advise you to not reveal it to anyone else until after you have progressed beyond being a protégé."

"Why is that?" I asked.

The corners of Qadir's lips lifted in a slightly amused smile. "Until you have received your protégé training, you will be ill-prepared to defend yourself against those who would do you harm.

"Whatever name people know you by is soon known by many others. Word gets out about your name, especially once you start interacting with demons. They are quite tenacious, seeking to discover the birth and Soul Names of their enemies.

"If a demon knows your birth name, with a lot of digging and persistence, they can find all about your life back in the human sphere of existence.

"With that knowledge they can try to hurt you or your family. They can influence and use an inhabited person to try to hurt you or your loved ones physically.

"Almost as bad, they can warp the minds of even uninhabited people and cause them to be unjustly angry with you. Their anger can propel them to slander you, to spread false tales about you, to sue you in court, and actively seek to ruin your life. It is somewhat of a challenge to be effective during your night travels when your day life is a shambles."

"That makes sense," I said nodding my head in understanding, "but what has that to do with my Soul Name?"

Qadir held up his right index finger. "Aha! If they know your Soul Name, your problems can be much worse!

"Your birth name only gives them information about a few decades of your life to plot ways to hurt you in the physical sphere.

"Your Soul Name gives them knowledge about who you really are. Using that name, demons and any creature that knows advanced magick, even humans, can create spells against you far worse than anything someone could do to harm your physical body or reputation.

What Qadir was saying made sense but was still somewhat confusing. "What changes when I am no longer a protégé?"

Qadir gave me a friendly slap on my shoulder. "If I have done my job well, you will know quite a bit of potent magick by then. Once you can magickally protect yourself and your family, having demons or other malevolents knowing your Soul Name is irrelevant. The more they try to hurt you the more they will injure themselves while you will remain unscathed."

Qadir's answer was reassuring, but it also brought up another question. "If my family can be magickally protected, and you are my mentor, why don't you just protect them while I am your protégé?"

"If only it was that easy," Qadir replied with a sigh.

"Long lasting protection is powerful magick. One of the necessary components of the spell is to have a deep love for those that are being protected and concealed. It is nothing that I, or anyone else could accomplish for someone else's family members.

"While you are in the early stages of your education, before you can do it yourself, I can put a temporary spell on you each time you interact with demons to prevent them either physically or psychically, from following you back to your residence.

"However, if demons knew your Soul Name, they would be able to counter my spell and put a trace on your Soul Essence. I will teach you how to nullify those types of spells and to protect your family with a Devotion Spell. But it will take some time for you to become proficient."

Contemplating what Qadir had told me about the

dangers of demons learning either my birth name or Soul Name, my choice was easy. "How about for now, I just go by Trevallion?"

Qadir slapped his hands together in approval. "A most judicious choice!" He held out his hand and I met him with a handshake. "Very pleased to make your acquaintance Trevallion."

I pointed to the crystal lie detector he was still holding in his hand. "Will that work if I use it on you?"

Qadir handed me the crystal. "By all means, please do so. If we are to have a fruitful relationship, it must begin upon a foundation of trust. This crystal has been enchanted rather than spelled. It will work faithfully for anyone who holds it."

I touched the crystal to the top of Qadir's hand.

"Is your name really Qadir?"

"Yes."

The lie detector crystal turned white.

"Is that your Soul Name?

"No, it is my birth name."

The crystal changed again to pure white and then back to clear.

"Are you really a mortal human?"

"Yes."

Once again the crystal turned white and after a few seconds reverted to clear.

"Do you have any intention of hurting me in any way?"

"No."

Again the crystal affirmed that he was telling the truth by changing to white then back to clear.

"Do you really want to make me your protégé, and will that be a good thing for me and those that I love?"

"Absolutely yes!" Qadir answered with enthusiasm. Once again the crystal turned white confirming the truth of Qadir's reply.

"What will I be a protégé to become? Tell me that you will not be training me to be an evil wizard or anything that would hurt or take advantage of people."

Qadir paused in thought for a moment. "That was a two-part question. I can really only answer the first part. You will be my protégé to fulfill your destiny as a Taz and become a Demon Hunter. We are dedicated to helping those who are tormented by demons.

"As for the second part, I will be teaching you powerful magick that is far beyond what is commonly known or can be employed by those who can only physically exist in the human Earth realm. Like any powerful tool it can be used for good or evil. I would not have chosen you to be my protégé unless I believed the light dwelt largely within you. But ultimately it is in your own hands whether you choose to be a good wizard or an evil one."

Once more the crystal turned white affirming Qadir's veracity. His last answer had brought up an unexpected question.

"What is a Taz?"

Qadir's face beamed with delight. "That is what I am, what Genavieve is, and some others whom you will meet, and what you are in the process of evolving to and becoming.

"You have started the natural evolution process prematurely, before you have met your catalyst, the person, place, or experience that will enhance the activity of all of your energy centers. That is unusual but not unheard of.

"Unfortunately, it means you are half in and half out of being a Taz. You have gained some of the abilities of a Taz such as having a body of physical substance in the 2nd and 3rd Dimensional worlds, or when you encounter Demons in our 1st Dimensional world of Earth. But you lack some very vital Taz abilities, primarily any ability to protect yourself or banish demons.

"Also, your ability to have a physical presence in the invisible worlds of the 2nd and 3rd Dimensions is only partial. When you travel at night now, it is like you are a half-breed. Part of you is still the simple immaterial Night Self that every human has, which is not constrained by time or space and cannot be injured by anyone or anything.

"But a part of you has begun evolving into a Taz, which for the time being gives you a body that can be physically hurt in the invisible worlds of demons, but not physically killed because it is not yet fully present, as it will be when you have completed your evolvement into a Taz."

Qadir's explanation immediately brought to mind my first face-to-face encounter with a demon named Gilgore who stabbed me in the heart with a sword. I felt the pain and the sword sliding through my body, but it didn't kill me. Was I to assume from Qadir's words that if I had fully been this Taz he was referring to, that I would have been slain by Gilgore?

I wanted to ask that question, but Qadir continued talking before I could interject. "For your protection and that of your friends and family, it is necessary that you either become a protégé, or stay completely away from the demon world until you have experienced your catalyst, which will subsequently cause you to have natural and rapidly evolving special abilities."

I had no idea what Qadir was explaining to me about being a Taz or my catalyst, but the crystal showed he was speaking the truth.

"I have many more questions," I told Qadir, "but I only need to ask one more with the enchanted stone.

"If I am not using this truth stone and just ask you questions as we are going along in our relationship, will you always tell me the truth?"

Qadir hesitated before answering my last question. "I will always tell you the truth as long as I deem it to be in your best interest to know the truth."

The crystal showed white once more, but Qadir's answer was less than reassuring. I held the crystal against his hand one more time.

"So you will lie to me if it suits you?"

"Only if I feel a lie would be more beneficial to you than the truth."

Once again the crystal turned white letting me know that though Qadir's answer was not exactly what I wanted to hear, he was still speaking honestly.

I handed the crystal back to him and he returned it to his vest pocket. "Thank you for answering my questions. As I said, I have many more but I don't believe I will need your truth stone any further."

Qadir put his arm affectionately around my shoulder and I felt a kind of son to father affection for him.

"Let us go to a more pleasant place and you can ask as many questions as you like."

Without any movements or magickal tools, Qadir spoke just a single word, "Lercedel." For a bare second, everything went black. The very next moment we were standing in exactly the same position with his arm over my shoulder, but in a beautiful sunny location with a deep blue, cloudless sky.

The pleasantly warm air was wafting with the sweet aroma of flowers, as they were growing everywhere around us in great abundance, with many varieties, most of which I did not recognize.

A soft, balmy breeze felt delicious and faintly swayed the several tall weeping willow type trees nearby.

We were on the edge of a large inviting green meadow. A stone-walled village with the thatched roofs of at least three to four dozen two-story buildings cresting above the wall stood off on the right side of the meadow, separated from the verdant grassland by a rushing creek.

At the far end of the expansive meadow, I saw what at first glance appeared to be over a dozen brightly colored small horses or ponies. But upon closer scrutiny, I saw that they were unicorns!

I pointed at them in excitement. "Are those really unicorns?" I asked in disbelief.

"Oh yes," Qadir replied. "Although on this world they are called leialli. You should know that any creature of myth you have ever read about actually exists. Most of them are here in the 2nd Dimension. You just need to know where to find them. Occasionally, humans from Earth will visit this dimension during their Night Self travels and see leialli, dragons, and other astounding creatures. Thus are the mythical beasts of Earth lore and legends born."

Out of nowhere, about a dozen short, but very handsome and beautiful people, with pointy ears, dressed quite quaintly, suddenly appeared and swarmed around us with exclamations of glee. "Qadir is here!"

"Yay! Our hero has returned!"

"Make a feast! Call in the clans! Let's celebrate!"

Everyone was jumping with joy and making happy exclamations all at once. Some were elatedly embracing Qadir. Without exception they all ignored me as if I wasn't even there.

I looked over at Qadir. "What is going on? I asked in bemusement.

Qadir laughed. "These are davos. They are like elves of Earth foklore but taller, with fine features and exceedingly good looks! They are pretty exuberant I must say. A few years ago I banished a horde of demons that had been capturing, torturing and killing the davos and terrorizing their villages. The davos of course were very grateful and never cease to give me a hero's welcome when I visit, as if I had just liberated them yesterday."

He looked over with a cheery glint in his eyes. "Being well appreciated is one of the perks of helping folks with their demon problems. Whether they are davos, humans, akara, leialli, or even glash, they are all grateful, and will always count you as a friend thereafter.

"And invite you to dinner!" he added with delight.

"However, you may want to respectfully decline dinner invitations from glash," he cautioned.

"I'm sure, like me, you would find their menu choices, which consists primarily of live food that is still frantically trying to get away and not be eaten, less than appetizing."

CHAPTER
Sixteen

True to Qadir's predictions, the davos invited us to share a meal with them.

Qadir introduced the davos that invited us as Oshlin, Baradon of the local clan of Siratol Davos, and advised him that we couldn't stay long, as we had pressing business elsewhere.

By the respectful way Qadir introduced Oshlin, I assumed that a Baradon was some type of head honcho like a mayor or chief.

Oshlin made a slight bow with his head. "Of course Demon Slayer, we understand," he answered deferentially.

After Oshlin departed to co-ordinate the festivities I glanced at Qadir with curiosity. "Demon Slayer? I thought demons were immortal."

"Yes, yes that is true," Qadir agreed. "But when we banish them, they are sent into Oblivion and remain there for at least 300 years and often much longer, depending upon how potent the banishment was.

"Even in the shortest instance, they will not return until all of these davos, and even all of us I dare say, will be long gone from the physical life.

"As they will never again be able to terrorize any currently living soul, they are effectively slain. Nor do I take the time to explain to the davos or anyone else that I help, that the demons are only banished for a few centuries. That would just give them needless apprehensions that their descendants might be menaced by the same demons."

"Where's Oblivion?" I asked with piqued curiosity.

"I have no idea," Qadir answered with surprising ignorance. "It is somewhere beyond any of the known dimensions. Where exactly it is located, not even the demons seem to know. That's why we call it Oblivion."

After Qadir had warned me about not accepting dinner invitations from glash, I had a few apprehensions about the foods that might be served at a davos celebration. But my worries were unfounded. The davos were gourmet vegetarians and the wide variety of amazingly prepared food they served were delights to every one of my taste buds.

I didn't recognize a single food item, but they were all delicious. Qadir told me later that though there were some similarities, almost none of the fruits and vegetables in the Davos Realm on the planet Sx were the same as those that are native to our Earth, with the important exception of dandelions, coconuts, and a few obscure herbs that contained both 1st and 2nd Dimension properties.

It continued to be disconcerting that I was unable to

strike up a conversation with any of the davos. Young, old, male or female, they all just ignored me as if I wasn't even there.

It was very strange. I always accompanied Qadir and he politely introduced me to every davos or group of davos we ran into. They would nod their heads in acknowledgment at me, but not one spoke a single word of greeting or asked me any questions.

Even when I would look right at them and ask a simple question like "how are you?" they would act as if they had never heard me and I wasn't actually standing right next to them. For all the excitement they showed to see Qadir, the level of rudeness they expressed toward me was unprecedented in my life.

When we had a moment alone, I queried Qadir about the davos' discourteousness.

"Not to worry," he assured me. "They are very standoffish to strangers. It's purely a practice of self-defense. Just like the wall protects their village, ignoring strangers is a wall protecting their hearts and mind and sometimes their lives as well.

""Until you have proven your mettle to them, they purposefully interact with you only as is minimally necessary for the situation. Once you have done at least three of them a selfless favor or service, and in other ways proven your sincere good intentions, then all of them will welcome you like a long-lost relative."

After our little feast was over, Qadir knelt down and was saying his goodbyes with hugs all around to the many davos pleading with him to stay. When what seemed to be by his stooped posture and long gray hair, the oldest davos in the clan came to say his goodbye, Qadir pulled him over in my direction.

"Loxadol, I want you to meet Trevallion. He is my new protégé."

The elderly davos glanced at me for the briefest second, then looked away. I did not take offense as I now understood why the davos acted this way.

Looking at me Qadir pointed at Loxadol. "Do remember this fellow Trevallion. Davos are the most ingenious of God's creations and Loxadol is the greatest of them all.

"Starting with nothing, they can invent marvelous and powerful magickal devices and non-magickal ones as well.

"It is why the demons were attacking them in days past. They demanded that the davos make some magickal tools for them. The davos refused and they paid a terrible price for their defiance before I arrived to banish the foul monsters."

Hearing this made me recall the words of the demon Ugar when he revealed to the demon class that he had tortured and killed six davos from Farvely to induce the surviving davos to build a Yargon for him.

I looked at Qadir somewhat confused, as what he was saying did not make sense.

"If davos can make such powerful magickal devices, how is it possible that demons have any success bothering them at all? It would seem that they would be more than capable of defending themselves."

Qadir nodded his head in agreement. "So it would seem. But things are often not the way they appear at first glance or deduction. That is especially true when you are dealing with demons or anything magickal.

"Davos are the greatest inventors of magickal devices. They have no peers in that regard outside of the davos realm. If they wished, they certainly could create magickal devices that would completely foil any attempts by demons to harm them, but they fear the weaknesses of one another even more than the murderous demons.

"Over a millennia ago the davos had impregnable magick that protected their realms, but it could be employed offensively as well as defensively. The clans began using their most powerful magickal devices, seeking to conqueror, subjugate and enslave other clans. The destruction wrought almost annihilated the davos race from existence, at least on this planet.

"Because they are small and can be high-spirited and ebullient, it is easy to think of them with child-like qualities of innocence. Please do not make that mistake. Davos adults are smart, clever, and can be ruthless. They have a tendency to develop strong jealousies and envies against one another. They must constrain themselves to not become worst enemies of their own kind, much less, outside foes.

"Luckily, ages ago, when their own personal foibles and animosities almost led to their utter destruction, the wisest among the surviving clans made a pact to never again use magick that could harm or enslave a davos. It is the only offense for which the davos clans have a death penalty.

"Unfortunately, any magickal device they would create that could protect them from demons or other marauders, could conceivably be used against davos as well. Hence they refrain from using all but the simplest or inherently benign magick themselves, even though they have the know-how to craft potent magickal weapons and defenses."

I was somewhat incredulous at Qadir's explanation. "So they just allow themselves to be killed by demons? That would be like a person that had a gun, but refused to use it to defend themselves when an attacker was trying to kill them."

"Quite right if you look at it that way," Qadir agreed.

"However, perhaps thinking of your analogy a bit differently would help. How about if two friends that were also rivals, each had a gun and due to their sometimes rash nature, they were more likely to shoot one another with their gun than to use it to defend against a rare outside invader. Would the gun be a good thing or a bad thing to possess in that scenario?"

"When you look at it that way, it does present it in a different light," I admitted.

"Not to worry too much though," Qadir assured me. "The davos are far from defenseless. In the normal course of events, they use a wide assortment of non-lethal defensive magick when they are attacked by demons and other predators.

"For instance, they have a very effective device that surrounds this village that makes it appear invisible to most attackers. Even if an invader runs face-first into an invisible wall, the assailant will have no idea what type of structure they have encountered.

"Nor will they have long to contemplate it. The davos

can still see their foes and will take other measures, such as pouring boiling stink oil on them, to ward them off."

I shook my head still confused. "Sounds like even with their restrictions to protect themselves from each other, they still have potent magickal defensive abilities. So how do demons breach their defenses and torture and kill them?"

Qadir held up his finger for emphasis. "Most demons become comedies of futility if they try to harass davos. They will retreat with howls of laughter from the davos that activated their benign defensive magick.

"Unfortunately, upper-level demons are a different beast. Unlike most demons, the upper levels have not squandered their millenniums of existence.

"Think how much you have learned in your years of life. Now consider how much more I have learned than you because I have lived thirty or forty more years.

"Now think about upper-level demons that have stayed on a quest to gain more knowledge for thousands of years. For every feat of benign magick the davos know, for every benign magickal device they can create, for every mechanical defense they can devise, the upper-level demons possess a counter knowledge.

"In their several thousand years of existence, they have seen it all. There are no surprise defenses to them, and long ago they worked out the counters to any barrier that stands in their way.

"When davos or any other creature, including humans, are targeted by an upper-level demon, they are doomed, unless someone like me or you comes to their aid."

"Me?" I laughed aloud. "I don't know how to help anyone."

"I'm the one that needs help," I protested. "I have no doubt Genavieve saved my life. I don't even know why you want me as your protégé. Surely there must be many better candidates for the position."

Qadir looked at me with an all-knowing smile of bemusement. "Perhaps it is time you learned a little bit more about yourself and your place in this big universe."

He pointed to the far end of the meadow quite a distance away. "Let's walk over and greet the leialli. Along the way we can talk. You can ask questions, I can give answers, and you might come away from the davos domains far wiser than you arrived."

CHAPTER
Seventeen

Walking through the lush green meadow, I reflected on what questions to ask Qadir. I had so many it was a challenge to figure out where to start.

"I guess my biggest question Qadir, is just trying to understand everything I have experienced since I first encountered demons. I have been Night Traveling with vivid, lucid dreams for many years. I was very accustomed to being able to instantly go anywhere in the universe with my Night Self and not be constrained by any obstacle or injured by any danger.

"Yet my night travels were just dreams, even if I suspected in many instances I was perceiving real places. If something dangerous or scary began to occur, I could change the scene more to my liking just by willing it to be so. It was the pure essence of lucid dreaming.

"When I first encountered demons in my night travels, I thought it was just a new type of adventurous lucid dream with an opportunity to interact with interesting new characters. To my horror and complete confusion, I found that these fiends could inflict real physical pain upon me! Not only did my Night Self feel the pain, but so did my Day Self when I would awake in a fright back home.

"Now, no matter where I venture in my night travels, though I still have some of my lucid dreaming abilities, like instantly blinking from one place to another, almost all other aspects are either gone or radically changed.

"It is as if I really exist here with you now in some kind of physical form. I can smell and taste the delicious food that the davos make. I can hold the food in my hand, chew it in my mouth, and feel satiated when my stomach is full.

"My experiences now are far beyond what I used to think were the most vivid dreams. They are as real as my life when I am awake. Now, there is not one detail I cannot discern and that's great. However, there is also not one thing I can change simply by willing it and that's not so great.

"My lucid dreaming ability to alter a dream to suit my desire or preference is completely gone! Now things happen that I absolutely do not want to take place, and things I do wish to occur only do so if I initiate a physical effort to make it so.

"Honestly, I think I'm going a little crazy and can no longer discern dreams from reality."

"You are not going crazy," Qadir assured me. "But you are also no longer having a lucid dream, even though you still retain the essential ability of transiting as you noted.

"No, my young protégé, your night travels now take you to worlds that are as physically real as the Earth we both call home. However, the worlds you travel to exist in the 2nd Dimension, whereas our Earth home is in the 1st Dimension. The energies of the dimensions are different enough that they are imperceptible to one another, even though in many cases they occupy nearby space.

"Essentially, you still have just one soul, but it now shares twin bodies. Those physical forms may look alike but they are actually very, very different energetically. The Earth body you have always known is composed primarily of 1st Dimension matter, while the body you have here is composed primarily of 2nd Dimension matter. But there is a little bit of the energy of both Dimensions in each of the twins.

"Now, when your Earth body sleeps, your 2nd Dimension body awakens, and when this body in the second Dimension sleeps, your Earth body awakens. In time you will learn how to have both bodies animated and awake at the same time, but for now one has to sleep while the other is awake.

"Your travels during the night when your Earth body sleeps are no longer dreams; they are real, they are physical, and they can be deadly. If your physical 2nd Dimension body dies, your Earth body sleeping at home will also perish in short order, most likely from a heart attack. So do be cautious, especially with unfamiliar creatures and plants."

Frankly, Qadir's comments were not reassuring. "Can I just go back to the way my dreams used to be with vivid lucid dreams that were thrilling but couldn't hurt me?" I asked wistfully.

"No, I'm afraid not. It is too late now as you have made

the transference from what you were to what you are. This should not have occurred until you had resonance with your catalyst, and Genavieve assures me that you have not.

"I suspect the change has begun to occur because you are already in your thirties rather than your late teens or early twenties when the transformation usually happens, so we will have to make the best of it and get you up to speed quickly.

"Not to worry, I will teach you all you need to know to navigate these worlds. If you are an apt student, all will be well.

"And you best become an exceptional protégé," he warned with emphasis, "as I cannot retire until you are prepared to replace me in my stewardship."

With some surprise, I noted a key word that Qadir had just spoken that left me curiously confused. "What did you mean when you said I have made the transference from what I was to what I am? What was I previously and what am I now?"

Qadir smiled broadly at me and spread his arms expansively. "Previously you were just a normal human being, albeit a very psychic one. Now you are a Taz, or at least half a Taz. It seems there are still parts of you that have not completely made the metamorphosis."

It was beginning to seem that every answer Qadir gave brought up two more questions. I was still trying to wrap my head around the concept of different dimensions composed of dissimilar energies. Now trying to figure out what a Taz was supposed to be, what I was supposed to be, had been added to my mental overload.

"Whether I was a psychic Izbo or a Taz seemed to be

a question among the demons as well. Can you please enlighten me as to exactly what a Taz is and why you think I am one?" I asked Qadir earnestly.

"Certainly," he replied enthusiastically. "You, me, Genavieve, and four other individuals currently living on Earth in a physical life, are what are known as, Taz. There have been many Taz for innumerable generations before us, and hopefully there will continue to be many after we are gone. Usually there are five to eight on our Earth at any one time. But there have been times when there were less and times when there were more.

"We all began our lives as normal humans, but over time we developed unique abilities, gifts from God really, that gave us the tools and powers to fight and banish demons, such as no other humans or creatures possess.

"We can only do what we do because we have the ability to split our souls between our physical bodies in the 1st Dimension, which includes Earth, and our Taz body, which is a 2nd Dimension energy that exists in a tangible solid form here in the 2nd Dimension.

"There is an interconnectedness of active thoughts if both bodies are awake at the same time and desire to tune into their twin. You will not automatically be able to see what your twin is doing. That would be an overload on your poor brain to be consciously living two lives simultaneously. But you can choose to tune in and see the activities of your twin with exact detail if you choose.

"You will also have complete memory recollection between your 1st Dimension body and your 2nd Dimension body of what occurred with one while the other slept if you desire to review it. However, other than memories and the ability of one version to be aware of the other version's activities when both are awake, the bodies themselves are independent and unconnected. The exception is within a day or two of death, when in most instances one body dies and the other usually soon follows."

I was in awe of everything Qadir was revealing, but it brought up one huge question in my mind. "Where does the Taz body come from?" I asked without a clue to what the answer could be. "My 1st Dimension body was created by a union of my parents and I was birthed by my mother. How does a fully adult Taz version of myself suddenly appear?"

"Yes, I can see how that could be perplexing," Qadir admitted. "The reality may be a bit of a challenge for you to wrap your head around. You see you actually birthed yourself. In your case, you are still in the process of accomplishing that feat.

"Remember, your 2nd Dimension self shares the same soul as your 1st Dimension body. In both dimensions the body present is you. Nothing new was created. You simply manifested a 2nd Dimension aspect of yourself that was always present but dormant inside of you until you matured and began to initiate the transformation.

"You are actually like an alien among the people of either dimension. In the first dimension, almost all native organic items that a person can see and touch, with the exception of a few plants, is 1st Dimension energy. This includes all the people, animals and 99.99% of the plants.

"It is the same in the 2nd Dimension; other than a handful of plants, all native organic materials including people, creatures, or other items that exist and can be seen and touched are composed of 2nd Dimension energy.

"Taz are unique in that we are both 1st and 2nd Dimension energy, which is part of the reason we can manifest a physical form in multiple dimensions."

Qadir cracked a playful smile. "Interestingly, your Taz body actually could meet your Earth body in the 1st Dimension and I'm sure it will from time to time."

"How would that work?" I asked, my curiosity piqued.

Qadir was happy to explain. "Let us think of Dimensions like radio stations. Television stations work on a similar principle. The numbers represent various frequencies. When you are tuned into the correct channel frequency, the broadcast of that channel becomes clear. If you are not tuned into that frequency, you will hear or see nothing from that station. Sometimes, when stations have close frequencies, it is possible to see or hear both stations overlapping at a midpoint on the dial between the two frequencies.

"For this example, we will say that the 1st Dimension is 700 on the dial. The 2nd Dimension is 1200 on the dial. The 3rd Dimension where only demons dwell, is 1400 on the dial.

"You notice that the 2nd and 3rd Dimensions are very close in frequency. That allows denizens from either to have some level of substance if they are in the alien Dimension.

"That is why demons have substance when they are in the 2nd Dimension. However, it is not full substance; they are not fully solid when they are in the 2nd Dimension because that is not the frequency of their energy. Yet they are solid and substantial enough that they can do physical acts.

"Moving on to the 1st Dimension, demons are not so fortunate. 700 and 1400 are far apart on the frequency dial. Demons can exist quite well in the 1st Dimension and billions of them do, with several million right on our own Earth! However, their energy is so different that they are completely invisible and inaudible to any person or animal native to the 1st Dimension, unless they are strongly psychic. Even then, psychic humans of the 1st Dimension can usually only sense demons and not actually see them.

"Demons are not so constrained. Though they have no tangible physical substance that can physically interact with 1st Dimensional people, animals, or objects, they can see and hear anyone or anything in the 1st Dimension quite clearly. That is an unfortunate ability they possess as demons.

"Fortunately, as a Taz, you also have special abilities when it comes to interacting in multiple dimensions. Your Taz body is almost pure 2nd Dimension energy, but of a very unique type. Unlike the demons that lose some of their physical solidness when they appear in the 2nd Dimension, a Taz will not lose any of their physical soundness if they travel to the demon demesnes in the 3rd Dimension.

"Consider that last bit just for informational purposes," he quietly added as if in confidence. "I wouldn't recommend actually going to the 3rd Dimension unless you have preplanned your mission in every detail. If you go unprepared you might find it easier to get in than to get out."

"What can a Taz do in the 1st Dimension?" I asked.

"Not as much as we can in the 2nd Dimension, but still quite a lot actually," Qadir answered with some pride in his voice. "The most important thing is we can see demons and vanquish them by various magickal, and other means. They are physical to us and we are physical to them when we are both in the 1st Dimension.

"And like your earlier more primitive Night Self, your Taz body can transit with the speed of thought to any place in the 1st Dimension that you wish, with the added benefit that your transiting ability has expanded to the 2nd and 3rd Dimensions as well.

"Returning to my original explanation, just like your Taz body can wander about the 1st Dimension and observe anyone or anything, it could do the same with your Earth body; observe it that is. It would be pretty boring, but if you wanted to stand next to your Earth body while it was sleeping to see if it was snoring or whatnot, you could do it.

"The only truly useful purpose of having your Taz body ever be near your Earth body for brief moments on rare occasions, is to ensure your home remains a demon-free zone.

"Eventually demons will discover your Earth alter ego, but even upper level demons will give your Earth body and family a wide berth because they know if they did anything to harm your Earth body or family, the wrath that would be unleashed upon them by you and all the other Taz, would be of epic destruction and banishment.

"Well, that's all I have time to say about it for now. Is clarity beginning to manifest in your head?" Qadir asked a little in jest. I nodded in reply with a smile.

Despite what he had just said, Qadir continued his explanation with a more serious tone. "You must never forget that though as a Taz you have both a 1st and 2nd Dimensional body, it is still the same soul shared between two bodies. There are many intricacies to that, but imparting the knowledge will take more time than we currently have, so it will need to wait until later in your training.

"Be ever humbled and grateful for the good you can do because by some divine miracle you are a Taz. It is our sacred stewardship to use our special gifts to help others that are tormented by demons. Sometimes we are their only hope."

Before Qadir could explain further I protested. "Thank you for all that you have shared, but I think you may be mistaken Qadir. I'm not sure I am really a Taz. I certainly have no special talents for fighting demons. As you know they would have killed me if not for the intervention of Genavieve, and she was amazing! She definitely has special abilities! But not me.

"Even Ugar, an upper level demon, explained to his students that I was only a strongly psychic Izbo. Certainly that is a special ability, but not one that allows me to fight with demons, much less banish them!"

Qadir gave me his all-knowing amused smile again. "Well, I guess that just goes to show you that demons seldom speak truth. Whether from ignorance or merely to deceive his students, Ugar was obviously very mistaken."

I shook my head in strong disagreement. "Ugar's ignorance wasn't very obvious to me! From my perspective, he was killing me and there was nothing I could do about it!"

"Of course you couldn't," Qadir agreed dismissively, "You had not yet been trained and had not yet discovered what you are. That is why you are my apprentice. Next time you meet a higher level demon, the outcome will be more favorable for you and less for the demon."

He reached over and pinched my bare forearm. "After all, here we are in the 2nd Dimension. You are undeniably quite physical, and I dare say, quite more than a mere psychic manifestation.

"Any more questions or have I answered them all?" Qadir asked jokingly.

I had to chuckle at his comment. "Far from all," I replied. "I'm just getting started.

"I don't really understand the nature of my physical state around demons or exactly how it manifests. When I was tortured by Ugar it was as physically painful as anything I could imagine. The student demons had tied my body down to the floor and the restraints held me tight. Ugar said he made my body physical from my ethereal psychic state by the power of his magickal Yargon machine.

"The other instance, when the demon Gilgore stabbed me with his sword, I felt the thick blade enter my body, but why didn't it kill me even though it went right through my heart?"

"Excellent questions!" Qadir commended. "Let's begin with Ugar. He was mistaken because he did not know your true nature. His Yargon machine actually had no effect upon you as you were already in a body of substance around demons. He just assumed it had worked upon you as a psychic. Of course you felt the torture because your 2nd Dimensional body was in fact being tortured.

"It was a little bit different in your encounter with the demon Gilgore. That was the first instance, as far as I know, that you manifested physically with your 2nd Dimension energy around demons. At that point, you would have still been strongly in transition, a rare time when a Taz is first metamorphosing and the 1st and 2nd Dimension energies flicker out-of-sync. The 2nd Dimension part of you felt the sword pierce your body. However, because the 1st Dimension aspect of your body was still strongly present, you were not substantial enough to actually get killed or even be injured, and you were able to transit away back to your Earth body.

"Be warned that that will no longer be the case. Though there are still some Taz qualities you have not yet manifested, I have no doubt that your body here is fully integrated into its 2nd Dimensional form by now. Hereinafter, if a demon attacks you with a weapon, you will be physically wounded and could be killed."

Qadir looked ahead and pointed toward the leialli herd. "We are getting closer. There's only time for a few more questions this round."

I still had a long list of questions, but just blurted out the first one that came to my mind. "How did Genavieve know to come rescue me when I was being tortured by Ugar and his demon class?"

"You would need to ask Genavieve to know for sure," Qadir reflected. "I know she was tracking Ugar and may have just stumbled upon you. Or, she may have tracked Ugar to that location and sensed your 2nd Dimensional energies.

"Though they can exist invisibly in the 1st Dimension and with substance in the 2nd, the true domain of demons is the 3rd Dimension, and that is their auric energy. Genavieve would have been on high alert for a rescue if she had sensed any living 1st or 2nd Dimension energies in the classroom with the demons. In you, she may have sensed both."

The more Qadir told me, the less I understood, and the more questions I had that vexed me. But I didn't want to disappoint him by expressing my continued confusion, so I decided to just venture questions that would seem to indicate that I was grasping everything he was saying, even though I was not.

We were about halfway across the meadow walking toward the leialli. We stopped to rest in the shade of a lone tree in the middle of the meadow. It was similar to a pine tree from Earth with long, thin, green needles, but differed by the fact that each primary needle had several smaller needles growing out of it at about forty-five-degree angles.

After sitting down next to each other with our backs to the large tree trunk, I thought it would be appropriate to begin finding out more about my mentor, now that we had stopped walking and might have more time.

"What is the origin of your name Qadir? I don't think I have ever heard that name."

Qadir had picked up a small dead old branch and began tapping it on the ground now and then as he contemplated answering my question.

"My name is Arabic. My mother was a Muslim from Tangier, Morocco. It has always been a very international city and it was there that she met my father who was a red-haired Irish Catholic that traded in rare artifacts.

"It was very taboo for a Muslim woman to marry a non-Muslim man because in Islam the religious lineage flows through the father. It is less of a problem for a Muslim man to marry a Christian or Jewish woman because their children will be born and raised as Muslims.

"When they married, my mother's family disowned her and probably would have killed her if they had remained in Morocco; at least that is what my parents told me. They originally fled to my father's home in Ireland, but my mother was not well received by his family either, nor did she like the climate.

"To get away from both families and to be centrally located for my father's antiquities trade, they decided to settle near Montepulciano, a town in the Tuscany region of Italy. That is where I spent my childhood and encountered my first demon inhabited people."

"Are you married?" I asked.

"I used to be in my twenties," Qadir answered wistfully. "She was my sweet catalyst. Being with her lit a fire in me that helped transform me into a Taz. Sadly, she left me decades ago when I foolishly told her what I did while my 1st Dimension body slept. You would be wise to never tell your wife or anyone else about being a Taz or a demon hunter. They will either be scared of you or think you are crazy. Either way, they will shun you."

I nodded in understanding, though I hoped when I met my catalyst she would not run away if I told her about my secret life.

"What about Genavieve? I wondered. "I noticed a diamond wedding ring on her finger."

"Yes, she has been happily married for somewhere around twenty-five years," Qadir answered. "Surprisingly, her husband is a lay minister or some type of religious fellow. Of all people, he was her catalyst. She has two teenage children I believe and she and her family have happily lived in the same house in France for many years.

"Genavieve says it is because of her love for her husband and family, to protect them and the world that they blissfully think of as normal, that she accepted her gift as a Taz and her calling as a demon hunter, but none of them even have an inkling of what she does while they sleep. She was wiser than me," he said in a sad, trailing voice tinged with longing.

Qadir quickly recovered his normal cheerful demeanor and looked over at me with a grin that caused the radiating wrinkles at the corner of his eyes to stand out. "Your questions seem to be drifting to the mundane. See if you can come up with a question that is more pertinent to your stewardship as a Taz."

"Alright then," I began. "When I was spying on the demon classroom, before Ugar came, there was a mid-level demon instructor named Thalgin. He had a bag full of what he said were dried human skins with writing on them in human blood. If that is what they truly were, how would a demon be able to physically possess human skins? I thought something from the 1st Dimension would be without substance to a demon. Even more important, if the skins were real, how would a demon obtain them?"

"Now that is a good question!" Qadir said with exuberance. "You are correct that normally a demon would be incapable of physically holding anything from the 1st Dimension. The most likely answer is that the demon Thalgin did not really possess human skins. More likely they were the skins and blood of some animal from the 2nd Dimension. Demons are serial liars and deceivers, especially among their own kind.

"However, there are a couple of ways a demon could obtain and hold human skins. If the skins are from the 1st Dimension, it would require the assistance of a developing Metastasis Demon, one that had accepted to be a demon, but to outward appearances still remained a human. They could continue to physically interact with humans in the 1st Dimension, as they had not yet died and passed into full demon auric energy. A serial murderer or rapist would be a likely choice.

"This warped individual would murder and skin a human, or dig up and skin a very recently deceased corpse.

"The higher level demon would appear to them and provide a magickally enchanted container to hold the bloody human skins. The container would be taken to the 2nd or 3rd Dimension, where the skins themselves could be enchanted to physically exist in realms outside of the 1st Dimension. This type of magick would only work on very small items from the 1st Dimension, but it would be possible with dried skins.

"The second, equally sinister possibility is they are real human skins from residents of Sx or some other 2nd Dimension planet that were killed by demons."

"I looked up with great surprise at Qadir's last comment. "There are humans on Sx?"

"Of course," Qadir quipped, as if the fact should have been obvious to me. "Humans are the most numerous higher life-form in the universe. There are not many here on Sx, probably less than a hundred thousand. But on some worlds there are billions of them, as there are on our own Earth."

"When can we go meet them and see their towns?" I asked with excited anticipation.

Qadir waved his hands back and forth across each other below his waist in negation. "No, no, no, that would be very unwise. Interacting with humans can lead to relationship complications that pull you away from your Taz duties. And humans in the 2nd Dimension do not like the Taz very much by and large."

"Why is that?" I wondered.

"Magick. We have it, they want it, and no matter what they do they cannot obtain Taz magick."

I cocked my head without saying a word and just looked at Qadir not understanding his meaning. Seeing my confusion, he elaborated.

"Most humans on Sx, or any of the magickal worlds of the 2nd Dimension, are obsessed with wielding magickal power and madly jealous and envious of anyone that has more magickal power than they do. They do not choose wise, caring, and good administrators as their leaders, but solely follow those that can exhibit the greatest magickal abilities.

"However, as you will discover, the magick even the greatest human sorcerer of the 2nd Dimension can wield, which is far greater than any 1st Dimension sorcerer, is still feeble next to the skills of a fully trained Taz and their Dragon Sword. Hence, there is always a lot of envy and ill-will when Taz interact with humans, especially their leaders.

"I advise you to stay away from them here on Sx unless you need to visit their realms to dispatch a demon to Oblivion. Anything else will end up being an unwanted distraction at the least or an unnecessary confrontation at worst. That's all I care to say about 2nd Dimension humans," Qadir said abruptly, leaving me to wonder if there was some hidden animosity between him and the humans on Sx.

Though I was very interested in hearing more about the Sx humans it was obvious Qadir didn't want to talk further about them, so I asked another question I had been curious about. "Tell me about some of your earliest encounters with demons. It might help me have a better understanding of what to expect."

Qadir waved me off. "Sorry, that is a long story and will have to wait until another day."

I nodded my head in understanding, but followed with another of the questions I had planned to ask.

"What exactly are demons?"

"That is another long answer," Qadir objected. "Don't you have any other questions that will require only short answers?"

I shrugged my shoulders and smiled at Qadir, hoping he would still answer my question.

"All right then," he began. "My explanation may trample over your personal religious views, but the truth cannot change to accommodate delusion.

CHAPTER
Eighteen

"O f course you do believe in God," he asserted as if it was an obvious fact.

I nodded silently in agreement and then added, "but I don't affiliate with any church or religion."

"So much the better," Qadir asserted. "You are a book whose pages are yet to be written, so with care, fallacy can be avoided.

"Let me testify to you most solemnly that there is a God, but not in the sense that most religions teach.

"Over half the population of the world belongs to one of the three Abrahamic religions, Judaism, Christianity, and Islam, and their offshoot sects. These are monotheistic religions that believe that there is only one God and that God is some form of a male being or energy.

"Among the other religions of the world, a little over twelve percent are Hindus and they believe in quite a number of Gods, both male and female.

"About five percent of the people of the world count themselves as Buddhists and their beliefs are somewhat confusing. On the one hand, they do not worship any particular God and most Buddhists feel worshiping a God or Gods is not the point of their religion. On the other hand, they have quite a number of deities and devas, both male and female that they venerate.

"Several religions have a doctrine that attests that there once was a war in heaven and a great number of angels rebelled against God. As a punishment, these fallen angels were cast out of heaven and became demons. I'm sure you will hear that fairy tale from time to time.

"However, the only part of it that is correct is there was a rebellion against God, but it was not by angels in heaven."

Qadir stopped in the middle of his explanation to ask me a question.

"What are your beliefs about reincarnation?"

"I don't really have a belief one way or the other," I replied. "Maybe there is and maybe there isn't. I haven't thought about it enough to come to a conclusion."

Qadir held up both hands palm up as if unveiling a big surprise. "Poof, there is no reincarnation for most people, at least not in the way they think of it with the same soul returning for many lifetimes into a different body."

"Wait a minute," I protested gently. "Live and let live is my motto. I really don't care what people believe in their various religions. As long as they don't believe in interfering in my life and dictating how I should live it, I'm good. Are you sure this tangent is necessary and has something to do with demons?"

"Most definitely," Qadir assured me. "You must be aware of this essential foundation or it will be impossible for you to comprehend what demons are, what powers they wield, and why they are motivated to do the dastardly things they do to hurt people."

"Sorry," I mumbled apologetically. "Please continue."

With a smile, Qadir resumed his explanation. "Before you can understand the rest you must have a more complete understanding of God, because the concepts of God that all the various religions believe are all incomplete. They each have a part of the truth. Now I will reveal it all to you in its sublime simplicity and logic.

"How do I know that my version of God is true and complete? The same way you will know. Look deep inside and ask yourself in all honesty what your mind thinks of my explanation, for it must make sense, and how your heart feels about it, as it must feel right.

"Whenever your heart and mind agree, it is a true path. That is wisdom to remember as it will aid you in all aspects of your life.

"Let me ask you. Can a man make a baby without a woman, or a woman make a baby without a man?"

"No," I replied.

"How about a dog, a cat, or a horse? Can they create a new life with just a male or just a female?"

"Obviously they need both a male and a female," I answered.

Qadir smiled, pleased I was grasping his simple points.

"We are made in the image of God. The scriptures of

many religions say it is so. God is our template."

Qadir reached over and gently hit me on my arm with the back of his hand. "Now you and I are men. It is easy to see how we are made in the image of a male God, but how are females made in the image of a male God? They have far more shapely figures, their facial features are more refined, they do not mature as large or muscular, and thankfully they do not grow bushy beards."

"That does seem to be a conundrum," I admitted.

Qadir continued. "Would it not seem more logical that if God is the creator of all that is, as many religions attest, that God would have to not be just one male individual?

"If God is our template, if we are made in the image of God, and all higher life is a creation of God, then it is only logical that there must be a male God that is the template for men, and a female God that is the template for women, and from the union of their energies, all creation has sprung into existence. "Together, they are the God of our universe.

"What does your mind think about that concept?"

"It makes sense," I admitted. "It is logical to think that the nature of God would not be different than the template they made for all other life."

Qadir nodded his head with a beaming smile, obviously very happy to see I was not having trouble with his explanation.

"Good, your mind is satisfied. Now let us look to your heart. What feels right in your heart, that your soul and spirit were created by a single male God, or that your eternal soul was birthed by the loving energetic union of your Celestial Father and Celestial Mother?"

I have to admit, when I heard the words Mother and Father in relation to God, my heart did beat a little faster, and I told Qadir of the immediate feeling that washed over me.

"Excellent!" he exclaimed. So you understand this very important foundation. Let us now move on to the next. Henceforth, when you hear me refer to God as singular, remember I am talking about both our Celestial Father and Celestial Mother together in the plural. They are two distinct individuals, but they are united as one in all things when it comes to their stewardship.

"Next point," Qadir continued, "All of us have lived a much longer time than our minuscule mortal lives. Before we came into this physical world, our souls were created by God and placed into spirit bodies.

"Spirit bodies are not like ghosts, they are not flesh and blood, but they do have a physical substance, similar to the difference between first and second dimension bodies. They both have physical substance in their realm.

"All the people that have ever lived upon our Earth and every other Earth-like world in our universe, were first created as spirit bodies in the premortal existence, before they were born into a body of flesh and blood on their physical world.

"Very importantly, this also includes demons. They were not created any different than anyone else, but devolved into becoming demons because of their very poor choices."

That brought up a question, but Qadir held his hand up in a silent sign to wait, and he continued his explanation.

"In the premortal world we had friends and even platonic romantic relationships. We attended schools and lived lives free to pursue our interests without the worries of having to make money to buy food and pay for shelter. Nor did we have to worry about sickness or diseases of any kind."

"Sounds like paradise," I interjected.

"For hundreds and often thousands of years of premortal existence it probably was," Qadir agreed.

"But at a point that differed in time for each individual, everyone eventually experienced limits to the growth of their soul in a spirit body. There was knowledge to gain and experiences to have, that could only be attained in a physical body.

"That is the point where everyone has to come down into a mortal body and experience a physical life with all of its travails if they wish to continue growing and expanding in knowledge and abilities, and gain a greater capacity for important emotions like love, empathy and compassion.

"Even something as simple as understanding what salt tastes like is knowledge that can only be gleaned with a physical body tasting salt.

"Of course there are so many other physical delights to experience, from the endless variety of delicious foods to the bliss of a loving sexual union, to the joys of being married and raising children.

"With all the joys, there are also many pains, hardships, and cruelties that can be experienced. However, as difficult as some of the challenges of physical life can be, whether we succeed or fail at the challenge, we still benefit. Just having the experience makes our eternal soul greater than it was before.

"We can learn and grow as much from our pains and failures as we do from our delights and successes. Often we grow even more from our failures, as why they occurred is seared into our consciousness and that memory serves us well in similar situations when they occur in the future.

"Our mortal life is very brief. Of course, when everyone departs the premortal world to go down to experience physical life, their fondest desire is to return to an immortal life enhanced and expanded because of their physical experiences."

I couldn't help myself. I just had to interrupt and ask a question. "Qadir, are you sure this is right? I don't remember even one iota of a premortal life. If I had lived for hundreds or thousands of years in a life before the one I am living now, I think I would remember it, or at least the most memorable parts."

"And I still don't see how this has anything to do with demons," I added.

"It would be a curse to remember," Qadir replied dismissively. "To prevent this curse, a veil of forgetfulness is put over our minds at the moment our spirit leaves the premortal worlds. The memories of our former life and relationships can be recalled with special techniques, but for the most part they are only brief glimpses of the past, and anything more would be impediments to our eternal progression.

"There are three reasons we come into a physical life.

"One: We are here to gain knowledge and experiences that can only be gained with a physical body.

"If we could fully remember the ease of our premortal life, we would long too strongly for it when faced with the challenges of a physical life. That longing would be a curse that prevented us from making our best effort to live our physical life to the fullest. We would neither grow nor expand our soul and our short physical life would be squandered.

"Two: We are here to build our character, to become better souls by making choices of significant goodness and benefit to others. We are here to embody all the virtuous qualities that demons hate.

"With each trait of light we fully live, we increase the powers and abilities of our soul, and that is of wonderful benefit, in both our physical life and our immortal life to come.

"It is by living through the challenges of physical life that our character has the opportunity to grow and develop. How we interact with others from family, to friends, to people we do not even know, how respectfully we treat them, how lovingly, how positively, how helpfully, all adds to our character.

"That was easy in the premortal life when there were no pressures, no illness, and no need to work a loathsome job for money to exist. However, making those good choices under the many stresses of mortal life are the building blocks of a noble character.

"Lastly: We come into a physical life with the Veil of Forgetfulness over our minds so we can develop faith.

"If we could fully remember our premortal life and

hence unshakably know that we are eternal beings, we would not be bothered so much by the challenges of physical life, because we would know that just like so many religions teach, there truly is an eternal life to come.

"Therefore, what would be the point of being concerned by the blink of an eye brevity of our physical life? We wouldn't be bothered so much by our physical life challenges, but neither would we have the motivation to gain knowledge or improve our character. It would be easy to think about just cruising through that microsecond of eternity that is our physical life."

"This is why we have the *Veil of Forgetfulness*. Because we cannot remember our premortal existence, when religions of the world teach of the immortal life to come, we have no way to know that what they preach is true. We can only develop a faith that it is so.

"That faith in inheriting a greater glory through the good physical life we lead becomes the motivation to take actions that demonstrate love for ourselves and for others."

Qadir stopped and took a deep breath, then let it out slowly. "Here is the most important part as far as your progress as my protégé goes. Faith is literally a power. Though it is almost always associated with religions, it is the greatest of all magickal powers.

"In the coming months I will be teaching you many magickal formulas, spells, enchantments, and words of power. You will learn fighting and banishing techniques so you can walk among demons unafraid while they will quake in your presence.

"But the greatest of all powers I cannot teach. It is something you must gain completely on your own, and that is faith.

"You are connected to all the energy of the universe. The power of the sun, of all the suns, is at your command, if you but have the faith to command it."

Qadir looked down at the ground for a moment then looked back at me and continued speaking.

"I confess that though I have an abundance of faith, I am still working to gain even greater faith. I have not yet arrived, but I can clearly see the destination and ever strive to get closer to it.

"There will come a time, more than once I am sure, where all the magickal and demon banishing knowledge you possess will be useless against a foe or foes you cannot defeat. The moment may be as overwhelming as an attacking horde of upper-level demons, or as inconspicuous as ingesting an unknown deadly poison, bacteria or virus.

"In your most desperate strait, when all hope would seem to be lost, if you have faith, you can call to you anything you wish and need to aid you in overcoming your foes.

"It will be like when you lucid dreamed and could change any scene into any variation you desired. Faith gives you that power for real, not just in a dream."

Qadir stopped speaking, but I was so raptly immersed in what he was sharing that I stared at him blankly for several seconds before it registered in my head that he was no longer talking.

"I am speechless," I finally stammered. "There is so

much to learn and know. It is almost disappointing that our physical lives are so brief. In our short time here, can we even learn a thimbleful of all there is to learn?"

Qadir chucked. "No need to worry about the limitations of learning in your physical life. You will have all of eternity for that. Just focus on gaining the knowledge you need to better navigate this life and fight demons."

"How did you learn all of this knowledge of the foundations of life?" I asked, somewhat in awe.

Qadir paused for a moment reflectively and then answered while steadfastly holding his gaze upon me. "Just as I am sharing this knowledge with you, it was shared with me by my Taz mentor, whose name was Barasel. He learned it from his mentor, who learned it from his mentor, and so on back countless generations.

It is said that the first group of Taz were visited together by an angel of God named Gabriel, who revealed the knowledge I have just shared with you and much more. The angel told them who and what they were, explained their stewardship and revealed the nature of their eternal adversaries, the demons.

I shook my finger at Qadir in a playful way. "After all you have shared, you still haven't told me much about demons."

CHAPTER
Nineteen

Hearing my continued light-hearted comment about how he still had not gotten around to more specifics about demons, Qadir chuckled jovially. "Only because there is so much to tell, my young friend.

"In the physical world, if people believe in demons at all, they just see them as some ill-defined evil caricature of a being. They are much, much more complicated and nuanced than that simple concept.

"Listen closely now," Qadir admonished, "as this is the part of my explanation where you will learn how demons came to exist.

"There actually was a great schism in the higher spirit realms. It is what some religions refer to as the war in heaven. It was not a war, after all how could angels, spirits, or any other creature expect to win a war against the all-powerful God that created them?

"It was a rebellion of malcontent spirits, instigated

and led by a spirit being named Lucifer. Some religions refer to him as a fallen angel. Lucifer was never an angel; he was just a cunning spirit being who was too full of himself. He was a persuasive speaker and succeeded in leading many of our spirit brothers and sisters down a dark and dreary path.

"In a nutshell, God had established the opportunity for all of the spirit beings to gain a physical body when they were ready to leave the premortal dimension of existence, and use their physical life to grow and expand their soul in ways that could only be achieved in a physical body.

"A spark of divine light is placed within every soul, even demons, because we are all creations of God.

"No matter how far someone falls down the path of darkness, the divine light in their soul will always be a small, quiet part of their consciousness that lets them discern right from wrong and good from evil.

"They can push the discerning light away; they can justify their despicable actions; they can numb their heart and mind to the light by repeated acts of darkness. Yet no matter how evil someone may become, they can never fully extinguish the light of truth in their soul. They still innately know right from wrong.

"With that divine light in every soul that could not be extinguished, God granted everyone the freedom to make their own choices in their physical lives.

"With every choice of significance we make, some good, some poor, we either gain or lose light in our soul. That was the part of God's plan to which Lucifer objected.

"Lucifer correctly pointed out that if someone

repeatedly made bad choices, when they died and passed from their physical life, they would have less light in their soul essence than before they were born into a physical life.

"If they made many horrendously awful choices, they could end up losing so much light from their souls that they could no longer manifest as beings made in the image of God.

"God did not dispute anything Lucifer claimed, but merely agreed that eternal progression could at times involve regression if someone made poor choices and took actions that were hurtful to themselves or others.

"Lucifer told God that he had a better plan. With Lucifer's plan, every person would still come into a physical life and have the opportunity to have those experiences unique to a physical body, but they would not be allowed to make any choices or take any actions that would be detrimental to themselves or others.

"They would be forced to only behave in ways that did not take away light from their soul's essence. Hence, at the very least, none of those that took a physical body would have to worry about departing their physical life with less light in their soul essence than before they were born.

"Lucifer was extremely proud that he had devised a plan that was superior to God's, at least in his mind.

"Being the persuasive fellow he was, Lucifer convinced almost one-third of our brothers and sisters of spirit that he had a better plan than God. In mass, they marched to the throne of God and demanded that God implement Lucifer's plan.

"God patiently explained that it was only by giving them the freedom to choose right from wrong in their physical lives, along with an inner light that could never be extinguished, that they would truly be able to benefit and progress from a physical life that made all the travails they would experience worthwhile."

Qadir stopped for a moment and took a deep breath, slowly letting it out. He looked intently into my eyes.

"It is very important that you understand the essential concept of freedom to choose right or wrong. It is the bridge from wherever you are to wherever you want to go.

"If you did not have the freedom to make a bad choice, you would not have the opportunity to build your character by wrestling with yourself about what course to take, and then choosing the path that lifts you and others up.

"If you never have the option to take a wrong action, or travel a dark path, you would never have the possibility of developing faith, because you would already know your inevitable future.

"If you never developed faith, you would fall short of gaining the greatest power in the universe and your soul would be unable to progress beyond a certain point.

"If you could only do good and never err or make mistakes for which you needed to make amends, your life experiences would be stale and boring.

"You would gain knowledge in your mind, but knowing that your future was predestined, would make your heart empty and passionless; your life would lack ambition, and your sojourn in the physical life would be rendered a fruitless waste of time.

"Without passion and with no possibility of making foolish errors that you can then apply the balm of reconciliation, your relationships would be unfulfilled and your life would be dull and uninspiring.

"Knowledge combined with passion is the spark of creativity and genius from which all the innovations of life spring. Without passion, knowledge alone is severely handicapped at best, and impotent at worst.

"God explained all of these truths to Lucifer and his horde of followers, but to no avail. Lucifer imagined that backed by all of the misguided souls that followed him, that his power was greater than God's. He insisted that God throw away his plan and follow the plan Lucifer decreed.

"His horde of minions all shouted out in agreement, demanding that God follow Lucifer's plan.

"It was at that very moment in eternal time, when they rebelled against God's most sacred plan for the eternal progression of all spirit children that Lucifer and all of his followers devolved into demons.

"They lost massive amounts of light from their soul essence by their ultimate defiance and rejection of God's love. The light of their souls was no longer bright enough to sustain them in the higher realms of spirit. It was no longer bright enough for them to be born into a physical body or worthy of having one.

"Most of them devolved into demons; some even lesser creatures. They have substance in the 2nd and 3rd dimensions, but cannot manifest corporeally in the 1st Dimension.

"By their stupendously stupid actions, they cursed themselves. They condemned themselves to not have the opportunity of living a life in a physical body; to not be able to enjoy all of its pleasures, or grow the light of their souls from physical experiences.

"This is why demons hate everyone that has a physical body. This is why they invest so much of their time and abilities to get people to abuse their bodies in every conceivable way a body can be abused and misused, and cause as many human lives as possible to be wasted and squandered."

I was like a sponge, soaking up all of the wonderful knowledge of the bigger picture of the world I never knew. I started to ask Qadir a question when we were startled by a loud commotion coming from the direction of the leialli herd.

The leialli were suddenly moving about frantically. What sounded like discordant musical horns, blasted loudly in the air.

Qadir leaped to his feet staring at the leialli commotion about one hundred yards away.

DEMONS! He yelled angrily. A long-bladed sword similar to the one that Genavieve had wielded suddenly appeared in his right hand pointing toward the sky.

"Remain here!" he ordered. Without another word he blinked away to join the fray.

CHAPTER
Twenty

Heeding Qadir's command to remain where I was and being mindful of my complete lack of ability to defend myself against demons, I moved behind the thick tree trunk to remain as hidden as possible. I peered around the trunk just far enough to watch the battle unfolding.

I was stunned by what I saw. There had to be at least fifty demons fighting with the small leialli herd! I could see Qadir slashing his sword in a whirlwind around him. He seemed more on the defensive than offensive, but I guess that could be expected being outnumbered 50 to 1.

The leialli were in even worse straights. Unlike Qadir's sword, which could be maneuvered in any direction despite which direction he might be facing, the leialli were limited to using their horn as a spear solely in the area in front of them or to their side, leaving them vulnerable from a rear attack.

Initially, the leialli formed a defensive circle with all

of their tail ends facing in toward a small center circle, and their sharp-pointed horns facing out, with at least one young foal protected in the center. But their defense failed as demons quickly blinked into the inner circle and some onto the backs of the leialli, scattering the startled herd.

When the herd split their defensive formation apart, I saw a young foal flee from the inner sanctuary where the adults had been protecting it. Two adults broke with it and ran away from the battle with the foal running between their bodies for protection. Six demons yelling like maniacs pursued them.

More demons tried to take up the pursuit, but the remaining adult leialli blocked them, and along with Qadir, furiously engaged them in mortal combat.

I didn't have long to watch the main battle as the foal and two adult leialli were heading right for me with the six-pack horde of demons right behind them!

Suddenly, one of the two adults fleeing with the foal stopped and turned about abruptly, instantly impaling an onrushing demon with its long horn. In the space of a breath it flipped the lifeless demon over its head and unerringly impaled another charging demon.

To my horror, before the leialli could kill a third demon, the remaining four monsters rushed at it from all sides, their wicked sharp-edged weapons whipping around without mercy.

The valiant leialli was stabbed and sliced all over its body, but still managed to impale one more demon with its horn before it fell on its side mortally wounded, and was gruesomely decapitated by one of the demons.

My blood boiled when I saw that. I hadn't hated demons before, I just despised them. But seeing that utter cruelty, a wave of fierce anger welled up inside of me such as I had never experienced in my life.

One of the pursuing demons threw a spear and it embedded deeply into the haunch of the other adult leialli. Its one back leg became useless, and rather than try to continue fleeing, like its mate it turned to face the oncoming demons.

The foal stopped for a moment when the adult was speared and looked at the larger leialli in confusion. The adult gave the foal a brief loving look, then jerked its horn around to face the demons that were upon it.

The last gaze from adult to child must have included an unspoken message for the foal to continue running, because it immediately turned and continued heading straight for my tree with all the speed it could muster.

Sadly, the remaining leialli did not have as much success fighting the demons as the first one. Already wounded and immobilized by the spear in its haunch, the other demons were able to mortally wound and then decapitate it without ever coming within reach of its deadly spiral horn.

During the, less than a minute, it took for the second leialli to be killed, the baby foal made it to my tree. I expected it to continue fleeing right past me, but instead it leaped right into my arms quivering in fear.

The remaining three demons were charging toward us swirling their weapons and screaming like banshees.

I should have felt abject fear at my own imminent demise, but that is not what I felt. Having watched in helpless horror as the two courageous leialli had been slaughtered, and now having the baby leialli leaning deeply into me shaking with fear obviously hoping I would protect it, I stood up in front of the tree with grim, resolute anger to face the three onrushing demons. The baby leialli cowered behind me with its other side against the trunk of the tree.

The demons obviously saw me as easy prey. They slowed to a walk and surrounded me in a half-circle, mocking me. "Oh look!" a huge, hairy brute in front of me taunted. "This little Izbo wants to fight us."

All the demons laughed at the first one's hilarious comment.

"He can't fight us and we can't kill him," an ugly female demon proclaimed.

"He's just one of those weird psychic Izbo apparitions. He's not really here. Just grab the brat. We have what we came for."

As the demons were about to find out, I did in fact have substance in these worlds. I didn't have weapons, but I vowed to myself that they would feel the fury of my fists before I fell to their inevitable death blows.

The big hairy demon bent down to reach through what he thought was my immaterial body to grab the baby leialli. I balled both of my fists together and raising my hands above my head, brought them swiftly down hoping to knock him out before he could grab the foal.

To both mine and the demon's shock, what came down on the demon's head was not my clenched fists, but a mighty razor-sharp sword that split the demon's body in half. The carcass immediately vaporized with a slight wisp of dirty smoke.

The other two demons looked at me in abject horror as I lifted the point of the sword toward them. The female frantically yelled out a warning in extreme fright, TAZ! TAZ! There is another Taz!

And that was it. Those two demons immediately blinked out and they were quickly followed by all the remaining demons that had been fighting in the main battle.

For a moment there was deathly silence. Qadir blinked over to stand beside me, but he did not say a word. After a couple of minutes, the surviving leialli also came over and stood around me and the foal. No one spoke, no one moved, and I was uncertain of what would come next.

CHAPTER
Twenty—One

When the leialli stopped in front of me, the little foal left my side and scurried over to the adults. They closed ranks and stood shoulder to shoulder facing me, with the foal standing between the two adults in the center of the line.

Qadir took a few steps over to me and touched the hilt of my sword, which I was holding with the point embedded slightly into the ground.

"Nice sword," he complimented. "It looks almost like mine. However did you get it to come to you?"

I looked at Qadir with some exasperation.

"I don't mean to be disrespectful Qadir, but I do not know the answer to your question. And talking about this sword seems a trivial subject at the moment, considering the tragedy we have all just been a part of. What in the heck just happened?"

"Quite a lot for such a short period of time," Qadir noted calmly. "Let me see if I can encapsulate the events for you."

He pointed to the leialli. "These wonderful creatures, which exude only love and would never injure another being except in self-defense, were as you know, attacked by a greedy, blood-thirsty horde of demons."

He pointed to the little foal. "They were after that young one.

"However, one young leialli alone is useless to them. So regardless of whether they succeeded or failed here today, they will continue to make raids on leialli herds until they achieve their goal of capturing two young foals of the opposite sex. They will treat them well and raise them together in a large, spacious high-fenced enclosure in a pleasant meadow, with comfort and amenities until they are adults.

"Despite the comforts the demons provide, the leialli will know that they are prisoners. If the leialli fall in love, which the demons futilely hope they will, they will not mate as they would never accept having their offspring born as a prisoner of demons.

"The demons do not actually care whether or not the leialli have offspring. They just want them to fall in love, which is fairly inevitable when they are the only leialli the other ever sees.

"Once they are deeply in love, the demons will begin to use them for the actual purpose they captured them for years earlier.

"You see leialli have very special healing magick. Most creatures think that it is their horn that is magickal, but that is not the case. Their spiral horn merely acts as a wand to focus and magnify the magickal power that dwells within the leialli.

"A few ignorant, unscrupulous inhabitants of this world, mainly the glash of the Glahscat Clan, who are mentally challenged due to generations of inbreeding, kill these lovely creatures to cut off their horns and grind them into a powder so they can sell it as a healing balm to gullible louts. And it is all for nothing as the horn has no healing magick! The same type of heinous act is done on Earth with Rhino horns.

"True leialli magick bestowed by a loving, living leialli, will almost immediately heal even the most grievous physical injury and banish even the most formidable diseases.

"However, their magick is powered by the love that issues forth from their living, beating heart. The leialli has to feel the emotion of love for the power of its magick to come forth.

"Their horn is just keratin, the same stuff your own fingernails are made from, just compacted into a more dense form.

"It is so sad for me to see these lovely, loving creatures killed to have their horn sawn off and ground into a useless healing powder. Their murderers should just grind up their own fingernails and sell that powder. The healing effect would be the same and the cost of lives and effort far less.

"Demons are smarter than most creatures. They know the leialli' healing power comes from the leialli itself and not from their horn.

"Being locked for all of their life in a small enclosure by demons engenders only anger and even hatred for their captors. You would think that captured leialli would be of no use to demons.

"However, that assumption would be wrong. Demons are cunning; they use the love of the leialli for each other to ensure their healing magick issues forth when needed.

"Though demons are immortal and can self-heal, severe injuries can take several days to heal and the pain they feel during that time can be excruciating. Demons cannot feel physical pleasure of any kind, but they certainly feel physical pain. However, the loving touch of a leialli takes all their pain away in a moment and heals their injury at once.

"Demons are constantly fighting, most often pitting one horde against another. They suffer horrible injuries on a regular basis. A horde that possesses a mated pair of leialli for healing, owns a very valuable commodity."

I was confused by Qadir's explanation. "How could the leialli ever have love for the demons? Their healing magick would never work, so what would be the point of the demons capturing and keeping them?"

Qadir held his index finger up. "Ah yes, that is the vexing question. Remember, I said demons were cunning. They are also very, very cruel.

When a demon needs to be healed, if one of their leialli objects, they will separate them. One, usually the female, will be put into a small, restrictive cage that does not even allow them to move. This cage will be placed directly in front of the cage of their mate. The caged leialli will then be tortured - nothing that would cause them permanent injury, but diabolical inflictions that cause them terrible pain.

"Because of their great capacity for love, the very first scream of agony from their caged mate will cause all the love in the heart of the uncaged leialli to come rushing forth.

"To save their mate any further pain, the unharmed leialli will agree to heal the demons, ignoring the hate in its heart for them, and thinking only of the love for their mate, so the healing magick will work.

"It only takes a few torture sessions before the leialli meekly acquiesce whenever they are called upon in the future to heal a demon. They know they cannot escape their captivity, so for the love of their mate, they will do whatever they must do to keep them safe.

"The demons, in turn, reward the leialli for their good behavior with regular treats of favorite foods and leave them alone to live their lives, except when they are called upon to heal."

I looked over at the little foal. I certainly had love in my heart for that young leialli. Even though our moments together were very brief, they were emotionally very intense since it had sought my protection as its last hope. Ultimately I was willing to die trying to defend it.

"Why go to all the trouble to try and capture young leialli? I asked Qadir. "It would seem far easier to capture an adult."

Qadir nodded his head in agreement. "Easier yes; helpful no.

"Adults have already mated for life soon after they reach maturity. They are not like horses that have one stallion for a herd of mares.

"Demons have tried to put two unmated mature leialli together in the past, but they were defiant and could not be tamed. Without exception, despite any torture inflicted upon them, they would rather die than submit to the will of demons.

"Sadly, demons being demons, when the leialli would not submit to their will, they would be slowly tortured to death over a period of days. Even demon hordes that are normally enemies would declare a truce to come watch the spectator spectacle of a leialli torture.

"The pleasure demons derive from seeing the suffering of others can never be understated. Because they are such fiends, none of the Taz that oppose them has any qualms about ending their despicable current existence and dispatching them without mercy to centuries of cold and loneliness in the realm of Oblivion."

Qadir smiled at me and patted me on my shoulder with his palm. "And I was obviously right to choose you as my protégé. Both Genavieve and I saw the distinct gold sparkle in your aura that only a Taz will have.

"She thought you first needed to be uplifted by your catalyst before the gold band would expand and allow you to call the Dragon Sword and fulfill your stewardship as a Taz. I thought the same. Obviously, we were both wrong, but in a good way."

Qadir gestured over toward the leialli that had been quietly standing and listening as attentively to his words as I had been.

"You have made lifetime friends of the leialli. Cherish them; for a bonded friendship like this is very rare and you have been found worthy by your actions today.

"Don't ever endanger their lives by bringing them into the 1st Dimension, even if it is for what you might perceive as a worthy cause such as healing an injured Taz. Leialli hate having magick used on them and transporting them to the 1st Dimension would be a grievous injury to their mental health. Even worse, in the 1st Dimension they would be easy prey for demons. They would also feel forlornly hopeless and alone in a world that cannot see them and one in which they can have no interaction with anyone other than with demons or Taz. The energy of their resonance is here in the 2nd Dimension as part of a herd, and in this world, you will never find more steadfast and loyal friends."

I nodded to Qadir in silent understanding and pivoted to look directly at the band of leialli. I bowed deeply to them to show my respect and love. In turn, each of the adults bowed their heads and touched their long, spiral horns to the ground.

Unexpectedly, I clearly heard, *friends*, as words spoken in my mind repeated several times, with varying inflections. It is a difficult challenge to describe what words that are not your own sound like when you hear them in your mind. It is somewhat like silently talking to yourself, but you know the words are coming from somewhere else.

I looked over at Qadir a bit confused and he sensed the source of my bewilderment.

"Ah yes, I forgot to let you know that leialli are telepathic as are most denizens of Sx, when they desire. It's really a marvelous form of communication.

213

Just look directly at the leialli you wish to speak with telepathically or see them clearly in your mind," he explained."

Qadir spoke very matter-of-factly as if telepathy was just an everyday experience. I supposed it might be on Sx, but it was wondrously amazing to me.

I smiled broadly, thinking about the freedom and possibilities of telepathic communication, but quickly turned my thoughts and attention to the young foal that had stepped away from the adults and came over to nuzzle my hands with affection.

After a minute or so, he returned to stand with the adult leialli, but kept his head up and eyes on me.

Unsure of the protocol, I hesitated for a moment, but ended up not being able to stop myself. I stepped over to the band of leialli, and one by one, I wrapped my arms around their necks and telepathically told them that I loved them and was so sorry for their losses.

To my humble delight, as I embraced each one around their neck, they blew a happy musical note through their horn, and telepathically in my mind I heard each one say their name and the words *I love you*.

The first leialli I hugged was a large, vivid red and blue streaked male that the foal had gone over to stand next to.

Despite having just been introduced to telepathy, I was still startled when I clearly heard him say his name, *Dorsavel*, in my mind and then the words, *I love you*.

I turned to smile at Qadir with what I'm sure was a look of child-like wonder on my face. He immediately perceived the source of my delight.

"Ah, I can tell by the rapturous look on your face that you are becoming quite enamored of telepathy and leialli."

"Yes," I nodded serenely in acknowledgment.

"As you will encounter a myriad of telepathic creatures in the magickal 2nd Dimension, I suppose I should tell you a bit about what you are experiencing."

I continued to hold onto and softly rub Dorsavel's neck while Qadir explained the intricacies of telepathy to me.

"You see there are two types of telepathy," he began. "If you are communicating with a being that speaks any of the languages you may know, such as English or French, then you will hear the words they are thinking clearly in your mind, just as if they had spoken them aloud."

"However, if you are communicating with a being or creature whose language you do not know, such as the leialli here, then the communication will be more primitive. This is because, for the most part, they will be conveying thoughts rather than words, or usually a melding of thoughts and words.

"For instance, what did you just hear telepathically?" Qadir asked.

"I heard a name, *Dorsavel*, and the words *I love you*, I replied.

"A perfect example!" Qadir exclaimed. "When Dorsavel said his name, he thought the name in his head and you heard it in your head exactly the same and understood that you were hearing his name. The fact that you do not speak Leialli was irrelevant because your mind understood it was a name that you were hearing.

"When Dorsavel told you, *I love you*, he thought those words in his mind, but those would not be words your mind would understand from the Leialli language.

"However, your mind and heart did understand the feeling that was being telepathically conveyed, and your mind translated that feeling into the words *I love you*.

"Perfectly clear?" Qadir asked expectantly.

"Perfectly clear," I agreed. "Thanks for the explanation."

I proceeded to similarly embrace each leialli, and like Dorsavel, each leialli said their name and then said, *I love you*.

After my first experience with Dorsavel and hearing Qadir's explanation, I reciprocated the greeting with each subsequent leialli I embraced. After they introduced themselves and said *I love you*, I in turn told them my name: Trevallion, and added with deep sincerity, *I love you*.

The marvelous magick of unconditional love also began to work in my heart. With each *I love you* that I heard, and with each one that I in turn said, I started to feel an ever-increasing bond with the leialli that became overwhelmingly powerful and familiar, like I had known and loved these beautiful leialli all of my life.

When I knelt down and embraced the young one, he surprised me with the melodious little musical sound coming out of his horn. I had no idea yet what his real name was, but hearing his musical exclamation I couldn't help affectionately giving him a nickname.

"I'll miss you most of all Little Toot, but I'll see you again before the passage of another day."

In response, I heard him say in my mind, his name and then he expressed his affection, "*Bilsobe. I love you Trevallion!*"

I gave him a big hug around his neck and telepathically told him, "*I love you too!*"

I looked at him eye to eye and asked aloud, "You don't mind if I call you Little Toot do you?"

Bilsobe looked at me blankly without answering.

"You have to ask him telepathically for him to understand," Qadir interjected. "He doesn't comprehend spoken English."

"Of course," I nodded in realization. I repeated my question telepathically and Little Toot responded enthusiastically, kicking up his heels and blowing a pleasant note through his horn.

Qadir brought his two palms together as if he were praying.

"A good ending to a tragic day. It would have been much worse if you had not unexpectedly manifested your Dragon Sword and the demons chasing the foal had not been so dim-witted that they didn't stop and stand still for a few seconds so they could transit in front of the fleeing leialli, instead of chasing behind them.

"I have much still to share with you my young apprentice. As fast as you have advanced, you are still nothing more than a naked babe in the woods. However, it is time for your Taz body to slumber so your Earth body can awaken, which I imagine is quite ready to arise.

"Simply desire your Taz twin to transit to Corsalain and to sleep. So it shall immediately be as you desired, and then your Earth body in the 1st Dimension should awaken."

I was a bit bewildered by Qadir's explanation. "Where's Corsalain?"

"Ah yes," Qadir said absentmindedly. "That's my home here on Sx. It will be your home as well until you build your own. There's a bed there waiting for you.

"Off with you now. Meet me here again tomorrow when your 1st Dimension self once again slumbers. I will take you to my home on Earth near Montepuliciano and we will begin your real training."

It was true; I could feel the inexorable pull of my Earth body ready to awaken. I looked at Qadir, my mind still overwhelmed by all he had taught me in a single night while my 1st Dimension body slept.

"Thank you my friend, my day will not be able to go by fast enough, so anxious will I be to see you again."

With that parting, Qadir blinked away and I closed my eyes and willed my Taz body to my bed in Corsalain, while simultaneously looking forward with excitement to waking up in my bed on Earth and remembering all that had just happened.

To my shock and confusion, when I opened my eyes it was not in my bed back home and it was not my Earth body eyes that opened. I was in a spacious, dimly lit room, looking about in confusion, trying to understand exactly what had happened and where

I was. I tried to move, but once again, as when I first encountered Qadir with Genavieve, I was completely immobilized.

The unpleasant answer to my predicament was soon revealed. A tall, slim man, dressed smartly, though a bit eccentrically, came and stood in front of me.

"Welcome to my home in the 3rd Dimension Trevallion. Please allow me to introduce myself. My name is Hamerac. I am a Level 12 demon, and I am so looking forward to getting to know you better."

CHAPTER
Twenty—Two

My eyes went big with disbelief that I was once again immobilized! First it was by Qadir and now by the demon Hamerac. This sure seemed to be a popular bit of magick.

I looked about for my sword, but apparently it did not make the trip with me, not that it would do me any good, as all I could do was blink my eyes.

Hamerac circled around me a couple of times like a hawk circling its prey before pouncing and tearing them to shreds, piece by piece.

"Not to worry young Taz," Hamerac assured me. "As long as you do nothing to attack or hurt me, I will reciprocate and not do anything to harm you in any way. I just want to talk to you and get to know you a bit. Give me a few moments of your time and I will release you from the paralysis binding so you will soon be free to return to your 1st Dimension body."

I just glared at Hamerac and could do nothing else

as my lips were sealed shut. Hamerac saw my dilemma.

"Just blink your eyes rapidly three times if you agree to my terms of a truce."

I readily blinked my eyes as he directed, reasoning he could have easily already killed me in my defenseless, paralyzed state if he wished. Obviously, my immediate death was not his goal, and being free of my bonds would allow me to at least have some ability to defend myself.

True to his word, as I blinked my eyes three times I felt the constraint of the paralysis immediately fade away.

Hamerac waved his hand and two comfortable-looking easy chairs popped into the room beside us. Hamerac sat in one of the chairs and motioned for me to sit in the other. I looked at the chair with great suspicion. I didn't trust Hamerac at all and I was already envisioning sitting in the chair and then being engulfed and suffocated by it.

"I assure you the chair is just a chair and will do you no harm," Hamerac promised.

Rather than take his word for that I decided sticking around was a bad idea. I smiled at Hamerac, then willed my Taz self to go to Corsalain to sleep so my Earth self could awaken back home; but of course, nothing happened!

Hamerac perceived my failed attempt. "Sorry there Taz junior, I released you from the paralysis binding, but I'm afraid I am still blocking your departure from my hospitality.

"None of your powers are viable here in my home. In my domain, I am surrounded by all of the magickal objects that I have collected and enchanted over the millennia. This is the place of my greatest power in the entire universe. I am God here! Not even Lord Lucifer would dare challenge me in my realm.

"As difficult as I'm sure it is for you to comprehend, I merely wish to talk with you for a few minutes. I know you must consciously return to your Earth body soon or people in your world will call the medical authorities when you don't wake up.

"Please sit down, be comfortable and spend a few minutes in conversation with me and I promise I will let you return to Earth with no strings attached, as they like to say on your world."

What choice did I have? I certainly couldn't think of one at the moment, so I reluctantly sat down in the chair. Like the matching chair Hamerac was sitting in, the foot panel rose up from the bottom with my feet on it, and the back slightly tilted, like a Lazy Boy chair, leaving me actually in a very comfortable semi-reclined position.

Hamerac put his two hands together interlocking his fingers. "There now, isn't this cozy?"

I wasn't for a moment fooled by his pleasant ways and remained silently glaring at him, rather than answering him. He didn't seem disturbed by my obstinacy and just continued talking.

"I'm sure you are wondering why a high-level demon, like me, is being so nice to you. Undoubtedly, you would like to hear that I am a different sort or demon, or that I just want to be your friend. But the harsh reality is, a demon does not get to the 12th level by being nice to anyone, particularly Izbos, and especially a Taz.

"Please have no illusions. I am very proud to be

ruthless, heartless, and as cruel as any demon you will ever encounter and I intend to be even more so in the future.

"Nevertheless, I can help you and you can help me, and as long as that is a workable and mutually beneficial arrangement, you have my word that I will do you no harm.

"The benefit to you is, you will have an invaluable source of information about the demon world. I can provide you with a wide range of knowledge, including magickal knowledge that you will be unable to obtain from any other source, including the other Taz.

"When our goals are not opposed and have any mutual benefit, I will even help you to banish other demons, as long as they are not from my horde."

At his last foul utterance I could hold my tongue no longer. "What makes you think I am so stupid that I would ever trust the word of a demon? A demon's word is an oxymoron. The very fact that you offered to help banish other demons is obvious proof that you are lying."

Though I spoke with contempt and even vehemence, it did not affect Hamerac's genial way of replying.

"I forgive you your angry tone. I know in your mind it is justified by the bloody slaughter you just witnessed with the leialli at the hands of demons. Typical of an Izbo, you are merely displaying your own ignorance, of both the bigger picture and smaller pictures.

"You are a curiosity Trevallion. For some odd, thus far inexplicable reason, as I've gleaned from conversations between the Taz Qadir and Genavieve, you gained your Taz powers before you had encountered your catalyst.

"I have seen this a few other times during the last couple of thousand years. Those Taz always became particularly great problems for the demon world for the short time they lived in their physical bodies.

"I should point out to you that the efforts of all of the Taz from the beginning of time until this day have actually been an exercise in futility.

"Even if you manage to live to a ripe old age of say 100 years, that is a pittance of time compared to the immortal lives of demons. And anything you manage to do to thwart demons during your very short physical life, including banishing them, is only a temporary measure.

"Because of our ability to reconstitute from wounds, and return from banishment within several hundred years, the Taz are merely a form of entertainment in our lives. Nothing any of you can do has any lasting damaging effect."

Perhaps foolishly, I was not feeling threatened at the moment and felt safe speaking my mind. Hamerac really did seem to just want to have a conversation for the moment. I still had to mentally pinch myself to accept that I was sitting in an easy chair casually talking with a high-level demon.

"I know you have been around for thousands, and maybe even tens of thousands of years Hamerac. Your knowledge must truly be vast, but your understanding of humans seems to still be lacking.

"The fact that I am a Taz means little. Whatever that actually entails is still a mystery to me. But I am a human, and I believe that most humans, at least if they are not being influenced or possessed by demons, have an inner light that motivates and prompts them to be kind and helpful to others.

"Humans will not refrain from doing good just because the good might be undone at some point in the future. If it is helping in the moment, it is a worthy endeavor.

"If a demon was hurting another being, whether it was a human or a magickal, mythical creature from another dimension, and a human could do something to stop it in that moment, unless they were a coward, or under demon influence, they would do what they could to help.

"They wouldn't think, Oh well, why waste my time, or risk my life or treasure helping them now, when their problem will just return again in the future.

"You pointed out our short lives compared to your immortal ones. That is actually a good comparison worth remembering, but not for the reason you might suppose.

"If I am ever fortunate enough to banish another demon, that demon will be eliminated for the entire lives of everyone it had been tormenting. Every person or creature that demon had ever plagued will be free of that demon's harassment for the rest of their short mortal life and their lives will be happier because of it.

"The reality that the immortal demon may return in a few hundred years is irrelevant. None of the people or creatures the demon had ever tormented will be bothered by them again in their lifetime, so as far as they are concerned, they have been freed forever."

Hamerac slapped his hand on his leg with enthusiasm.

"That's what I am talking about! Though I had figured that aspect out over four thousand years ago, it was still excellent to hear you explain it from your perspective.

"Now it's your turn. Feel free to ask me any question."

I had a long mental list, but the most pressing one was, "How did you bring me here?"

"Oh, that's an excellent question," Hamerac complimented.

"Any upper-level demon has the ability to see and hear anything happening in the dimension that they tune into, as long as they are not magickally blocked. We use an enchanted crystal gazing ball for this purpose.

"With my crystal ball, I watched the fight with the inept mini-horde that attacked the leialli. Before that, I observed and heard everything that transpired with you in the davos village.

"I quickly deduced you were a newly fledged Taz when I heard Qadir introduce you to the davos, Loxadol as his protégé, and I saw you eat food establishing that you had physical substance in the 2nd Dimension, and were not just a strongly psychic Izbo.

"Once you have been trained for a couple of years, you will know how to prevent demons, or Izbos wise in magick, from intercepting you when you transit from one location to another. But for now, you do not. So I waited until you tried to return your active consciousness to your Earth body, and used the rare opportunity to bring your Taz body here as my uninvited, but very welcome guest."

Hamerac paused and started to ask his next question, but I interrupted him. "You did not actually answer my question of how you brought me here."

Hamerac laughed, not in a pleasant way, more like a cackle with an evil tone and forced smile - so that his laugh seemed more threatening than jovial.

"I will not be revealing my magickal methods to you young Taz. That would not be in my best interest. You will have to learn that secret from your mentor, if he ever gets around to revealing it to you."

Hamerac rubbed his hands together in gleeful anticipation. "My turn again. How did you call the Dragon Sword to you? By your surprised reaction, it was obviously your first time. Had you tried previously and failed? Or, have you been practicing and finally succeeded at precisely the most opportune moment?

"Demons can materialize any weapon they have an affinity for, but even Lord Lucifer cannot materialize a Dragon Sword. So how did you do it?"

I looked at Hamerac indignantly. "You won't answer me a simple question about how you brought me here. A question you have already told me I can get the answer to from Qadir, yet you expect me to tell you one of the greatest secrets of a Taz?"

Hamerac put his hand to his chin pondering my words for a few seconds, then blurted out, "Alright, I will tell you, as long as you reciprocate and answer my question."

"Agreed," I acknowledged.

"It was a magickal summoning spell. It only works on beings and creatures that are not innately magickal. So it will work on an Izbo, a davos, and most higher creatures of this world, but it will not work on creatures where magick is part of their physical being, such as a leialli or an oosas.

"One of the essential components of the spell is, you must know the name of whomever you are summoning. As lower creatures do not have names, at least not ones we are aware of, we cannot summon them by this spell. However, they can still be summoned by a different type of spell. It is only innately magickal creatures that are entirely immune to summoning spells.

"Tell me now, how did you summon the Dragon Sword?"

I shook my index finger in the air. "Nope, you still have not answered my question. I want you to tell me completely how to do this summoning spell so I can do it myself."

"Oh, alright!" Hamerac spat out. "You are exasperating. Are you this much trouble to the Taz Qadir?"

I just lifted my palms in a silent 'I don't know,' and let Hamerac continue.

"I will reveal the complete spell to you, with your promise to not leave out one detail of how you summoned the Dragon Sword at the precise moment you needed it."

I promise I will tell you every detail," I assured him.

Hamerac took a deep breath, exhaled slowly, and then continued his explanation.

"There are three essential ingredients you must have before doing the spell. You must know their name, recognize their face, and be ready to act at the exact moment that they try to transit somewhere.

"The last requirement makes this an almost impossible spell for anyone except a high-level demon, or another type of being that has a very great repertoire of magickal skills.

"For instance, I will tell you how to do this spell, but you will not be able to do it without an enchanted crystal ball that allows you to observe someone's every word and movement.

"Even then, transits most often occur as an instant reaction to a threatening situation, or in a silent thought of the being that is transiting. Even if you are carefully observing them, it is only occasionally that you will be ready to act at the very moment they initiate the transit in their mind.

"Usually the opportunity arises when the being announces that they are leaving, such as you did. That unaware but thoughtful forewarning is an alert that they will be transiting in moments.

"To prepare the spell, you must place a picture of them under the crystal ball. It can be a drawing, a photograph, or a painting, but it must be a good representation of their appearance. Their image will show through the crystal ball.

"As you are observing them, and you see them preparing to transit, you merely say their name once and the magickal word of power *Ulqwizar* three times. When they try to transit anytime during the next seven seconds, they will come to you instead of to their intended destination.

"There, I have fulfilled my part. It is now your turn. How did you call the Dragon Sword?"

I was sure Hamerac was not going to like my answer. "Actually, I had never even heard the term Dragon Sword until Qadir said the name to me after the demon raid was over. As I'm sure you observed watching us in your crystal ball, he also wanted to know how I got the sword to come to me.

"The truth is, I would like to know too. I had no thought whatsoever of calling the sword, and as far as I know, I said or did nothing to summon it. The sword just appeared in my hands. I was as surprised as everyone else."

Hamerac eyed me warily. "I have a grain of admiration for your sly answer. That was very tricky, almost demon-like in leading me to believe I would receive much more than you knew you would reveal.

"However, I hope you are not too disappointed to learn that you actually fully answered my question to my satisfaction. I now know something about you, and about Taz and Dragon Swords that I did not previously know.

"True to my promise to let you return home, I will answer one more question for you and then you will be free to go."

I had many questions, but it was hard thinking about them as I was trying to figure out how the little bit that I had told Hamerac about summoning the Dragon Sword could have had any value to him. And I was worried that I had somehow revealed something that would cause me or other Taz harm in the future.

In retrospect, there were more valuable answers I could have sought with my last question, but I still was happy I asked the one I did. It would help me in the future to have a better understanding of my adversaries.

"Explain to me the organization of the demon world. You say you are a Level 12 demon. I also encountered a Level 13 Demon named Ugar. How does all of that work?"

"You met Ugar and survived? That seems quite impossible. I promised to let you return to your 1st Dimension body after this question. But how you escaped from Ugar will be my first question on our next meeting."

In my mind, this was going to be my first and last meeting with Hamerac, but I didn't tell him that and let him continue with the answer to my question.

"Lord Lucifer set up the demon hierarchy and the rules for advancement. It is easiest to understand if you start at the top and work down.

"Level 13 is the highest level and its members are Lord Lucifer's most valued demons. There are only thirteen demons at that level.

The numbers of demons in Levels 12 through 5 increases exponentially as you descend and multiply the level number by the next exponential number sequentially increasing. So my level 12 is multiplied by the power of 2 or squared (12 x 12), to give a total of 144 demons at this level.

Level 11 is to the power of 3 (11 x 11 x 11), resulting in 1,728 demons at that level.

"It continues like that, so Level 10 is to the power of 4 (10 x 10 x 10 x 10) and has 10,000 demons. By the time you get to Level 5 it is to the 9th power exponentially and there are 1,953,125 demons at that level.

"Levels 4 through 1 are chaos levels and have no set

number, but there are billions of demons in those levels.

To advance in levels 1-4, a demon merely needs to challenge a demon at the next level up to combat. If the challenger prevails, they advance up to the next level, while the defeated demon must go down to the lower level.

To advance to Level 5, or any of the higher levels, a demon must first pass the tests for that level that have been created by Lord Lucifer. These will include both academic and practical tests, such as demonstrating specific magickal abilities.

"The practical tests will always also include tasks that must be accomplished: everything from something simple at lower levels, such as proving their ability to transit, to something more challenging at mid-levels, such as enslaving a formidable creature like a glash or a hokrok, or inhabiting an Izbo. At higher levels there is always one test that is the same: a horde must be formed and successfully directed on an important campaign.

"The attack on the leialli herd was certainly the effort of a 10th or 11th level demon to qualify for advancement. Happily, they failed miserably; one less competitor," Hamerac gloated.

"Seeing demons aspiring for upper-level status fail is very satisfying. If they had succeeded in the last step to achieving their upper-level status, they would need to defeat a demon like me at the next level up in combat.

"When the incompetents fail at their campaign test, they never have the opportunity to challenge an upper-level demon to combat. We are therefore spared the wasted energy of having to defeat them.

"And because they failed with their campaign, other demons will no longer have confidence in them and they will not be able to convince lower level demons to follow them again, hence they will remain stuck in their current level for at least several hundred years.

"Off you go now Taz junior. You are free to return to the 1st Dimension. I look forward to our next conversation."

That abruptly, my coerced time with Hamerac was over and he blinked out of the room. Simultaneously, and without any intent on my part, I was blinked back to the meadow of the leialli.

I appeared right next to Qadir in a different part of the meadow than I had departed from. He looked over at me with surprise and did not look happy to see me.

CHAPTER
Twenty—Three

W hat are you doing back here? Qadir asked impatiently. "Never mind, I don't want to know! Your Earth body is supposed to be awake by now and your Taz body needs to be resting.

"Please return your consciousness to your Earth body so your 1st Dimension version can have its ordinary day. There is nothing you need to tell me or do that cannot wait until your Earth body sleeps again."

"As you wish," I replied nonchalantly. "I guess my long, in-depth conversation with the Level 12 demon, Hamerac is probably just a run-of-the-mill day for a Taz. I'm sure I will learn to keep things in better perspective as I gain more experience."

"What did you say?" Qadir asked with concern in his voice. I knew I had caught his interest, and couldn't help teasing him just a bit more.

"It's nothing important, just mildly interesting. Forgive my ignorance. I didn't realize how vital it was to let my Taz body rest, and for my Earth body to wander about in the mundane world."

I smiled at Qadir and gave a friendly little wave goodbye. "It was all new to me so I will have a couple of questions for you when we meet next. See you then!"

Suppressing a chuckle I closed my eyes pretending I was going to blink away, fully expecting the reply I knew was coming.

"Wait!" Qadir exclaimed. "What is this nonsense about talking with Hamerac? I know of that terrible demon, and if he had you in his clutches you wouldn't be here to tell the story. Generations of Taz have been trying to banish that one.

"What game are you playing with me Trevallion?" Qadir asked perceivingly with a wily smile of good humor.

I held my hands apart showing he had caught me at my jest. "I confess I was playing with you a bit just to lighten the moment. But I really did have an eye-opening conversation with Hamerac."

Qadir immediately forgot all about having me blink back home so my Earth body could awaken. Now he earnestly encouraged me to reveal all that had transpired with Hamerac. So I told him everything from the moment I found myself bound in paralysis to the moment I reappeared in the meadow next to him.

When I finished recounting my experience, Qadir seemed shocked and almost disbelieving.

"I doubt the demon you met was really Hamerac," he said shaking his head in negation.

"Hamerac has been trying to kill a Taz for at least the

last five hundred years, and we have been endeavoring just as intently to banish him to Oblivion.

"Killing a Taz is a sure ticket for a 12th Level demon to qualify to battle for a spot on the 13th level. If a 12th Level demon had you in his power, he would have brought you before his entire horde so they could witness your slow torture and death."

Qadir shook his head back and forth even more and curled up his lower lip, obviously seriously disturbed by my encounter.

"No, you most definitely did not encounter Hamerac. But it still must have been, at least a mid-level demon to have the magickal ability to intercept and redirect your transit back home.

"That being true, it is an even greater mystery. While it would be a great coup for a 12th level demon to capture a Taz, it would be the pinnacle of triumph for a mid-level demon to do so.

"In either case, neither a 12th Level nor a mid-level demon would just let you go. The fact that you were allowed to depart indicates that something more sinister is at work. You must have had a spell or a hex put upon you, but to what end?"

Qadir put a hand on my shoulder and looked at me intently with his dark brown eyes. "It is not safe for you to return to your Earth body until this is fully investigated and you are cleared of any magickal entanglements that you have likely had placed on you.

"We must call a Circle of Power to deal with this."

From within the same small vest pocket that he had withdrawn his truth crystal, Qadir now pulled out a beautiful pendant. At its center was a deep green emerald. Three concentric circles of silver or platinum supported at least twelve radiating rays of gold with each terminating at a different colored gemstone.

Qadir noticed my look of admiration at the beautiful piece of jewelry. "This is an enchanted beacon. It is called a Vazaron and it is used to call Taz. It has other helpful magickal summoning powers as well."

I reached out. "May I hold it?

"You may not," Qadir replied curtly, gently slapping my hand away. "You will have an opportunity in the coming years to fashion and enchant one of your own. For now, in your ignorance, who knows what unpleasant surprises you would call up by randomly touching the enchanted gems?"

"Aren't you afraid it's going to fall out of your little vest pocket?" I wondered with a sincere hint of worry. "You don't even have a zipper or button to secure your pendant and the truth stone inside it."

"Not at all necessary," Qadir explained. "This pocket is powerfully enchanted. It is like a mini-safe. Fireproof, crushproof, hex-proof, and the only way anything comes out is if my hand reaches in to pull it out."

He pointed to the large emerald at the center of the pendant. "This gemstone is me. For the enchantment to work, the center stone must be of exceptional quality.

He pointed to the outer ring of gemstones at the end of all the little golden rays. They were all different. "Each one of the eleven gems at the end of the gold rays that are in active use is synchronized to the soul of a Taz.

"Our auras can change from day-to-day, depending

upon our moods, health, environment, and the actions we choose to take, but every person's soul is constant and unique to them. It never changes.

"If you press three times firmly on a Taz gemstone, the gemstone that represents you will vibrate in the similar pendant that the Taz you are calling possesses. They will know you are calling them and they will come to your aid as rapidly as their current situation will allow, which sometimes is not as quickly as you would like."

"Is there significance to the number twelve?" I asked.

"Indeed," Qadir acknowledged. The greatest number of Taz that have been alive at the same time from our Earth during the last few hundred years, is twelve, so including the center stone there is a gemstone for every possible Taz.

"Currently we have six, plus you make seven. You can choose from any of the inactive gemstones for the one you wish to have represent you."

"Can I choose now?" I asked.

Qadir shook his head. "No I'm afraid not. Until we determine what black magick you may have been infected with, you cannot be allowed to interact with any tools of the Taz. Once you are cleansed, you are welcome to choose the gemstone to which you feel most drawn.

"So let us get on with it without delay," Qadir said as he began putting pressure three times on five of the gemstones.

I made note of the gems he pushed on so I would know which were still available for me to choose to be my calling gem in the future.

Though Qadir had mentioned that sometimes the

Taz did not respond in a timely manner when they were called, it wasn't so on this day. In less than five minutes, four of the other Taz had appeared around us.

The first to materialize was a very wise-looking, late middle-aged black man. His short-cropped hair was beginning to gray. Qadir went up and gave him a warm embrace. "Thank you for coming so quickly Nkosi."

"Of course my brother," Nkosi replied. "I know you would not call unless it was urgent."

Qadir turned to look at me and pointed at the new arrival. "This is Nkosi. He is a proud member of the Xhosa tribe in South Africa and calls Cape Town home when he is not gallivanting around somewhere else, fulfilling his stewardship as a Taz."

"Pleased to meet you Nkosi," I said respectfully.

Qadir introduced me next. "This is Trevallion, my new protégé. He seems to have been inflicted with a demon hex or spell. I asked you and the others to come today to form a Circle of Power so we can find out just what the problem is, and get rid of it.

"Time is somewhat of the essence as it is time for his consciousness to be back united with his Earth body."

"Yes, I see," Nkosi nodded gravely. "You were right to call us. We must remedy this problem with haste."

While Nkosi was speaking, Genavieve popped in. She gave me a nod of recognition, but was not happy at all when Qadir told her why he had called her.

"I told you it was too early to take him as an apprentice," Genavieve lamented. "It has only been a couple of days and already we have to assemble a Circle of Power to extradite him from demon magick?

240

"You should have let me send him home and bar him from these realms until his powers were fully activated by his catalyst."

"Hmm, I don't think I acted prematurely," Qadir said confidently. "He has already manifested his Dragon Sword and has already banished a demon."

"Really?" Genavieve exclaimed in astonishment. "That is remarkable," she admitted hesitantly. She cocked her head a bit and looked at me as if seeing a strange oddity for the first time and not sure what to make of it.

Her focus on me was broken by another Taz blinking in. This woman seemed to be about my age and was obviously East Asian. She was dressed all in white with somewhat baggy pants and a loose-fitting top. It contrasted remarkably with her jet black hair that was braided in a long ponytail that trailed down to the small of her back. Her straight-cut bangs enhanced her delicate facial features.

Genavieve went over to meet the new arrival and greeted her with a tender hug. "Jenji, it is so good to see you again."

"And you dear sister," the newcomer replied with equal affection. "Who is this?" she asked pointing at me.

"He is the reason for our gathering," Genavieve replied. "This is Trevallion, Qadir's new apprentice as of just a few days ago. He has barely begun his training, but already has manifested his Dragon Sword and banished a demon. However, with his extreme inexperience he has also managed to get hexed or spelled by an unknown demon. We are here to cleanse him of his black magick restraints and hopefully identify the demon that did this."

"He has already manifested his Dragon Sword? Jenji said with surprise. "I didn't know it could be done so quickly. Qadir must be a very good mentor indeed."

Hearing his name spoken, Qadir joined the conversation. "Oh no, I had nothing to do with it. I had not even told him yet about Dragon Swords. It is a complete mystery to me how he was able to summon his."

It is most peculiar," Jenji mused. "If a demon captured a Taz, even a new Taz such as this one, I am surprised he was not tortured and killed. There must be some hidden nefarious purpose for sure, that he was allowed to live."

"That is what we hope to determine," Nkosi said, joining the group.

It was kind of funny because nobody had introduced me to Jenji and everyone was talking about me without including me in the conversation as if I wasn't even there. It was uncomfortably reminiscent of my recent visit with Qadir at the davos village.

I was about to speak up and ask to be introduced to Jenji, when another Taz materialized among us. He looked to be in his late forties or early fifties, slim and muscular with an olive complexion, dark wavy hair, and a mustache. His brow was furrowed and he seemed a bit angry even before he spoke, and definitely after he spoke.

"This had better be important! I was right in the middle of a great fight with a mini horde that had been tormenting an entire neighborhood near Lisbon. I still had a half dozen to vanquish and now I will have to track them down all over again!" he declared with frustration.

Qadir lifted his hands up a bit and waved them in a downward motion toward the newly arrived Taz. "Calm down Marguese. You know I would not have called you if my need was not important and urgent."

He pointed at me. "This is my new protégé, Trevallion. He is a fast learner and shows good promise, but has become entangled in some devious magick of an unknown demon of some power.

"The fact that he was not killed when he was captured leads me to believe something quite foul is at work. It is more than I could fathom on my own and time is pressing. This matter requires some haste as his full consciousness must return as soon as possible to the 1st Dimension, so his Earth body can awaken."

"Alright," Marguese grumbled, "I can see calling a Circle is warranted, but let's get on with it. You know how bored I get with all these types of tasks that do not involve fighting, vanquishing, and banishing."

Marguese looked around at everyone except me with a much friendlier demeanor and a smile on his face. "Hello everyone, it is good to see you all again."

They all expressed their happiness at seeing him as well and Genavieve came up and gave him a hug.

They waited another five minutes or so for the last Taz to show up. Marguese paced around in circles impatiently the entire time; it seemed with greater restlessness with each step. He reminded me of a bottle of soda being shaken up getting ready to pop, and finally he did.

"Enough! We do not need to wait any longer for Aurora. You know she is probably lost in meditation in her red hills of Sedona. Likely wasting time as usual, contemplating what should be done to banish demons, instead of being out there actually fighting and banishing them.

"We only need three for a Circle of Power and we have five, so let us do it now.

"Please," he added politely when no one reacted immediately.

Everyone looked about at one another and nodded in agreement.

"First we must split his soul more completely," Qadir announced solemnly.

CHAPTER
Twenty-Four

Yikes! I shuddered with apprehension at Qadir's declaration that the Taz were going to split my soul more completely! The image of a sharp knife slicing a cake in half came immediately to mind and I timidly lifted my finger to object.

"Excuse me; I thought my soul was already split with my Earth body, but in a friendly joint tenancy way. I'm sure I would like to keep my soul from being split any further."

"Nonsense," Genavieve chided. "It is not a painful procedure. It will be over before you know it, and it is for your own good."

"Sorry Genavieve," I protested a bit meekly. "I really need a little more information. Right now it sounds like a doctor telling me he is going to cut off my leg, but not to worry because I won't feel a thing."

"It really is a quick little spell," Jenji assured me. "All of us use the magick regularly. As you begin assuming your Taz duties you will find splitting your soul into two autonomous twins on more than a daily cycle is really a necessity if you hope to fulfill your stewardship and also have a life in the mundane world."

"We really should change the name," Nkosi ventured to the others.

His eyes caught mine. "We are not really splitting your soul; more like magickally cloning it and separating it into two different dimensions for an extended period.

"You see without soul splitting, either your Taz body is physically active in the 2nd Dimension while your Earth body sleeps back in the 1st Dimension, or the opposite, and your Taz body is asleep while your Earth body is awake and going about its daily activities in that world.

"In your case, because you are so inexperienced, your Taz body must remain sleeping here on Sx while your Earth body is awake and active. Until you have personally mastered soul splitting, your soul and active consciousness can only be in one awake body at a time.

"That is an untenable situation for a Taz. For instance, you cannot be in the middle of a fight with demons and hold up your hand to tell them that you have to pause the battle and depart, as your Earth Body is awakening.

"Many times it is possible to have a regular cycle of your Taz body only being active while your Earth body sleeps, with your Earth body living a normal life with usual hours of sleep and awake time. But sometimes, circumstances in other dimensions do not allow that luxury, hence the Soul Splitting spell and subsequent enchantment. Is it clear now?"

I nodded my head hesitantly. "Somewhat, but how

does it work?"

Marguese looked at me with his eyes slightly bulging with frustration and impatience. "Never mind how it works. You will find out as you gain experience and then you will be able to do it without our assistance!

"For now, lay down, we will stand over you, invoke the Soul Splitting Spell, and then we will not be pressured to get you back to your Earth body so quickly. Now lay down!"

Qadir came over to me and held on to my arm. He directed me toward a nearby spot of lush green grass.

"Kindly lay down on your back here," he directed. I did as he asked, and then he explained a bit more about what was going to happen.

"We need to do a Circle of Power spell to invoke the initial magick of prolonged Soul Splitting."

He put a small, transparent crystal, the color of blood, in my open palm and used his hand to curl my fingers around it. It was surprisingly heavy in relation to its small size.

"Hold on to that crystal tightly as we coalesce the magickal energies. The magick will be imbued into it and mated to your soul.

"The crystal will only work for you. Keep it safe. It is a part of you, and can therefore go wherever you are in any dimension. You may leave it at your home here, or take it to the 1st Dimension if you like. It will split your soul so that both versions of you can be awake and active at the same time. Either one of your two bodies can activate the magick; whichever one possesses the crystal. However, I advise you to keep it with your Taz self in the

2nd Dimension, where your enhanced magical abilities will be a better bulwark to protect the crystal from harm.

"Whenever your Taz twin needs more time for your Taz duties, but your Earth twin still needs to awaken and go about its day, you will be able to hold the crystal and be empowered by its magick to be fully conscious and active in both bodies, simply by saying a single Word of Power. However, we will wait until we have cleansed you of your demon infection before revealing that word to you."

Alright, this was making a lot more sense now and actually sounded pretty cool! "OK, I understand, please continue," I encouraged everyone.

They started to gather around me in a circle when something Qadir had just said jumped into my consciousness.

"Wait a minute! I have a home here on this world?"

Everyone looked at one another with some exasperation at my continual delays.

"You will have," Qadir answered calmly. "As I mentioned you will be sleeping for now at my home at Corsalain. We all have homes at various places in this dimension, most of us here on Sx. But please save your questions." He glanced over at Marguese rapidly moving his intertwined fingers with obvious impatience.

Marguese, the shaken bottle of soda, popped once more in exasperation at my lack of focus. "Enough with the chit chat! Some of us came here from urgent business elsewhere! I'm sure we all would like to return to what we were doing before Qadir summoned us. Let's get on with it that we may return quickly to our own lives and duties."

I felt chastened by Marguese's words and heartfelt request. I nodded humbly and quietly asked them to please continue.

The five standing Taz formed a tight circle closely around me. They joined hands intertwining their fingers. I saw all of their mouths start moving as they were speaking in unison, but I could not hear any of the words they spoke. After about ten seconds my vision also blurred and I could no longer distinguish any of them as anything other than indistinct obscure shapes.

Their spellcasting went on for about five minutes and it was quite odd to experience complete silence, and see them only as hazy shapes the entire time.

The silence was broken when they suddenly became crystal clear once again. I saw all the Taz release one another's hands and Qadir addressed me.

"We have enchanted your Soul Splitter and your physical Earth body is now awake and going about its day while you remain here, also awake and active. Isn't magick wonderful?" he asked with reverent glee.

I nodded my head in enthusiastic agreement, but to the dismay of the gathered Taz, I also had a question. "Are you sure it worked? I have no awareness of what my Earth Self is doing. I don't see or hear anything except what is here, and there are no images in my mind's eye either."

Marguese rolled his eyes upward in annoyance. "Yes, yes, that is another enchantment. You do not need to be aware of your 1st Dimension Self for the moment; he can get by just fine on his own for now."

Qadir held up his hand to stop Marguese from speaking further, as he wanted to say something as well.

"We also did a Dampening Spell followed by a Circle of Protection Spell. As I'm sure you noticed, you were unable to hear the words or see us clearly while we did the spells. Until we have resolved your demon problem, we wanted to ensure that a demon could not hear through your ears, or see through your eyes."

I knew it wasn't going to get a good reception, but I just had to ask another question, as at least in my mind, it seemed eminently important.

"If you are afraid of demons learning our magickal secrets, how can we ever use magickal words to help us fight or banish them?"

As expected, Marguese was very upset that I had the temerity to ask another question. "Can you please keep quiet! We are here for one purpose; supposedly a very quick purpose. Save your questions for your mentor at another time. This is not your Taz 101 class. If you ask one more question I will personally put a silence hex on you!"

"Now, now," Qadir tutted. "It is a reasonable question Marguese, which in respect to your time my friend, I will mostly defer answering, to another day."

Qadir looked at me soberly. "Almost all of the magickal words and procedures we use for spells or enchantments only work for a Taz because the source of their power is from within us, or from a source of light that cannot be coalesced or utilized by beings of darkness.

"So in your battles with demons, you will not need to worry whether or not they hear the words of power you use.

"We initiated a block today for a couple of reasons. First, because it humors us to know that suddenly being deaf and blind to our activities will greatly enrage and frustrate the demon that may have hoped to hear through your ears and see through your eyes. Demons work so diligently to make human lives miserable, the least we can do is to reciprocate in kind whenever the opportunity presents itself.

"Second, after we have come to a conclusion about your situation, we don't want a demon to be able to spy on us through you as we plan our retaliation.

"Now we are all within the Circle of Protection, so nothing undesired, material or immaterial, not even words or thoughts, can pass in or out of the circle until we have disbanded it. Only magickal energy that we call and coalesce can enter or leave the circle, so we shall proceed."

Nkosi bent down and held up a small, rounded, chatoyant, semi-clear white stone for me to see.

"This is a Discovery Stone. It has been enchanted to create a three-dimensional holographic projection of your memories. Whatever you saw through your eyes and heard through your ears, we will be able to observe as if we were present.

"This should allow us to determine what hex or spell was cast upon you by the demon, and ascertain the identity of the demon, if he is known to any of us.

"Once the Discovery Stone has merged with you, we will use its coalescing words to activate its magick so the truth may be revealed."

Nkosi placed the Discovery Stone on my forehead and I felt a series of strange sensations. At first, the stone felt quite cold, but after just a few seconds it began to heat up, close to the point that it would be too hot to bear. Thankfully, it rapidly cooled back down until it seemed to match my body temperature so perfectly that it was difficult to even feel it was still there.

Then to my surprise and a little worry, it felt like it was passing through my skin and sinking into my skull! But soon it once again felt like nothing at all was there.

In unison, the encircling Taz spoke aloud the words *Hweth, Qwargon, Zwasal*, three times. I assumed these were the words Nkosi has spoken of to activate the enchanted Discovery Stone.

As soon as the Taz had finished their third repetition of the words, I saw the face of the demon that had captured and bound me in paralysis, staring right at me in the empty space above my prone body.

It was uncanny, I was seeing him exactly as my eyes had first seen him, as were all the Taz who were observing. Though there was a slight translucency to the image, the replication was exceptional, with all the colors and fine details that I had witnessed with my own eyes; not just the face of the demon, but the surrounding room as well.

The last scene showed the demon blinking away and me reappearing here in the leialli meadow next to Qadir. At that point, Nkosi stepped over and removed the Discovery Stone from my forehead and gave me a hand to help me stand up.

Genavieve was the first to speak. "Remarkable. That

certainly was Hamerac, or a demon masquerading perfectly as him."

Jenji affirmed Genavieve's conclusion. "I agree. I barely escaped with my life last year when Hamerac led a small demon horde to ambush me in the Quorthian Forest where I had gone to protect the wood felaci.

"I will never forget his face. I was bringing my Dragon Sword down upon his head and he somehow froze it in place for a couple of seconds, which was enough time for him to transit away to safety. He looked me in the eye and laughed at me before he departed."

Nkosi interjected. "Whether it was or was not Hamerac perhaps is not as important as the fact that we saw no evidence that Trevallion was hexed or spelled in any way by that demon. Perhaps we all rushed here to be of assistance, which was not actually needed, at least not in the way we initially assumed.

Marguese looked doubtful. "He was in the power of a demon. That was not just to have a conversation. I have never encountered Hamerac, but if that was truly him, or any other high-level demon, and he did not kill, spell, or hex Trevallion, it could only be because he felt the time spent with him was more useful in some other way than his death."

"What we need to ascertain, is in what other way?" Qadir interposed.

I raised my finger requesting to speak. I felt like the only student in a group of teachers, which I guess I was at the moment. Everyone looked at me a bit annoyed or bemused, but remained quiet to give me an opportunity to offer my opinion.

"Maybe, it was after all just what Hamerac said it was: an opportunity to gain knowledge that would help him in his battles in the demon world."

"Hmf!" Marguese grunted dismissively looking at me with disparaging scorn. "What useful information do you think an upper-level demon that has been gaining knowledge for ten times more years than all of us have been alive combined, could possibly glean from a newly minted Taz that does not yet know even a pinch of what it means to be a Taz?"

Genavieve shook her finger disapprovingly at Marguese. "Stop it Marguese. You are being too hard on him. Yes, he is naïve and ignorant of our worlds, our lives, and our stewardships, but he is one of us.

"I did not want him to be here yet, but he is. We must all help him in our own ways to grow as quickly as possible so we can stand as seven Taz and not just six, against the horrors the demons inflict on every race and creature of many worlds and dimensions."

"Hold that thought," Qadir interrupted. He fished in his tiny, bottomless vest pocket and pulled out a large gelatin capsule about the size of my thumb. He stepped over to me and instructed me to swallow the giant pill. I gagged just looking at it.

"I can't swallow that!" I protested. It's way too big and I don't even have any water to try to help it go down."

"Oh, no worries there," Qadir assured me. "It is self-lubricating. Now open up. This will let us know without a doubt, whether or not you are hexed or spelled. Once we are certain, one way or the other, we can devise a firm course of action."

Very hesitantly I opened my mouth and let Qadir drop the enormous pill inside. I closed my mouth, reluctant to try swallowing the pill, but as soon as it was in my mouth, it easily slid down my throat seemingly under its own power.

Everyone was quiet as they stared at me intently, apparently waiting for a reaction. After a couple of minutes, I must have somehow passed the test because Qadir exclaimed, "OK, no hexes or spells. What course of action does everyone suggest we take next?"

I was relieved to know I wasn't under magickal demonic compulsion, but was curious as to how swallowing the pill had definitively made that determination and ventured to ask that question aloud.

Qadir was happy to answer, I think in a teasing sort of way just to see what my reaction would be.

"If you had been under any type of harmful magick from a demon, within a minute the Purging Pill would have done its job and rid you of your magickal infection. You would have also had a violently upset stomach and would have been puking the demonic infection, and a lot of other unpleasantries, out of your body."

Everyone chuckled contemplating the scene Qadir had described.

"But nothing happened, so you are fine and are not under the influence of harmful magick. Which returns us to the question of why the demon was so interested in talking with you? What did he hope to gain?"

"This is enough!" Marguese said abruptly. "I am leaving now. Our presence is no longer needed for the purpose that we were called for as he is not infected. Let me know when it is my turn to mentor him and I will teach him how to fight better than any of you."

Marguese gave the group a little two-finger salute. "Until we meet again my friends, may you banish many demons, Tchau," and then he blinked away.

He was soon followed by all of the other Taz, until I was once again alone with just my mentor Qadir. He put his hand on my shoulder and looked at me with a friendly smile.

"Despite our Soul Splitting Spell, I believe it would be wise for you to return to your Earth body. As this was your first time you don't want to leave your awakened consciousness split into two independent versions for very long. As you gain experience, you will be able to do it for several days if necessary. But for now, a couple of hours is a safe boundary.

"It will be your first time remerging in full consciousness when your Earth body is not in bed and alone. Do be careful and don't act too startled. Who knows what your Earth self may be up to."

"I feel unfulfilled," I complained. "We went through a lot of motions, called in all the Taz, did a lot of magick, but I don't feel anything with that demon is more resolved than it was before everyone went through all the effort."

"It is and it isn't," Qadir said obliquely. "We determined that you are not infected, and that to our surprise the demon likely is Hamerac. Beyond that, your meeting with him is a mystery, which means you must meet with him again, so we can learn more of his motives."

"That's not going to happen!" I objected.

Qadir just smiled and then without forewarning or

my consent he sent me back to the 1st Dimension, just like Hamerac had blinked me back to the leialli meadow without a word of warning.

When I opened my Earth body eyes it seemed I had come back just in time, as the ocean was getting ready to swallow me up!

CHAPTER
Twenty — Five

Returning to my Earth body it took a slightly terrifying moment to grasp where I was, as I found myself holding on to a thick braided metal wire with one hand, while standing on a narrow perch that was plunging down toward a vast expanse of water below.

With a resounding smacking sound and a spray of water, my perch almost submerged, then came roaring back up. After a second, I realized I was standing on the bowsprit of the 48-foot sailboat I shared with my adventure partner, Skye.

It was a gloriously, warm, sunny day off the Florida Atlantic coast and I quickly gained my senses and knew where I was and why I was there. Skye and I had just recently left the west coast of Florida near Naples and had sailed through the Florida Keys and up the South-Eastern coast.

We were nearing our destination of St. Augustine on

259

the far Northeast corner of Florida where we planned to drop anchor out in the bay to explore the oldest continuously inhabited town in North America.

I looked back at Skye in the wheelhouse masterfully piloting our sailboat through the tossing seas unerringly to our destination. Skye was a very New Age woman and I reminded myself again how much she would love to hear about my recent Taz adventures and I was oh so tempted to tell her.

However, remembering the admonition of Qadir to not share anything about my life in the other worlds, even with those close to me, I held back once more and said nothing. Over the years that followed, I came to understand the wisdom of that advice. Despite that prudent necessity, not sharing my other life with Skye and later with my wife Sumara, was one of the most difficult choices I ever had to make, and the internal turmoil it caused never went away.

A small pod of dolphins were playfully racing our boat with frequent arching leaps out of the water in front of the bow. Their unfettered freedom and unabashed exuberance reminded me of the same happiness that had been enjoyed by the leialli herd before their peaceful world was shattered by the marauding demons. That memory helped steel my resolve to do everything in my power to thwart and defeat demons, even if it included keeping silent to protect the ones I loved.

I marveled how my 1st Dimension Self standing on the bowsprit of a sailboat, on a glorious Earth day, had all the memories of the events I had experienced as a Taz while on the planet Sx in the 2nd Dimension.

When my soul had been split so my 1st Dimension body could awaken and go about its day on Earth, even while my Taz self was still active in the 2nd Dimension, my Taz self on Sx had chosen to have no insight into what my Earth Self was doing. But with my active consciousness now solely in my 1st Dimension body, if I chose, I had complete memory of both worlds. It was really cool!

By late afternoon we had sailed into the sheltered harbor at St. Augustine. After dropping anchor in the bay, we motored our rubber dingy over to the guest dock at the nearby marina and walked in to explore the town of St. Augustine.

St. Augustine ended up being one of my all-time favorite towns. There are so many wonderful historic activities to see and experience. The old town is amazing as is the formidable Castillo de St. Marcos, which began construction in 1672 and is the oldest masonry fortification in the continental United States.

Skye and I loved St. Augustine so much that we decided to stay awhile. We both got jobs in town: she worked as a waitress at the Santa Maria restaurant, and I worked as a Tour Guide in town and a Bridge Tender on the famous Bridge of Lions that spanned the inner inlet and was the main artery from the town to the beach. We ended up staying in St. Augustine for over two years and it was an invaluable time for my education as a Taz.

It wasn't until the seventh night after Skye and I set anchor at St. Augustine that I willed my Taz body to go to Qadir while my Earth body slept. Unfortunately, my timing was very bad, or very good depending upon one's perspective.

I materialized inside a very large cavern that was dimly lit by what seemed to be natural irregular-shaped, luminous sections of the rocky ceiling and walls. The phosphorescent green glow they emitted was disquieting.

There was a ferocious battle raging all around me and it took a minute for me to organize in my mind who was a friend and who was a foe. About a dozen short, stout fellows with long beards were fighting with various weapons against at least three times that number of both male and female demons all over the cavern. There was quite a din of metal on metal weapons clashing. In the center swinging his Dragon Sword was Qadir.

My first instinct was to jump into the fray and help. That noble thought was immediately overridden by my next more prudent thought: how?

My Dragon Sword had appeared when I needed it during the fight with the demons trying to abduct the baby leialli Little Toot. To help in this skirmish I mentally pictured it and called it to me, but to no avail; nothing happened.

It didn't take long for a demon to notice the weaponless Izbo standing in the middle of the room. He immediately charged at me swinging a deadly spike mace on a chain.

In an attempt to deflect his attack I yelled out, "I am just a psychic Izbo apparition!" I assumed even a dimwit demon would accept that conclusion as why else would a defenseless Izbo be standing alone in the cavern?

Unfortunately, the demon either didn't understand English or he really was a nitwit. He didn't slow down even a step in his charge at me, whirling his mace around above his head with manically fury.

No matter how dexterous I might be at jumping or ducking to avoid being hit, I knew if I stood in one place it would not be long before that swirling ball of spiked iron found its mark. All I could do to stay alive was to retreat and try to find cover. So I turned and ran back toward the nearest cavern wall hoping to find a boulder or rocky outcrop I could duck behind as a shield.

My self-preservation instinct was good and I quickly came upon a rocky outcrop about the size of a small car standing on end that projected up from the floor of the cavern about eight feet away from the cavern wall.

The demon was right behind me but had to stop in his tracks once he was blocked by the rock outcrop. He tried a couple of times to move around it, but each attempt was thwarted as I moved in sync to ensure he was always 180 degrees opposite of me.

I was feeling momentarily secure when the demon suddenly disappeared and blinked in right behind me swinging his mace on a chain. I quickly ducked the onrushing ball of death and ran around the outcrop so he was once again directly opposite me.

He tried the blinking maneuver once more with the same failed result. As soon as I saw him dematerialize I instantly raced to a new location before he had fully rematerialized where I had previously been standing.

Remembering one of my lessons from the battle between the demons and the leialli, I made sure to keep moving. As long as I moved the demon had to move to follow me. And as long as he wasn't standing still for at least a few seconds he couldn't blink.

I was on the rear side of the outcrop with the cavern wall to my back when the demon tried a new tactic that quickly began to get me worried. As there was no place else for me to hide or run, he began swinging his mace and pounding the rock outcrop. With every impact of the mace, large pieces of the rock shattered apart. In less than a dozen swings the demon's assault on the outcrop had reduced it to a knee-high rock surrounded by a pile of rubble and dust.

With nothing else nearby to use as a shield, all I could do was duck as the demon swung his mace at me. That worked the first few attacks, but I knew it would only be a short time before he found his mark.

Unfortunately, that time came sooner than I feared, as when I last ducked the swinging mace, my heel caught on a small loose rock. I slipped and fell hard onto my back, hitting my head and putting me in a momentary daze.

Before I could regain my senses the demon switched the swing of his mace so he could arch it down with bone-crushing force onto my prone body before I could move. I had no time to roll out of the way and instinctively put one arm up in front of my face for protection, not that it would do any good. Thankfully it wasn't necessary.

Just before the demon could initiate his downward death blow a long sword came flying through the air. It passed right through the demon's body and embedded horizontally into the cavern wall. The demon vanished into a pile of dusty smoke the moment the tip of the sword touched him.

Qadir came running up and extended his hand to

help me up. "Are you all right?" he asked, as he hastily pulled his Dragon Sword free from the stone wall.

"Yes." I nodded humbly, embarrassed that I had been so defenseless and in need of help fighting off just one demon.

"Stay here," he ordered. "There are only a few more demons remaining so you will be fine." Without another word he leaped back down into the fray still continuing in the center of the cavern.

"Pretty spry for an old man," I thought to myself in silent admiration.

After a few more minutes the last demon was dispatched and Qadir beckoned me down to the center of the cavern and introduced me to the surviving eight bearded warriors.

They were all very sad and despondent because four members of their party had been slain. Only one came up to greet me as the other seven mourned over and attended to the bodies of their friends that had been killed by the demons.

The fellow that came forward to meet me was the largest of the bunch. He came up to about my chest height and was bald on the top of his head with short gray hair on the sides and back. His face was wrinkled and gray-bearded from what I assumed was old age, but his bulging muscles were still evident, pushing on the tight fabric of his plain brown tunic and trousers.

Qadir pointed to the old man, "Trevallion, this is Yzwerb. He is the chieftain of the Hollavoy clan of akara.

"Yzwerb, this is Trevallion, my apprentice."

The akara squinted at me and then looked at Qadir

very doubtfully. "He is a Taz?"

"Indeed he is," Qadir assured him.

Yzwerb seemed less than convinced by Qadir vouching for me. "If he is a Taz why did he run away from a demon and where is his Dragon Sword?"

"Hmm, yes, I can see how that would be a bit confusing," Qadir admitted. "You see he is very new to his calling. He still has much to learn about how to be a Taz."

"Including how to summon his sword," he added after a momentary pause.

"I'm pleased to meet you sir," I said respectfully to Yzwerb with a bow of my head. But he just turned his back on me with a disgusted look on his face and returned to the other akara to tend to the bodies of those that had been slain.

"I don't think I made a good first impression," I lamented to Qadir.

"No, I don't suppose you did," Qadir agreed.

"Akara greatly admire courage and equally scorn cowardness. I'm afraid they perceived the latter in you. They will all pretty much ignore you with some disdain until you can show them a fearless warrior side at some point in the future."

"What else could I do?" I asked defensively. "I tried to call my Dragon Sword, but it did not materialize. My only recourse was to find something to hide behind."

"Yes, yes, I understand," Qadir assured me. "I do not fault you for that. But I would like to caution you that in the future, do not transit to my location without an invitation. You never know what I might be up to from being in the middle of a fight like today, to having an amorous embrace with a lass and not wanting to be interrupted."

I looked at Qadir with surprise. "You do that?"

"Of course I do from time to time," he replied indignantly. "I am old, not dead!"

"But now that you are here, why are you here?"

I was a little confused by his question. It's been seven days since I last saw you," I pointed out. "I want to continue my training."

"That would be good," Qadir agreed somewhat nonchalantly.

"What have you been up to this last week?" he asked.

I told him about how, when he sent me back to reunite with my Day Self, I had appeared on the bowsprit of my sailboat, and how Skye and I had spent the last week getting to know the new town we were planning on living in for a while, St. Augustine, Florida.

He was aghast when I told him Skye and I had decided to settle for a time in St. Augustine.

"That place is full of demons!" he shouted. "And ghosts!" he added. "There are more demons in that town than there are humans! You can't live there; your Earth Self will be as busy keeping demons at bay as your Taz Self. You'll never get any rest!"

CHAPTER
Twenty—Six

I was surprised how upset Qadir seemed to be about me living in St. Augustine. "We cannot talk here," he grumbled as he pulled me along toward the center of the cavern toward the akara.

Qadir went up to Yzwerb and put his hand on his shoulder sympathetically. "I am sorry for your losses my friend, and sorry I did not arrive sooner to help."

Qadir reached into his bottomless vest pocket and pulled out three small glass vials. They had a deep green glowing liquid inside and appeared to have both ends of the vial melted shut so there was no stopper.

"Here are a few Roxars for you and your chief advisors. Next time you have a demon raid, just break one of these vials. Upon contact with air the liquid inside will immediately turn to gas. It is tuned to my aura and will act as a magickal beacon allowing me to quickly transit to your location if I am in this dimension at the time. I will come to your aid as soon as my circumstance will allow, which hopefully will be soon enough."

"Thank you Qadir," Yzwerb said appreciatively. "We look forward to seeing you again. Perhaps without that one," he said pointing dismissively at me."

I was embarrassed that the akara thought so little of me, but thankfully Qadir spoke up for me. "You did not see him on one of his better days that is certain. But I promise the next time you see him he will have more training and I am sure he will make a better account of himself."

Yzwerb, raised his eyes brows hopefully, nodded and turned away back toward the other akara.

Qadir held out his arm. "Hold on to my forearm. I will take you to Corsalain so you can begin real training instead of merely discovering your skills by accident while you are jumping out of the fires."

I reached out and lightly put my left hand on Qadir's right bare forearm. As soon as I made contact he spoke aloud the single word of our destination, "Corsalain."

I wasn't sure how much time elapsed between blinking from one distant place to another or from one dimension to another, but in my perception it seemed instantaneous, as quick as thought. You think or say where you wish to go, close your eyes for just a second, and when you open them again, you are physically at the destination you chose.

We appeared inside a tall octagonal tower that came up from a house-size building about three stories below. We were up on top of a lush green hill with many small trees. It gently sloped down in all directions to an extensive flat, green grassy plain with occasional groves of trees.

I could see three different herds of animals in the distance, but could not make out what they were. Beyond the plains in two directions were jagged mountains.

In the third direction, the plains seemed to turn into a dense forest in the distance. In the fourth, a large river wound sinuously across the plain and emptied into a vast expanse of water like an ocean or very large lake.

All in all the natural aspects of Corsalain were breathtaking. "Where are we?" I asked Qadir.

He beamed with enthusiasm. "We are at Corsalain. This is my home on Sx."

"Wow!" I exclaimed in admiration. "With a beautiful, serene place like this to come home to, it must be challenging to return to the mundane, non-magickal, strife-ridden world of Earth."

"Yes, yes, it would be," he agreed, "except I have little choice. My 1st Dimension body holds no allure for me, nor does my empty life on Earth. But I cannot permanently escape the curse, nor can you."

"The curse?" I asked worriedly, seeking a bit more information about what suddenly seemed to be an unknown threat.

"Yes," Qadir continued, "the curse of a Taz is we cannot simply live two independent lives with one twin in the 1st Dimension and the other in the 2nd. Always and regularly there needs to be this cursed time when one body sleeps and is physically inactive and consciously subdued, while the other twin is physically active and consciously alert.

"With diligent effort, with each year that passes, I have

been able to extend the blessed time of soul separation longer and longer, even into weeks of the two versions of myself living active and independent of one another.

"Sadly, the bliss of separation always has to come to an end and our Earth bodies must for a time have full possession of our consciousness. This is the curse of the Taz. We must forever submit to temporarily leaving our 2nd Dimension body sleeping and effectively dormant, so our soul can be fully reenergized in our Earth body.

"Without that regular renewal, both the 1st and 2nd Dimension bodies would soon begin to degenerate, become sick and die an early death."

I was fascinated by Qadir's explanation of the soul split twins of the Taz, but as always every question he answered just brought up more questions.

"What happens to the 2nd Dimension me when my soul is no longer split and is fully reunited within my Earth body. Does that mean my Taz body that is sleeping is then soulless?"

Qadir looked upward with his eyes for a moment as if considering his answer. "Yes, I suppose it does in a strange sort of way if you want to think about it like that."

"That's kind of spooky," I said with a little revulsion. "A soulless me."

"Nonsense," Qadir chided. "Remember, your Taz body is simply a manifestation of the 2nd Dimension aspect of yourself. You created your twin, but your twin is you! Though you can manifest two bodies in two different dimensions, it is all just you in one soul. It is like having two arms or two legs; though they can move separately and perform different activities, they are still both part of the one that is you.

"Enough self-reflection," Qadir said abruptly, reprimanding himself. "Let's get on with your education."

"Let's start with terminology. Though I have been as guilty as anyone of using longer phrases, from now on just say *Earth*, or the *1st Dimension*, whenever you are referring to the place our original bodies reside."

"OK," I agreed.

"And because you will occasionally be soul splitting to allow you to spend more conscious time in your Taz body, please henceforth refer to your *Day Self* as your *Earth Self, Earth body*, or *1st Dimension Body*, because when you have split your soul your Earth Self will be operating independently day and night, not just in the day hours."

"Next," Qadir continued, "you need to have an understanding of the world where we now are, all the layers, and how they connect and relate to Earth."

"Great," I exclaimed. "That will help a lot."

"Yes, yes," Qadir fussed. "Just listen and you will learn, although it may be a bit of a challenge for you to wrap your mind around the reality at first."

"Let's start with what you already know. You are of course familiar with the physical universe, the Earth as the third planet from the sun, the other planets, the Milky Way galaxy, and the fact that there are untold billions of other physical galaxies in our universe."

I nodded my head affirmatively. "Yes, I understand."

"All the planets and stars in the universe that people living a physical life on Earth can see, and all the life from a clump of grass to an elephant that we see with our physical Earth eyes, is properly called the 1st Dimension," Qadir explained patiently, "but there is more than one dimension of space and time," he added.

"How familiar are you with what scientists call the dark matter in the universe?"

"Not very," I admitted. "I've heard the term, but don't really know what it is referring to."

Qadir chuckled. "Then you are as enlightened as the scientists because they do not know what it refers to either, and none of their speculations or hypothesis are correct."

"The 1st Dimension world that our Earth Self lives in and can observe, from an eagle flying in the air on Earth, to a distant star in the galaxy, only comprises a small percentage of the total matter in the universe. The larger percentage is what Earth scientists call *dark matter*, and its cousin *dark energy*.

"They call it *dark* because they can tell it is there by the gravitational effects it has on visible objects and subatomic particles. But they cannot examine it by any means because it does not absorb, reflect, or emit any form of electromagnetic energy measureable by scientific instruments of the 1st Dimension."

Qadir lifted and straightened his arm and swept it around panoramically. "You see all of this beautiful land; the mountains, the plains, the rivers, the lakes, the forests, and all the wonderful animals and inhabitants that live here?"

"Yes," I nodded.

"This is all dark matter," he said solemnly.

He poked me with a finger on my chest. "Your Taz self

is dark matter, as is mine.

"Demons, davos, akara, leialli, oosas, and every other creature that is not in a tangible, physical body in the 1st Dimension, all live and thrive in the realms of the universe that Earth scientists call *dark matter*.

"People, from scientists to New Agers to science fiction fans commonly use the term *other dimension,* in reference to some nebulous place other than the world they live in that they really don't understand.

"Well all the worlds of other dimensions that are not tangible and perceptible to the 1st Dimension people of Earth are made of *dark matter.*

"I don't like the terminology *dark matter* at all. I just used it to help you grasp what I was speaking about as that is the common term on Earth, but there is nothing dark about it, or any of the marvelous worlds in this dimension. A more correct term would be *invisible matter*. At least it is invisible to the people and denizens of the universe that exists in the 1st Dimension.

"Obviously, there is a tremendous difference in the type of matter that exists in the 1st Dimension from the type of matter that exists in the 2nd Dimension. It would be incorrect to say that they are opposite energies. They are not at all opposite, but they are very different in their nature.

"The biggest difference is regarding magick. Magickal energies exist in the 1st Dimension and can be summoned and coalesced, but only to a minuscule degree compared to the 2nd or 3rd Dimensions.

"This applies to your ability to do magick as well. In the 1st Dimension, you can do it and you will, but what magick your Earth Self can accomplish is infinitesimal to the magick your Taz Self can achieve here in the 2nd Dimension.

"For your own safety it is wise to remember that here in the 2nd Dimension, virtually everything has one or more magickal properties or abilities."

Qadir pointed to a beautiful group of blue flowers down below in the nearby ground. "Those pleasing blue flowers appear completely innocuous. But were you to sit down near them for more than five minutes or so, you would fall into a deep slumber that you would not awaken from for at least a week or longer without a magickal counter.

"It would be akin to suspended animation as all of your body systems would greatly slow down similar to a bear in the 1st Dimension going into hibernation.

"The ability of that flower, which is called Auvis by the way, to induce deep sleep, is accomplished through magickal energy that it exudes. It has nothing to do with its scent, or its pollen, or touching it, which are all ways noxious plants and flowers might affect you on the 1st Dimension.

"So please remember when you are in this dimension that every being you meet has either innate magickal abilities, such as the oosas and leialli, or has acquired knowledge about how to control some aspect of the magickal energies that pervade this dimension.

"I would put almost all the mythical human-like characters of the 1st Dimension that all exist for real in this dimension in that category, including the davos and akara you have already met.

"And just as the Auvis Flower has innate magickal properties, the same is true for virtually every form of plant or animal life in the 2nd Dimension. Even many of the minerals, rocks and crystals, exude unique magickal energies.

"As you learn what the various magickal properties of these items are you will be able to use them to assist you. However, until you learn their properties, they very well could inadvertently hurt you. So do be careful everywhere you go, and make a diligent effort to discover what the magickal properties or abilities are for every plant, animal, and being that you encounter in this dimension.

"Remember, what you know can help you and what you do not know can hurt you."

"I will," I promised with deep sincerity. "And I truly look forward to discovering the magickal wonders of this dimension."

Qadir nodded appreciatively in acknowledgment of my commitment and continued with his educational talk.

"Now the interesting thing about matter from the 2nd Dimension is it exists everywhere in the 1st Dimension, but it is invisible and intangible to people from Earth because they are composed of an entirely different form and frequency of matter, as is everything of substance in the 1st Dimension.

"When people back on Earth reach out their hand into what may seem to be empty air, they may be touching space that is actually occupied by 2nd Dimension matter that is invisible and intangible to them on Earth, but exists perfectly visible and tangible here in the 2nd dimension.

"On a small scale, because the people and creatures in the 1st Dimension worlds of matter and the 2nd Dimension worlds of matter cannot physically interact with each other, they can simultaneously exist in a close proximity of space as different frequencies of energy. How close depends upon their mass.

"The governor of physics in all dimensions is mass and gravity, which often go hand in hand. A 1st Dimension person could stand right next to a 2nd Dimension person and neither would be perceptible to the other with any of the five standard senses. Nor would gravity or mass be an issue because people do not have enough mass to create a gravitational force.

However, such would not be the case with two planets, one of the 1st Dimension and another of the 2nd. Though both may exist in the same solar system and both revolve around the same sun, because of their gravitational mass they could not orbit too close to one another, else their gravity would draw them into a collision."

"And that would be bad?" I hazarded to guess.

Qadir looked at me as if I had a dunce cap on. "Well of course it would be bad! He said raising his voice and waving his hands in exasperation. "Two planets colliding together would be an unmitigated disaster! It would be the end of both worlds!"

I was really feeling stupid, but had to ask, "but wouldn't they pass right through each other? Isn't that the concept you have been teaching me that the 1st and 2nd Dimension energies are not physically perceptible to the other?"

Qadir held his palms out and took a deep breath, then exhaled slowly before answering. "That is not what I have been teaching you. Remember gravity and mass. Yes, a person from the 1st Dimension would pass through a person from the 2nd Dimension as if they were not even there. But if an individual from one dimension encounters a larger mass from another dimension, they will be able to interact with it even if they cannot otherwise perceive it.

"For instance, demons are creatures from the 3rd Dimension. There are millions of them on Earth. A demon can effortlessly pass through the wooden wall of a building, but they would be unable to pass through a building that had thick reinforced concrete walls. The thicker wall made of minerals and metal would have sufficient mass that it would act as a solid substance to the demon. It's the same effect that allows demons to walk around on the ground, which is really the surface of the enormous mass of the planet.

"Nor forget that the worlds of the 2nd Dimension are not in some other universe or galaxy. They share space within our universe and everything in it, including our Earth. It's all one universe; it just has multiple frequencies of energy. And the different energies become more capable of physical interaction as the mass and gravity increase.

"If Earth scientists were more diligent with seeking out and discovering gravitational abnormalities in space, they would be able to identify the location of 2nd Dimension worlds such as Sx, even though they could not see them or identify them with other scientific instruments.

"However, contrary to science fiction books they are by no means mirror images of the physical universe or Earth we see. This is not a parallel universe.

"For instance, we are on the planet Sx in the 2nd Dimension. It rotates around a sun that is hotter and about 30% larger than our Earth's sun. But Sx orbits at a considerably further distance from its sun than Earth does from the sun of that solar system. This allows us to have a year-round temperate climate in the mid-latitudes that is very pleasant.

Sx is in a different solar system than our Earth and is located in a different place in the Milky Way Galaxy. Happily, it also spins on an axis like Earth, giving this planet a similar day-night cycle.

"There are other planets in this solar system revolving around the sun of Sx as well. Some are 1st Dimension planets and others are 2nd Dimension planets, but they are all revolving around the same sun, which has aspects of both 1st and 2nd Dimension energy. Is this clear to you?"

I shook my head negatively. "I'm sorry Qadir, you lost me a little while back, talking about planets from different dimensions existing together in the same solar system with a single sun serving both dimensions. That would seem to indicate you could have planets in different dimensions occupying exactly the same space. I thought you said that they couldn't do that, but were only in nearby locations to one another."

"That is correct," Qadir said in a scholarly tone.

Chapter 26

"Planets from different dimensions do not share the same exact space any more than planets in the same dimension could. Yet they may still exist in the same solar system, and in countless solar systems they do.

"However, suns are different. They are a more pure form of energy. Every star in the universe, which all are suns, each emanates both 1st and 2nd Dimension energy, so they serve as the sun for both the 1st and 2nd Dimension planets in that solar system. Is all of this clearer to you yet?" He asked hopefully, before continuing his explanation.

"Keep in mind that though 1st Dimension and 2nd Dimension planets share solar systems and space in the universe, they are at different frequencies of energy, so neither exists in the other's reality by any visible or measurable means. At least that is normally the case."

"Normally?" I asked, curious as to what Qadir meant.

"Yes, well there are three circumstances where an abnormality prevails," Qadir explained.

"The first is you and me and all the other Taz. For some reason only God knows, we, or at least a different dimension duplicate version of ourselves, in most instances, are the only beings or creatures that can physically exist in both places.

"We have physical substance in both dimensions, we breathe and eat in both dimensions, we can be killed in both dimensions, and we are physically perceived in both dimensions by all the inhabitants.

"The second abnormality is a Nexus. They are very dangerous. No one knows what causes a Nexus to form or disappear. It seems to be a natural process.

"But like many of the aspects of this menagerie that we are a part of, from the Taz, to multiple dimensions, to the Nexus and the magickal creatures of this dimension, comprehending why or how it all exists the way it does is beyond the understanding of us mere mortals.

"We can explain a Nexus in all of its intricacies in exact detail, as I shall for you. But why it is, or why the Taz can physically be in both worlds, sharing a soul with two independent but connected mental thoughts and memories, can only be answered by God, the creator of all. And God does not communicate much.

"Anyway, a Nexus is a small place in the fabric of space where the physical energy of the 1st Dimension begins to blend with the different frequency energy of the 2nd Dimension.

"More often than not a Nexus will occur out in the middle of the vacuum of empty space where they are of no practical or useful purpose. However, on rare occasions, a Nexus will open a portal between a planet in the 1st Dimension and a planet in the 2nd Dimension, such as between Earth and Sx.

"It is like putting down a drop of red paint and a drop of blue with an empty space between them, then drawing a thin line of each color to that empty space where they form the blended color purple.

"When a Nexus forms, it connects two dimensions. For instance, if a Nexus formed between the 1st and 2nd Dimensions, anything from the 1st Dimension could pass through the Nexus into the 2nd dimension. Likewise, anything from this dimension could pass through to the Earth dimension.

"Many of the unsolved disappearances on Earth, from people to entire ships and planes, in places like the Bermuda Triangle, occurred when the people unintentionally and unknowingly went through a Nexus into this dimension or another. Once on the other side they either could not find their way back to that small portal in interdimensional space, or more likely, the Nexus closed up and disappeared, which they do quite often and unpredictably.

"Most curiously if a person from Earth was here on Sx no individual or creature from this dimension could see them, but the individual from the 1st Dimension would be able to see everything and everyone here on Sx quite fine, even though they would be unable to have any physical interaction with organic matter. It would be the same for a visitor from Sx to Earth. They would be able to see everyone and everything clearly but would be invisible to the residents of the 1st Dimension and would not be able to physically interact with them.

"So they are like ghosts?" I interjected.

"Essentially yes," Qadir agreed. "They are like ghosts that did not die to become a ghost. You will encounter them from time to time as you are a Taz and will be able to see them and talk with them. They tend to be very sad people, but they will be very happy whenever they encounter you and have someone to talk to after so many years of silence."

"Can't they talk to others like them that have accidentally passed through a Nexus?" I wondered. "And can't we help them by bringing them to a Nexus and send them back to Earth?"

Qadir nodded affirmatively. "Yes, there are other Nexus Ghosts and occasionally they find each other and some happiness because of it, but this dimension is as big as our physical universe in the 1st Dimension and where they come out when they pass through a Nexus could be anywhere, including an uninhabited planet, or even the emptiness of space, so it is not often that they encounter another like themselves.

"Sadly, we cannot help them return to the 1st Dimension. Other than a few upper-level demons that have figured it out and guard their knowledge zealously, when and where a Nexus appears is extremely unpredictable. Even if you knew where one was, you would need to then go find the person you wanted to help, and by the time you got back to the Nexus it probably would not be there anymore."

Qadir lifted his finger to make a point. "There is one way you can help any Nexus Ghosts that you encounter," Qadir added.

"Most of them quickly starve to death when they arrive in the 2nd Dimension because everything organic they encounter has too little mass and is something they cannot touch, including food. They can still walk upon the ground and drink water because they are not organic and in the case of the ground have great mass. But they cannot eat the dirt so they starve.

"If you are fortunate enough to encounter new arrivals, you can lead them to the rare plants that like a Taz have both 1st and 2nd Dimension energies, such as dandelions and coconuts. These are food they can touch and hold and they will sustain their life until the natural end of their days."

I was excited to hear that such amazing plants existed and looked at Qadir expectantly. "Please point all of those multidimensional plants out to me whenever we encounter them, as I would be very happy to be able to help Nexus Ghosts in some way. They are very unfortunate people and I have great empathy for them."

"Yes, yes," Qadir said rotating his hand in a circle indicating he wanted to get past the subject of the Nexus Ghosts.

"We help everyone as we can, but there is only so much of us to go around. You need to weigh the value of your time to ensure you can help the most people and creatures with every minute that you have available. Sadly, focusing on helping just a single individual takes away minutes that you could be helping many as a collective group."

Qadir suddenly seemed to have some impatience with the subject. "Let's get on to the third abnormality and that is demons."

CHAPTER

Twenty—Seven

A s you know, demons have never had a purely physical body in any dimension; they are a different type of energy, a different type of matter. In the 2nd Dimension they have considerable physical substance, and even more so in the 3rd Dimension. But in every dimension they lack the ability to feel pleasurable sensations and in the 1st Dimension they are entirely without tangible substance.

"Due to the peculiar nature of their energy, in the 1st Dimensions they can create perversions such as inhabiting a human, or any other creature for that matter, that is not possible for humans or any other of God's creations.

"Demons have their own dimension of space separate from 1st or 2nd Dimensions. The demon dimension is the 3rd Dimension. It is small and consists of only a single sun and one very large, rocky, mostly barren planet that has barely bearable high temperatures due to the proximity to its sun.

"There are some places on the demon world that are less gruesome than others, such as their university campuses and the territories of the higher-level demons. But most of it is a dreary and barren land.

"Many Earth religions have a concept of Hell as a fiery place that includes flaming lakes where the wicked are thrown to burn but are never consumed. While I do not subscribe to the religious doctrines, their physical description of Hell pretty much describes some parts of the demon world.

"I have no doubt that there have been humans that have inadvertently passed through a Nexus and ended up in the Demon Dimension. I assume they were fortunate enough to be able to pass back through the Nexus before it closed or disappeared. The description of the fiery demon world they shared upon their return to Earth clearly played a significant role in religions forming a visual concept of Hell.

"All of the Original Demons that were cast out of the Premortal World ended up in the 3rd Dimension on that single big planet. Coming from the paradise of the Premortal World to the hot barrenness of the demon world must have been quite a shock.

"Needless to say, few demons wanted to remain there and few did, at least not permanently, once they discovered they could transit to planets in the 1st and 2nd Dimensions through a Nexus.

"Demons being immortal, had a great deal of time to study and understand the nature of a Nexus. Some of the higher levels among them learned how to discern whenever a Nexus was about to open or was beginning to fade and close.

"Over many millennia they have been passing through Nexus openings to come to planets in the 1st and 2nd dimensions. Occasionally, they go the other way and return through a Nexus to the demon world in the 3rd Dimension for demon purposes such as attending the university.

"There are a handful of locations in the 3rd Dimension where demons have somehow been able to capture a Nexus. There is one at their university, and some of the Level 13's have their own personal Nexus for interdimensional travel.

"Luckily for us there are a couple of catches. As far as we know, in their dormant state the captured Nexuses are only about the size of a pingpong ball and far too tiny to be of any use. The Nexus can only be activated and enlarged by someone holding a Nexus Compass. These are powerful magickal devices crafted by davos, eons ago. There are less than a dozen known to exist and it takes a great deal of expertise to operate one.

"A demon that possesses a Nexus Compass and knows how to use it, can cause the captured Nexus to open for them connecting any two points in the interdimensional universe.

"Fortuneately, time is an additional limitation. The Nexus will only become enlarged and forced open by the Nexus Compass for about five seconds. That's barely enough time for one demon to pass through and ensures hordes will not be able to follow.

"As a Taz, you do not need a Nexus. You can transit with the speed of thought to anywhere in the 3rd Dimension, just as you can to the 2nd. But I strongly advise against going to the 3rd Dimension unless you have an extremely important purpose.

"In every instance, you should never go alone. Demons are terrors in all dimensions, but they have their greatest power on their homeworld.

"The frequency of the 1st Dimension is far from the frequency of the 3rd Dimension. Hence, demons coming to the Earth Sphere are entirely invisible and without physical substance.

"Their auric essence can inhabit the emotionally vulnerable. And they have telepathic abilities which allow them to be masters at influencing weak-minded people. But physically they can do almost nothing, at least not with anything living or organic. They can, with practice, have a very limited ability to physically interact with inorganic objects.

"However, here in the 2nd Dimension, they can manifest an almost solid physical form because the frequency of this dimension is closer to the frequency of the 3rd Dimension.

"As I have mentioned before, it is similar to two radio stations that have almost the same frequency, and with just a little turn of the radio dial, you can find a spot where you are hearing both stations at the same time.

"A very important point for you to remember is though demons may seem fully physical here on Sx, they are not. Anyone from the 2nd Dimension can see and hear them, and be killed by their weapons, but the demon bodies are more like a thick clay here rather than firm flesh and bone."

"Why is that important?" I asked.

Qadir looked at me as if perhaps I wasn't as smart as he had thought.

"It's obvious," he said matter-of-factly. "If they are less than fully substantial, they are easier to dispatch. It makes no difference to us as Taz, as our Dragon Swords will send them into oblivion in this dimension or the 3rd. But for the regular folks here, if they fight back, anything they do against the demons will be more effective.

"For instance, if a demon is sliced with a long knife on

the 3rd Dimension, where they have full substance and power, it would barely inflict a wound, and it would heal almost immediately. But here in the 2nd Dimension, when that knife encounters the demon's less than fully substantial body, the blade will slice through it deeply, severing an arm or maybe even decapitating the demon."

I held up my hand a little so Qadir would know I wanted him to pause for a moment. "Just so I am clear, there are three dimensions of space, our Earth, this realm, and the demon dimension, and these three actually exist in the same solar systems and galaxies, but not exactly in the same spot?"

"First part wrong, second part almost correct," Qadir affirmed. "There are actually seven dimensions of space, but we only concern ourselves with the three that you mentioned. And though we call them dimensions, we would be more correct to say there are seven frequencies of space."

"Seven!" I exclaimed incredulously. "Tell me about the others."

Qadir shook his head negatively. "That would be a lesson for another day, a day very far off as you have a great deal to learn about matters that will actually concern you. Those matters will only be occurring in the three dimensions I have spoken about."

"What about the other four?" I protested. There are no threats to worry about from those?"

"Quite the contrary," Qadir quipped. "There are bigger threats than demons from the other dimensions, but there are Earth Guardians that deal with those menaces."

Qadir paused a moment in reflection. "Well, at least there used to be multiple Earth Guardians. Now there is only one, but he is very adept at zipping around to all the trouble spots."

"Well let's help him," I proposed enthusiastically. "Surely if we have seven Taz to take care of only three dimensions we can lend a hand to the poor guy that has to take care of the other four all by himself."

"Qadir once again shook his head negatively. "No, you do not understand. Demons only exist in our three dimensions and demons are what we Taz have been blessed with special abilities to counter.

"Lazarus is the Earth Guardian who attends to threats from the other four dimensions. Our sole task is to contend with demons; Lazarus' task is to deal with everything else in all seven dimensions."

I was perturbed somewhat by Qadir's explanation. "That seems like a very unfair burden to put on one man. Why does it have to be that way?"

Qadir shrugged his shoulders. "Ask God next time you are having a Celestial conversation."

I brushed off Qadir's somewhat flippant answer and still ventured to ask another question. "Lazarus is an unusual name," I noted. "The only Lazarus I've ever heard of is the one from the Bible that Jesus resurrected from the dead."

"That's the one," Qadir affirmed. "He's been alive as an Earth Guardian ever since. Our paths cross from time to time, so I'm sure you will meet him someday, but for now, let's get back to your training."

"Wait a minute!" I protested. "Are you saying that Lazarus from the Bible story has been alive in a physical body for 2000 years?"

Qadir nodded his head affirmatively, "Yes, I believe that is what I said, but I do not want to talk about this subject anymore, so please stop. I'm sorry I mentioned it.

"You have a tendency to wander off on tangents Trevallion. Stay focused in your heart and mind on learning and perfecting your Taz skills and duties. That will keep you alive and helpful to others in our three dimensions. That is your stewardship."

Reluctantly I agreed. "Alright, what's next?"

"How about a little sword training?" Qadir asked.

"Seems kind of one-sided," I pointed out, "with my side having the disadvantage, as I have no sword."

Qadir looked around dramatically to the right and left. "Well imagine that, I don't have a sword either."

He held his right arm up at a ninety-degree angle and within a second his gleaming, long-bladed Dragon Sword was in his hand. He jestfully looked at his sword as if he was seeing it for the first time. "Well I'll be! Qadir exclaimed in feigned surprise. Will you look at that! I do have a sword now, and a mighty fine one it is."

He held it in both hands and swung it in a wide arc right for my head! I ducked but could sense how close it came to giving me a haircut or worse.

I knew Qadir was playing with me, but still a little slip or miscalculation, and it could have been my head instead of a whiff.

Qadir placed the tip of his sword down on the wood floor of the tower and slightly leaned on the hilt. "Alright, I have mine, where's yours?"

I shrugged my shoulders in ignorance. "I don't know. What's the trick? How do you get your Dragon Sword to come to you?"

Qadir whipped his sword around rapidly in a 360-degree forward circle then stuck the point back in the floor and once again leaned on the hilt.

"You just hold out your hand to receive it, and call out or even think its name in your mind, and poof it will appear whenever you are in the 2nd or 3rd Dimension where magick reigns.

"It also works marvelously to call it in the 3rd dimension if you have the misfortune of finding yourself there. However, it will not answer your call in the 1st Dimension as there is not enough magickal energy in that realm."

"But I don't know the name of my Dragon Sword," I pointed out.

"I think you do," Qadir replied coyly. "Your Dragon Sword appeared at just the right moment in the leialli meadow. It could only do that if you called it."

I thought back to that moment when I was going to bring my fists down on the demon's head. I was very angry at the demons and to find myself and the baby leialli Little Toot in such an untenable situation, where for both of us there seemed to be no escape from our dismal fate.

I know I hadn't said any words aloud and I couldn't remember even thinking any. I just remembered the feeling, the anger at the situation.

And then I knew. Like a rising wave that could not be denied it resonated in every fiber of my being. The name of my Dragon Sword was forged in the very instant of that dreadful confrontation with the demons; it could be no other.

I held out my right arm bent ninety degrees at my elbow, held at rib height as I had seen Qadir do when he called his Dragon Sword, and for the first time I said the name of mine aloud, "*Fury.*"

CHAPTER
Twenty—Eight

Qadir had a beaming smile when he saw me manifest my Dragon Sword. "I knew you knew!" he exclaimed.

I held Fury in my hand and marveled at it. Though the blade was long, at least three feet of gleaming steel in length, it seemed light and amazingly balanced in my hand. The hilt had a polished, spherical pommel. The grip had a slightly braided spiral that fit my fingers well. The somewhat ornate cross-guard was slightly curved outward at each end.

I loved it! The blade felt like it was a living part of me. It was truly amazing how harmonious and unified I felt with it, as other than that one brief instant when I split the demon in half at the leialli meadow I had never even held a sword.

"Let's not waste any more time!" Qadir declared. "Follow me down the stairs and we will practice in the living room."

Qadir lifted a large hatch on the tower floor revealing a long spiral staircase. I followed him down the steep, narrow stairs all the while trying to figure out what he meant by practicing in the living room.

I assumed we were heading to his house as he had already told me that we were at his home in Corsalain. Yet, the living room seemed a very odd place to practice sword fighting, especially when the grounds around the house below were so expansive and open.

To my surprise, Qadir actually meant the living room. Although I'm not sure that is what I would call it, as it was a very cluttered mess, and living in it, or even relaxing in comfort, would be a challenge.

There were numerous odd pieces of furniture scattered about from two desks of distinctively different design; to three different couches that were completely disharmonious in their upholstery and style. Plus, at least six end tables of various designs and sizes that seemed to have no thought for tasteful or even practical arrangement.

The entire far wall from floor to ceiling was a bookcase of many shelves, filled with books of all sizes, many of them askew or partially open rather than neatly stacked side by side. The bookcase also had spots on the shelves that held what appeared to be some type of scientific glassware, beakers, globes, tubes, and such.

A high-back, leather-like armchair sat somewhat in the middle of the spacious rectangular room. It had a large, square ornate wooden table in front of it piled high with papers, books, and various unknown apparatuses.

There were also large end tables on either side of

the chair and they too were piled high with disheveled materials. The only lamp I could see in the room was a tall floor lamp with a green glass shade that curved over the top of the chair to provide illumination to anyone sitting there.

Even the floor was cluttered with piles of books, papers, and strange apparatuses, so just walking through the room without stumbling over something was a bit of a challenge.

In the middle of the room, with both of us hemmed in by piles of papers, books, and scattered furniture and glassware, Qadir raised the point of his sword toward me, "En garde!"

"Wait a minute!" I protested, raising my hand for him to stop and keeping the tip of Fury pointing down. "I thought you were going to teach me how to fight with swords."

"Exactly!" Qadir replied enthusiastically. "En garde!" he repeated once again raising the tip of his sword toward me.

"Wait!" I objected again. "What am I supposed to do? How do I defend myself?"

"It will come to you naturally," Qadir replied casually.

I held my head in my hand and shook it for a second wondering if I needed to see if one of the other Taz would be willing to be my mentor.

I felt exasperated by Qadir's strange method of teaching. "How can something I have never done or even imagine doing, come to me naturally? At least show me a few defensive techniques or positions so I won't be totally embarrassed."

"Do you know how to dance?" Qadir asked as a seemingly random question.

"No, not really," I replied. "Actually not at all," I professed. "Honestly, I probably have the proverbial two left feet when it comes to dancing."

"No matter," Qadir quipped. "Just imagine you are the girl and have to follow the lead of the man. Wherever the man leads, just quickly move along in step and rhythm."

"What are you talking about?" I asked with some frustration, thinking that perhaps Qadir was a little daft. "The only men here are you and me. I can't dance with myself and you want to stick or slice me with your sword, so I don't want to dance with you either."

"Your sword is your dance partner," Qadir revealed. "As I attack you just let Fury defend you. As long as you do not let go of the sword, I'm sure you will be a fine dancer and swordsman."

And so it began. Once again Qadir lifted his sword and said, En garde."

This time I hesitantly lifted the tip of Fury to meet him and the tips of our two swords touched lightly. Then he disengaged and swung his sword viciously at my head. I ducked expecting his sword to go swishing over my head as it had done earlier up on the tower. Instead, I managed to lift up Fury and block his swing with a loud clank of metal on metal.

Our mock battle raged on for at least five minutes. We moved all about his living room. Amazingly, though all my attention was focused on sword fighting and defending myself from Qadir's blows, neither one of us ran into any of the furniture, piles of books, loose papers, or other ridiculous obstacles in his living room, or hit anything in the living room with our swords.

During the last minute or so I began to feel a confidence in my sword-fighting ability that should have been completely unwarranted. After all, the entire sum of my training was but a few minutes and I hadn't actually received any instructional training.

Nevertheless, I felt a great confidence welling up inside of me. I no longer just acted defensively and began taking swipes with Fury at Qadir when his motions presented an opening. Soon I had him back peddling defensively and that boosted my confidence even more.

"Enough!" Qadir yelled. He put the point of his sword down to the floor and looked at me with a happy smile on his face.

"Congratulations Trevallion, you have successfully completed your Taz sword training."

"What?" "That's it? You didn't teach me anything. All we did is hit blades against one another for a few minutes."

"No, no," Qadir corrected. "We did much more than that.

"You learned the name of your Dragon Sword. You learned how to summon it to you in an instant. And you learned to dance the dance of the sword, which is to say you let the sword lead you in the dance. That is all you need to know to be a master of sword fighting as a Taz."

He pointed at his cluttered living room. "Look around you. Not a single item was hit by a sword. You neither tripped, stumbled, or even bumped into a stack of papers in the room, all while fending off my incessant attacks.

"You see the Dragon Sword is an extremely magickal object; certainly one of the most magickal items in the 2nd Dimension. You do not need to know how to battle with swords when you possess a Dragon Sword that is bonded to you as yours obviously is.

"Your sword will magickally defend and protect you with greater ability than the greatest master swordsman that ever lived in the 1st Dimension. As long as you can keep ahold of it and keep up with the dance, it will weave its way through the thickest horde of demons, and almost nothing they can do will be able to pierce its shield or stop its wrath."

I was dumbstruck with awe at what Qadir had revealed about my sword.

I gently ran my hand over the smooth flat part of the blade. "Where did these amazing swords come from?" I asked in reverence. "Who made them?'

"They come from dragons of course," Qadir answered with a tone of high regard. "That is why they are called Dragon Swords."

"Real dragons?" I asked incredulously.

Qadir nodded affirmatively. "Yes, real dragons. As I told you when we first came to the 2nd Dimension, virtually every fairy-tale creature that exists in human folklore is real and dwells here in the magickal 2nd Dimension realms, although not all here on Sx.

"But even here, where magick abounds and is commonplace, dragons are special. Nobody but a fool bothers dragons. They are impervious to virtually any weapon or magick and their own magick is extremely powerful and potent."

Chapter 28

Qadir tapped the silvery blade of his sword. "You probably assumed the blades of our swords are made from steel, but that is not the case. They are made from the inner scales of dragons.

"In the mountain forests of Lartharn dwells a clan of davos known appropriately as the Dragon Clan. They are very famous makers of hand combat weapons. Indisputably, the finest weapons in the three dimensions of our stewardship are made by the Davos of Lartharn.

"Though the davos are master craftsmen, it is not solely due to their skill that the weapons they make are so extraordinary. Several dragons live on the high mountain peaks above the Lartharn Forest and they have formed a symbiotic relationship with the davos clan.

"Dragons love gold. I'm really not sure why, as they do nothing with it as far as anyone knows. They don't trade it or fashion anything out of it. They just hoard it. Many a foolish warrior has ventured into a dragon lair planning to become rich by stealing their cache of gold. Needless to say, none has ever returned alive, let alone with any gold.

"Yet for all their love of gold, the dragons have no way to mine and refine it. Even in this magickal realm, mining is mostly a physical effort. It is primarily done by akara and they are cunning traders. The only thing a dragon could trade with an akara would be protection from demons, but the akara relish fighting almost as much as mining, so they have no interest in dragons scaring off all the demons.

"Even though akara get killed by demons as you witnessed, they still love the battle. Their young men

301

grow up training for their first battle with demons. And their young women seek mates that are noted warriors more than those who are wealthy.

"Short of raiding villages and stealing a bauble here or there, or kidnapping a fair maiden or village chief and holding them for ransom, dragons have a big challenge actually acquiring the gold they so dearly love.

"Ages ago some wise davos of the Lartharn Clan struck a bargain with the dragons of the mountains. They proposed for the dragons to donate some of their thin inner scales, and use some of their magick to allow the scales to be hammered and formed into shapes and fabricated into parts of weapons.

"Once formed, the dragons use their magick fire to re-solidify and temper the dragon metal, but not quite as strong as the original dragon scale, as they do not want any weapons made with their scales to be able to be used against them.

"Even with that small caveat, the final products become weapons that are wonders to behold and truly worth more than their weight in gold. And gold is the only way a weapon may be purchased from the Dragon Davos. The gold that is paid is split 50-50 with the dragons and that is how those of the mountains serenely acquire their treasure of gold.

"Because of the high cost of dragon metal, the most common weapon made with it is a dagger, and then usually only the tip is dragon metal, with the rest of the short blade being steel. The dragon's fire melds the junction of the two metals so they become as strong as if they were one.

"With swords, the tip and the cutting edges are typically fashioned with dragon metal, but the majority of the blade is usually steel. Only an extremely wealthy warrior could afford the price in gold to have a sword made entirely of dragon metal."

Qadir pointed to my sword. Like him, I had the point down on the floor and was resting my hand on the pommel.

"The swords of Taz are different than all other swords or weapons of the three dimensions.

"You will find that every intelligent creature or being here on Sx is aware of the Taz even if they have never seen any of us in person. Everyone knows we have the ability to physically transit the three dimensions, and that our sole stewardship is to help those beset with demon problems, wherever we find those in need.

"No creature hates demons more than dragons. Why? I am not sure. Dragons are somewhat unfathomable. I don't know why they hoard gold that they don't seem to use for anything. Nor do I understand why they hate demons so much, but hate them they do.

"Because of their hatred for demons and their solitary nature, for millennium dragons have allowed Dragon Swords to be forged for Taz and Taz alone, so we can be out and about banishing the demons they hate, while they remain in their lofty, solitary homes, undisturbed by the antics of lesser beings.

"The Davos of Lartharn pound and shape the dragon metal, magickally altered by the dragons so it can be forged into the swords you and I and all the Taz possess. But that is only the beginning of the miracle that is the sword you wield.

"Once the Davos of Lartharn have completed a new Taz Dragon Sword, a message is sent out to the clans of all the magickal beings of the 2nd Dimension that are protected by the Taz. Each clan of Davos, Oosas, Leialli, Akara, Glash, Weiants, and every other intelligent creature or being that gathers into clans, tribes, herds, or flocks, sends their most magickally talented member on a journey to the land of the Dragon Davos.

"When they are all gathered together, they combine their magick and put a series of powerful enchantments upon the Dragon Sword that will bond to the next Taz, which in this case was you.

"Dragon Swords are created and given as a most precious gift from all the citizens of Sx. They are thanking you in advance for all the good they hope you will do on their world.

"A Dragon Sword is enchanted to bond only to a single Taz. If that Taz is killed, their sword will immediately turn to dust. It is enchanted to come immediately to the hand of the Taz when summoned. And most importantly, it is enchanted to banish demons to Oblivion with the slightest touch of its metal upon their bodies.

"The swordplay dance you have just been a part of with me is also an enchanted gift of the great magickal Adepts that gather together in unity, even those that are often enemies, to bless these swords, because the Taz defend them all from the demons.

"If you trained every day for fifty years you still would not have the skill magickally embedded in your sword. As long as you can follow the lead of your Dragon Sword, no creature or being in the 2nd Dimension will ever be able to beat you in one-on-one combat.

"Because it is such a formidable weapon that could even slay a dragon, one final enchantment is put upon the Dragon Sword by the assembled magickal Adepts. If anyone other than the Taz to which it is bonded, even another Taz, tries to pick up the sword, it will merge with the nearest mass of bedrock, and neither an army of men nor the strongest cauldron of magick will be able to lift it from the stone. Only the Taz to which it is bonded will be able to pull the Dragon Sword from the bedrock to which it has melded.

"Lastly, one of the fire-breathing dragons of the mountains will envelope the sword in an inferno of magickal dragon fire. They will strengthen the metal to once again be as strong as the original dragon scales. So great is the trust of the dragons in the Taz that they present us with a gift of the only weapon that could actually kill them.

"And only by the magick of a dragon could such blades ultimately be forged.

"The metal is so hard and so powerfully enchanted that it can slice diamonds like butter. No tool in existence can cut it or even scratch it. In turn, there is no substance other than the scale of a dragon or the blade of another Dragon Sword that can resist its blow. Whatever a Dragon Sword hits is severed.

"All you have to do as a Taz is to touch a demon, even lightly with your Dragon Sword and they will be banished to Oblivion for centuries. The same thing is true if a dragon touches a demon.

"Demons fear dragons even more than Taz. While we are not relentless in banishing demons and leave them alone as long as they are not causing trouble for other beings and creatures, dragons are not so merciful.

"If it were not for the fact that dragons tend to be hot-tempered, grumpy and disruptive neighbors, many of the creatures and beings of the 2nd Dimension would ask dragons to live nearby to insure demons would never come around."

"There is one small Achilles Heel to your Dragon Sword; a counterspell the magickal Adepts put on it to ensure no Taz ever became an unassailable tyrant that would try to rule over the inhabitants of Sx.

"If you ever try to use your Dragon Sword against any native creature or being of Sx, for instance against an enraged Glash, it will still be a mighty fine sword, one of the best in the land, but its ability to lead you in the dance of the sword will be nullified. You would have to rely solely upon your own skill for your defense."

I was literally brought to tears of gratitude while Qadir was telling me how my Dragon Sword was forged and magickally enchanted by the unity and common purpose of the citizens of the planet Sx.

Up until that point, my limited experiences and learning about being a Taz had been fascinating, but it didn't seem like my life's purpose. But on that day, in the cluttered living room of Qadir's house in Corsalain, I was greatly humbled by what he shared with me.

From that point on I felt profoundly in my heart that I had been blessed and trusted with a most sacred responsibility, and I determined that I would not let my world, or this world down.

Suddenly I felt very weak and fatigued. I actually had to sit down on a nearby table to rest. Qadir rushed over to me with concern.

"I have kept you here too long, he said with concern, hovering over me like a worried mother. "You are not yet practiced enough to have your consciousness separated from your Earth body for this many hours.

Qadir pointed off to the right toward an opening at the end of the room. "There is a bedroom down the hall that I have prepared for you. Go off and sleep now in this body and let your Earth body romp around with your full consciousness for a bit. Please do not seek to awaken your Taz twin again until I call for you. Spend some normal days on Earth with several good nights of sleep and we will meet again in about a week, OK?"

I nodded weakly in agreement. When I opened my eyes again I was laying alone in my bed.

I reflected for some minutes on all my recent experiences on Sx and the life I had just come back to on Earth. I had a good life in the 1st Dimension. There were many activities I enjoyed and relationships I appreciated having. Like anyone, I had some regrets and had bigger aspirations for the future. Unfortunately, the most impactful thought that hit me was how mundane Earth was and I was sad because I was having that thought.

I had never ever thought of my life on Earth in that way before. There were so many scenic and historic places I loved on this planet, so many incredible people I had the opportunity to know and meet and even share a portion of my life with. I loved the wide variety of foods and the assortment of outdoor activities available to enjoy from sailing to skiing.

But the comparison with Sx was dramatic and wide. On Earth, only a handful of people knew who I was, and the most likely good deed I could do would be to help a little old lady cross the street.

On Sx and other places in the 2nd dimension, I was a Taz, living in a world filled with powerful magick that could literally make a difference in anyone's life who had threats from demons. On Earth, with miniscule magickal abilities and without my Dragon Sword, I couldn't see how it would be possible to help anyone with demon problems, even though Qadir had hinted otherwise.

I thought it was surely a good thing that we could not stay separated too long from our Earth body, even with a Soul Splitting Spell, because most of the Taz would probably never come back to Earth after experiencing their life and abilities on Sx.

I fell asleep again with those thoughts in my mind and would only realize later after some more experiences and a lot more knowledge, how wrong I was about my life on Earth.

CHAPTER
Twenty—Nine

The week just living my normal life on Earth passed slowly. I kept remembering all that had occurred on Sx and I missed it. I was looking forward to returning very much. Each day that passed, I was increasingly more tempted to just return there on my own without an invitation from Qadir.

By the seventh night, I could wait no longer. Once my Earth Self was asleep and my Taz Self had materialized, I was on the cusp of willing myself to Sx when I was unpleasantly stopped by the appearance of Genavieve beside me.

"Hello Trevallion," she greeted me pleasantly. "Where are you off to tonight?"

I debated with myself whether to tell her I was going to Sx, or to make something up. Apparently, the few seconds I was considering what my best choice would be was too long of a wait for Genavieve as she quickly did away with the polite chit chat.

"Never mind, wherever it was, you will need to wait for another night," she said authoritatively. "Qadir asked me to help you learn some of the Taz tasks you will need to do here on Earth and how to accomplish them."

"OK," I responded with no enthusiasm.

I had really been looking forward to going to Sx and could think of nothing we could do on Earth that would be very interesting or helpful, as demons were insubstantial and very limited in what they could do here, and we too were fairly magickless and impotent.

Genavieve could see the disappointment in my eyes. "Had something more exciting planned did you? Not to worry, I'm sure you will find tonight less than boring."

She reached out to me. "Close your eyes and hold my hand. I want to take you back to my home near Dinan."

I obliged and closed my eyes as my hand made contact with hers. In a moment I opened them again only to find it was still fairly dark.

We were outside of a midsize country home that seemed to be built of stones. The moon was not quite full, but it was a clear night with sufficient moonlight to see several other homes nearby. They had a good amount of space between them as you are more likely to find in the country versus the city.

Genavieve held one of her hands forward toward the house directly in front of us. "This is my home, please come in and let me introduce you to my family."

I followed closely behind Genavieve and assumed she was going to pass through the wall of her home into the interior. She turned aside at the last moment just as I absentmindedly walked so forcefully into the stone wall of the house that I got knocked onto my backside in shocked surprise. I looked up at Genavieve with some confusion.

"Ouch, I thought our Taz bodies could pass through walls in the 1st Dimension."

"Whatever gave you that idea?" Genavieve asked with a mystified tone. While that might be true for some thin organic walls of recently harvested wood, it certainly isn't true for a wall of stone."

"Isn't that what you were going to do?" I asked meekly. "I was just following you."

"Obviously you were not," Genavieve replied sternly. "I approached the wall only to get on the little stone walkway that leads to my front door. Now please do get up and follow me into the house. We have much to see tonight and there is no time for loafing around."

After entering through the front door we appeared in a good-sized darkened room. The windows were shuttered and I really could see very little, other than vague shapes. The only light that was seeping in came from a hallway off to the right and it was toward the dim illumination that Genavieve walked.

There was a little night light plugged into a wall socket at the far end of the hall near the bottom of a set of stairs. We ascended the stairs and were met at the top by another very dim night light in a wall socket slightly illuminating the narrow upper hallway.

We walked to the left and passed through a closed door at the end of the hallway into what I assumed was the master bedroom. The windows were not shuttered and the room was illuminated sufficiently by the moonlight coming through the large windows that I could clearly see a man asleep on a queen-sized four-poster bed with spiral posts and a canopy.

Genavieve pointed to the man on the bed. The Earth body of Genavieve was sleeping beside him.

"This is my husband. He is just a mundane man of this world. There is nothing more you need to know about him other than I love him and look forward to the time I can spend with him during my days, and for my Earth body to be able to sleep next to him at night.

We turned and walked back through the door and down the hall to the two rooms on the other end. In one a teenage girl was sleeping. The other had a sleeping teenage boy.

Genavieve introduced them as her two children, again without revealing their names.

"I brought you here Trevallion to help you understand that though we are more limited on what we can do against demons in the 1st Dimension, there is still much that we can accomplish to help our world to not devolve into a demon hell, and it is more than worth our time to make that effort.

"I love my children and my husband, just as I know you must love your family and billions of other people in our world love theirs. "I do what I do as a Taz so my children and my husband and others like them in homes across the land, can have peace from the machinations of demons."

"Our stewardship as Taz takes us to many worlds. Sx is only one of countless inhabited worlds in the 2nd Dimension and there are many other demon infested worlds here in the 1st Dimension as well.

"I'm sure you have already become very enamored of Sx and all the amazing creatures that live there and all the marvelous powers you possess there. But in fulfilling your stewardship as a Taz, please don't forget the world you come from Trevallion. You may have few of your Taz powers here, but you are not powerless as you shall see. This is where my family is, this is where your family is, and our world needs the help of the Taz as much as Sx or the other worlds of the 2nd Dimension.

"Though the demons are less of a threat here because they are insubstantial, they can still be a great scourge upon the land. And unlike the citizens of 2nd Dimension worlds, the people here on our own home planet are almost defenseless."

"I understand," I said nodding in agreement with a new perspective.

Genavieve reached out and took my hand again. Without further comment, she blinked us into a room where a woman that appeared to be in her late thirties or early forties was fitfully sleeping on a bed. Wisps of smoke were still rising from a cigarette in an ashtray on the nightstand by the bed, indicating the woman had only recently fallen asleep.

A small television was playing on the dresser in front of the bed and the show was in French, so I presumed we were still in Genavieve's native country. She pointed to the women on the bed.

"This is an unfortunate soul named Claudia. She has been inhabited by a demon for the last six months and it has destroyed her life in that short time. She is always either drunk from alcohol, or high on drugs. Her mind and memory are scrambled. Due to her debilitated state, she lost her job as a bank executive four months ago.

She used to have a longtime boyfriend and a good relationship with her three children that live with the husband she divorced some years ago. But her children choose to not see her now. They are too embarrassed by the drug/alcohol stupor she is most often in. Her boyfriend left her when she became promiscuous.

"How do you know so much about this woman? Do you know her in your Earth body life?" I asked.

"I do not know her personally," Genavieve replied. "I was made aware of her plight and some of the details by a demon I captured and threatened to banish."

"What?" I exclaimed. "How did that happen?"

Genavieve held her index finger up to her lips. "Hush. Stay focused Trevallion. Focus is a key to the power of a Taz. For now, I just wanted you to see and understand how devastating a demon inhabitation can be and how it can quickly and utterly destroy someone's life. I will answer your other questions at another time."

"Well, how do we get the demon out without our Dragon Swords?" I asked.

"Normally, we would not get this demon out," Genavieve replied with an answer that truly surprised me.

"There are tens of millions of demons on our Earth and certainly several million wretched souls that are inhabited.

"We are only seven Taz and we must divide our precious time between multiple worlds in two dimensions. As much as it pulls on the sympathy of our hearts, we cannot take the time to remove demons from individual people.

"Plus, when we banish demons in the 1st Dimension it is very draining on our physical bodies. Your Earth body will usually require a full day to recover and recuperate. You can often feel like you had just endured several rounds in a boxing match.

In the 2nd Dimension banishing a demon is virtually effortless thanks to the magick of our Dragon Swords. But here in the 1st Dimension, it is literally hand-to-hand combat and the demons will fight violently to try and escape being banished.

"When we are in the 1st Dimension we must choose our battles wisely to those minutes in time when we can banish many demons in one instance, without physically draining ourselves too severely. Or, when we can banish high-level demons, such as Ugar, because they do great damage by leading and guiding hordes of lower-level demons to evil. However, with upper-level demons, when they are in the 1st Dimension, it will require the combined efforts of three Taz to banish them, because our magick is so weak in this dimension."

I understood what Genavieve was saying. It made sense that we had to make the best use of our time, couldn't afford to have our Earth body be physically drained for a day, and couldn't help all of the people that were demon inhabited, but I was having anguish in my heart thinking about leaving and doing nothing to help the lady still thrashing in a light sleep on her bed.

Genavieve must have read the turmoil in my eyes.

"We are here, so we will help this one," she said with soft compassion.

"Watch what I do Trevallion. "Remember to the regular people of this world, unless they are great psychics, they cannot see us, hear us, or feel us. We are as invisible to them as the demons.

"But we can see and hear each other, as well as the demons because our Taz body is multi-dimensional energy, so watch and learn."

Genavieve reached her hand out toward the woman. As her hand made contact between the women's breasts, it passed right into her body! She moved her arm up toward the women's throat and suddenly her hand began shaking.

In a moment her hand withdrew from the woman's body and she was holding a muscular female demon with bright red skin tightly by her throat. With surprising strength, Genavieve lifted her arms aloft and the female demon was left thrashing her feet and arms in a frenzy to get away from Genavieve's unrelenting grip.

The demon was reaching out with her clawed fingers trying to gouge Genavieve's face and rake the claws of her feet against Genevieve's stomach and upper legs, but the demon's vicious counterattack was to no avail. It was as if Genavieve had an invisible shield that protected her body from the poisonous rakes of the demon's claws.

From the moment Genavieve withdrew the demon from Claudia's body I could see she was squeezing its neck. Tighter and tighter she squeezed with both of her hands, and after about thirty seconds the demon just vanished in a small poof of grey smoke exactly like they did when they were banished by contact with a Taz Dragon Sword.

Genavieve wiped her hands together several times and a small cloud of powdery grime puffed off of them. "Demon dust," she said noting my curious look. "This method is somewhat messy, more involved, exhausting, and time-consuming. Quite commonly our Earth body will need a day to rest and recover due to its energetic connection to our Taz body, but it has the same end results on Earth as our Dragon Swords do in the 2nd and 3rd dimensions, which is one more demon banished to Oblivion."

"How come you were not injured by the demon raking its claws against you?" I wondered somewhat mystified.

"Demon shield," Genavieve answered simply. "Like most of the magick we can use in the 1st Dimension it requires an enchanted amulet made by Nkosi. But it is an absolute essential if you are going to banish demons in this dimension and not get ripped to shreds by their claws in the process. Unfortunately when they punch you, it still hurts. The shield is right against your skin. It's useful to prevent claw rakes, but it does little to limit the impact from a blow of a fist."

"One more thing Trevallion," she added. "It is usually not proper to transit into a person's home, especially their bedroom, as they may be involved in private matters they do not wish others to see. I only did so this time as I knew the woman would be asleep and it was necessary for you to understand her state of deterioration.

"In the future, if you ever need to banish a demon by strangulation while in the 1st Dimension, it is best to force them out of the body by a magickal incantation and summon them to you from a nearby location.

"However, this method only works sometimes, mostly with lower-level demons. The demon is still connected to the person they are inhabiting and will be drawn back to them like a stretched rubber band snapping back if you do not dispatch them quickly. You usually will only have one to two minutes to fight and banish them before they return to the person they were inhabiting."

"That's awesome!" I said enthusiastically. "How do I do it?"

She reached out and took my hand. "That will have to be a lesson for another time. Our agenda is already full tonight," she said with a friendly smile as she casually blinked us to a new location.

It was still night and we appeared in a glade in a forest. Even with Genavieve by my side, I had a little trepidation when I saw we were surrounded by well over a hundred demons!

They were all quite surprised to see us, as everyone leaped up in menacing anger. They encircled us and began to tighten the circle ever smaller and smaller.

Abruptly, a tall thin demon with an Amish-type black beard held up his hand and yelled out, "STOP!" in a loud voice.

He cocked his head slightly and looked at us through snarled lips. "You are not psychics, you are Taz. Why are you here? You have no power over us in these numbers in the 1st Dimension. One on one we avoid you, but now we will just ignore you.

"Or, maybe kill you," he added with a malicious grin.

Despite his threat, the demon turned his back and started to walk away. Most of the other demons milled around in confusion, not sure if they should attack us or walk away like the other demon.

"Wait," Genavieve called out. "I just came to talk to you for a moment Barzas."

The demon walking away turned with a surprised look on his face. "How do you know my name?"

Genavieve looked at him sternly. "As you noted, I am a Taz."

Barzas nodded his head in grudging acknowledgment, so apparently Genavieve's brief answer spoke volumes.

"What do you want to talk about lady Taz?" Barzas asked angrily.

Genavieve got right to the point. "You and your horde have been terrorizing the local townspeople. Many have been inhabited and the others tormented by the wicked thoughts you put in their heads. Your demon corruption has pitted children against their parents, and set adults in angry schisms with one another. People are drinking and abusing their bodies into an early grave, cheating on their spouses and abusing their children."

Barzas smiled a wide, wicked grin. "Thank you for acknowledging the wonderful work we are doing. We are quite proud of the success we have had with these Izbos."

Genavieve glared at Barzas with a fierce stare. "All of this must end tonight and all of you must leave. I will return here tomorrow to verify that you are gone and check up on this town from time to time in the future. Any demon I encounter shall be sent immediately to

Oblivion."

Her words elicited a range of reactions, from nervous laughter to some demons taking some fearful backward steps. But Barzas just smiled his confident, wicked smile and shook his head in denial.

"You cannot bluff me lady Taz. You are little more than a regular Izbo in this dimension. While it's true that we can't kill you without far too much effort, there's not much you can do against us either without your Dragon Sword."

Barzas waved his two hands toward us using the tops of his hands. "So scoot on back to whatever hovel you two Taz came from, or stay and watch as we degrade and torment the helpless Izbos in this town."

Genavieve ignored Barzas and spoke to all of the other demons. "I hope all of you are not as foolish as Barzas. This is my final warning. Leave this place now and never bother these people again, or embrace a very long visit to Oblivion, because in Oblivion is where you soon shall be."

Barzas began laughing a loud and grating laugh. Many of the other demons joined and it was an almost painful chorus of cackle to hear. Human laughter is contagious and buoys your spirit, but demon laughter is frightening. I actually felt a chill run down my spine as I heard it.

Barzas finally stopped laughing and pointed at Genavieve. "Poor little helpless Taz, thinks she can fool us into believing she has power in the 1st Dimension. Just ignore her and the other one. Without their Dragon Swords or 2nd Dimension magick, they are nothing."

Without another word, Genavieve slapped her two

hands together. It was like a fourth of July sparkler had ignited between her hands. A spray of tiny bits of light burst forth. The sparks all zipped away and an individual single spark pierced into the body of almost every demon as far as I could tell.

At first, they were all afraid she had attacked them with some unknown magick or weapon. When they realized that none of them had suffered any visible harm, they all began their rasping laughter again.

Barzas started to make another demeaning comment, but Genavieve cut him off.

"You were right Barzas; without our Dragon Sword and the magick of the other dimensions, our Taz abilities are very diminished. So I will just have to bring all of you to the 2nd Dimension where we can meet under different circumstances."

Her words had caught everyone's attention and now Barzas looked at her with some concern etched on his ugly face.

"What do you mean!" he exclaimed angrily.

Genavieve was only too happy to explain. "Each of you has been embedded with a Summoning Bur. There is nothing you can do to remove it. You are now marked for the entirety of your eternal existence. If I or any other Taz ever activates your bur, you will be summoned immediately to our presence wherever we are, in any dimension.

If I find anyone of you here again, or hear that any of you are bothering any of the humans again, I will summon you to the 2nd Dimension and you will arrive impaled on the tip of my Dragon Sword for a very, very long trip to Oblivion."

CHAPTER
Thirty

Without another word to the demons, Genavieve reached out her hand to me. As soon as I took it she blinked us back to the tiny bedroom in the forecastle on my sailboat where my Day Self was sleeping.

I was excited to hear the details of what she had just done.

"That was awesome!" I exclaimed. "I thought we couldn't do powerful magick here in the 1st Dimension. I can't wait to learn how to make a Summoning Bur. When can you teach that magick to me?"

"Never I'm afraid," Genavieve replied instantly deflating my excitement and hopes.

"In truth, I do not know how to do the magick myself," she added to my great surprise.

Seeing my blank, uncomprehending look, Genavieve elaborated.

"It was actually a magickal amulet that I invoked, but

I do not know how the magick works.

"That particular amulet was just a tiny geode; a hollow, small walnut-sized rock of the mineral quartz filled with tiny crystals inside. From the exterior surface it looks like a plain, uninteresting rock. If anyone other than a Taz saw it, they would not give it a second glance.

"However, when a Taz touches one, it will feel hot. You could blindly reach into a bag of identical, non-magickal quartz geodes and easily feel the one that had been magickally enchanted.

"Nkosi makes these invaluable tools for all of the Taz. He is our enchanted amulet specialist. Because of his personal talent for coalescing and imbuing magickal energies into objects, we encourage him to leave the demons to us, and instead, stay in his lair on Table Mountain to craft the little wonders that give us at least some limited magickal advantage to fight demons here in the 1st Dimension."

I was somewhat confused about how the amulet Genavieve described could work and gave her a puzzled look.

"How does your Taz body, which you said is 2nd Dimension energy, hold on to a physical object from the 1st Dimension?" I asked with some bewilderment.

"This is only possible due to our peculiar nature and the magick of Nkosi. Even so, it is only on a very small scale," she replied. "Nkosi's ways and means are mysterious. The very fact that he can create any magick at all in his Table Mountain lair that incorporates 2nd Dimension energies is amazing. He learned the secrets decades ago from his mentor and someday when he takes on a protégé, he will pass on the Arcanum of interdimensional magick.

"Nkosi explained to all of us once, that his enchanted amulets are only able to be imbued with magickal power because beneath his lair is the greatest source of magickal energy on Earth. He believes the true origin of the power is a continuously open interdimensional portal to the 2nd Dimension, but he has never been able to locate it.

"Nkosi's amulets will only work in the 1st Dimension for the Taz. Though we think of our Taz body as 2nd Dimension energy, and our Earth body as 1st Dimension energy, we have an ability to harmonize with both, or those of any other dimension as well. That is unique among all the beings of the multi-dimensional universe. There is a link between our twin bodies because they share a multidimensional soul that is beyond mere conscious awareness of each other. We are essentially one individual with two different bodies that coexist in perfect harmony.

"Thanks to that peculiar juxtaposition, Nkosi is able to craft magickal amulets and other small items that take advantage of that exotic merger of interdimensional energies. He imbues his enchantments with both 1st and 2nd Dimension energies that are kept in separate parts of the enchanted item. When the amulet is crushed, or by some other means the two energies merge, the magickal power is released, but only when it is done by a Taz. We are the catalyst that makes the magick possible.

"You will certainly find Nkosi's amulets helpful, especially here in the 1st dimension, and would be well advised to arrange a visit to see him sometime soon.

"As you are just beginning to learn how to coalesce magickal energies and really can do nothing yet on your own, you will find it very helpful to have a few enchanted amulets on hand that require nothing more from you other than to invoke or crush them to activate the magick.

"When you want to visit Nkosi, just call out to him and he will answer you telepathically. You may need to try several times, as he will not communicate if he is in the middle of crafting an amulet or other magickal item."

Genavieve turned to hold my gaze for a moment. "Goodbye for now Trevallion. I'm sorry I was hard on you initially and reluctant to have you take on your Taz duties so quickly. You obviously have excellent potential.

"But you still have a very great deal to learn to be fully effective in your stewardship and the world of demons can be deadly, even for us. Knowledge and skill will keep you alive."

"And a few magickal amulets from Nkosi will help as well," she added in a humorous tone.

"Stay humble and grateful Trevallion for the good you have been blessed to be able to do. Think of yourself as a sponge and use every conscious minute of your time, in both the 1st and 2nd Dimensions, to learn more about everything and anything than you did the minute before. All knowledge, however irrelevant it may seem at the time, can come in very handy someday in the future.

"Adieu, until we meet again." Before I could reply in turn, she blinked away.

It was still the middle of the night in St. Augustine so I decided to go explore the town with my Taz body. I had been delighted by everything I had seen during the day, walking through the town with Skye, especially in the old town with its stone buildings, quaint shops, and colorful residents.

As it was after midnight I didn't expect to see too many humans out, but Qadir had warned me the town was filled with demons and ghosts. I wanted to see how accurate that was and to determine if there were any situations of demons troubling humans that I might be able to help.

I had never knowingly encountered a ghost and wasn't sure I would be able to see them like I could demons, but I blinked into the old town to see what I would find.

As I first appeared by the gate to the old town and contemplated the demons I might encounter, I made a mental note to make sure the next time I saw Genavieve, that she explained how she had reached into Claudia's body and pull out the demon by the throat, and then banish her, just by squeezing her neck with her hand.

Observing the demon-fighting techniques of other Taz was certainly helpful, but if they took the time to explain exactly how they did what they did, it would be even more so.

I didn't have to look far for demons once I blinked to the old town. There was one standing right near the gate, less than five feet away when I blinked in, and I could see several more wandering the main street of the old town.

The fellow by the gate opened his eyes a little wider when he saw me pop in, but his face soon regained a calm non-concerned look that was a little disquieting.

He was about my height and a bit rotund for a demon.

He had a close-cut mustache and was dressed in overalls with a straw hat like a country bumpkin. If he had been a human, you certainly would never have noticed him in a country crowd, but he would have really stood out in a group of sophisticated city dwellers.

He neither seemed threatening or concerned by my appearance, so I ventured a friendly greeting.

"Hello," I said simply.

He looked over and smiled a slight grin and helloed me back.

"First time to St. Augustine?" he asked cordially.

"I just recently arrived," I acknowledged. "I've seen the old town during the day. I wanted to check it out to see what it felt like at night."

"Ah, night is my favorite time," the demon swooned. "All the Izbos go to bed and we get this little piece of pleasure all to ourselves."

He looked over at me with a little more scrutiny. "You're not a demon, so you must be one of those psychic Izbos, off on a Night Travel to do some sightseeing, eh?"

"Not exactly," I answered hesitantly. This demon was being entirely too friendly and I didn't really know what to make of it. In any case, he entirely ignored that I told him I wasn't a psychic Izbo.

"You are a lucky Izbo to be able to Night Travel around the world," he said appreciatively. "I've lived in St. Augustine for over four hundred years and I still love it. I would be happy to show you around and tell you some of the history that you will never learn on an Izbo tourist tour."

Honestly, I was flabbergasted by the demon's cordial demeanor and offer to be my tour guide. I was reminded of the non-threatening behavior of the upper-level demon Hamerac and concluded that at least some demons were not in a constant frenzy to kill, torture, and debase Izbos.

On the other hand, they were demons. I suspected that this demon, just like Hamerac, had a devious alternative motive and that his friendly manner was just a means to a less friendly end to our relationship. But for the moment I decided to go along with his offer.

"What is your name?" I asked.

"I'm Mateo," he replied happily. "I never had an Izbo ask me my name before," he said somewhat amazed.

Mateo pointed at me. "You're not the first psychic Izbo I've encountered, but I never met one that wanted to know my name.

"The others were all holier than thou. I tried to talk to them, but they just walked away with their noses stuck up in the air like I was smelly garbage left too long in the sun. Why are you so nice?"

I gave Mateo a little smile. "I could ask the same of you. I've encountered a lot of demons, but I've never met one like you."

Mateo looked down and humbly pushed the palm of his hand up into the air as if I was giving him too much credit. "I'm just like all the others here in St. Augustine. Most of us have not been demons very long and most of us wish we weren't.

"We love this town. Many of us lived here at one time or another when we were Izbos. We made some awful choices in those days of life; horrendous deeds too terrible to atone for. Now we are cursed to be demons for all eternity. But what little is left of our hearts does not want to hurt Izbos anymore. We hurt them enough when we were one of them."

If demons could cry, I think Mateo would have then. It was a bit of a challenge for me to not feel empathy for him. I had to keep reminding myself that he was a demon and that there was a reason he was a demon. As he admitted, he devolved into a less than human form because there were atrocious things he had done when he was a human that were too terrible to atone for.

I still found myself trying to cheer him up as he had lost his earlier spunk as soon as he started to reflect upon being a demon and the heinousness of his past.

"I'd like to take you up on your offer," I said cheerily.

Mateo looked up at me with heavy, sad eyes. "What offer?" he asked blankly.

"To be my tour guide, of course."

"Oh yeah, we can do that," he said with slightly more interest.

"It really is a lovely town," he acknowledged. "I just wish I could experience it physically again without having to inhabit an Izbo."

As soon as he spoke about inhabiting Izbos, my internal warning radar sounded an alarm.

"Have you inhabited Izbos before?" I asked, doubtful that he would answer truthfully.

"Oh yes," he replied frankly, to my surprise, "not a lot, just once since I've been a demon. And I never tried to make him do anything bad to himself, although he always did anyway.

"I like to think I actually helped him. The guy I inhabited was initially very suicidal; that's why I was able to inhabit him because he was feeling so worthless.

"Of course I didn't want him to commit suicide because that would end my pleasure of enjoying his body, so I talked him out of it and was able to spend many years with him.

"I just missed being in a physical body on this Earth so much, and the temptation was too hard to resist when I encountered a distraught Izbo. When they get into those negative spaces in their heart and mind, it is like they are holding out a sign for a demon to come inhabit them.

"He was lucky I got into him before some other demon that wasn't from St. Augustine did. A demon from any other place would have done their best to destroy the Izbo's life. I just wanted to share it, to experience pleasurable physical sensations again."

I was very tempted to get into a moral discussion with Mateo, beginning with inhabiting a human's body was never OK. Pointing out that harm was surely being done whether he realized it or not; even if it was not his intention. I didn't see a demon inhabitation, even a friendly one, as being any different than a parasite, like a tapeworm claiming it was doing no harm, just sharing a little food.

However, he did stop the man from committing suicide. I didn't give that as much weight as I probably should have because after all, Mateo was a demon and I didn't really trust the truth of anything a demon said, especially using it to justify their demon activities.

In the interest of learning as much as I could during my nighttime visit, I made no comment on his statement about inhabiting a human and deferred the moral lecture for another time. Instead, I changed the subject.

"How about the tour you promised me?"

Mateo definitely seemed less enthusiastic than when he originally greeted me. "I suppose we could do that," he drawled out kind of slowly. "Follow me," he said, turning to walk down the street.

As we walked down St. George Street, I was following a step behind Mateo. He continually pointed right and left to indicate various places where atrocities occurred: rapes, murders, robberies, beatings, slavery, suicides, deaths from floods, deaths, and destruction from fires, horrible deaths from multiple plagues, but never any of the normal historical points of interests.

Along the way, we passed many other demons walking by. I started counting them but eventually gave up as there were too many to keep track of.

I passed one young human couple out for a late-night walk and laughed to myself, realizing they were oblivious to the dozens of demons walking by right next to them, especially as I was now very aware of demons and could spot them even if they were at the far end of the street.

For many demons, their totally crazy style of dress was a big giveaway. No humans dressed so non-sensical and incoherently. While an occasional well-dressed demon might be encountered, they certainly were not the norm.

Demons also have an aura with a large gray band that is never seen in humans. So regardless of how they dress, speak, or present themselves, a demon cannot hide from a Taz.

Several of them gave me a second glance, but none even said hello to Mateo. I wasn't sure if demons were typically just that standoffish and unfriendly with one another, or if Mateo was some kind of outcast who was being shunned.

Eventually one of the demons stopped us to ask Mateo who I was. It was something I had expected to occur sooner.

A stocky, swarthy demon with curly black hair that fell to his shoulders and a bushy beard, dressed like a pirate, including a patch over one eye, stopped us by standing right in front of Mateo. Two other demons soon stepped beside him.

"Who is this Izbo you are leading through our town? he asked in an unpleasant voice. "We don't like Izbos that can see us. Send him back to Izbo land. He is not welcome here."

To my surprise, Mateo stood his ground. "He is my guest Jobar, so just you never mind about him. He can't hurt us and we can't hurt him, so go find someone else to harass. He will go when I am done with my tour."

I imagine life was usually pretty boring for these St. Augustine demons, as in less than half a minute this little tiff drew a crowd of many spectators. And that's when things began to get a little dicey.

I was standing off to Mateo's left. We were in the middle of the street and most of the demons were facing us, but as the crowd grew, the available space began to shrink and many demons started congregating all around us on all sides.

One demon that had been in the back decided to move up to the front. Unfortunately, like everyone else, he thought I was a psychic Izbo without physical substance, so he tried to walk through me rather than around me. I felt him collide with my back and turned around to see a look of great surprise on his face.

"This Izbo has substance!" He yelled out in disbelief.

Jobar looked at the demon angrily. "You are such an idiot Yipbid! No Izbo has substance. It's dark and you obviously bumped into Mateo."

"I did not!" Yipbid said defending himself.

"Why are we even talking about something so ridiculous and stupid?" Jobar asked dismissively.

He reached out toward my body. "Here, see my hand passes right through...." He never finished his sentence because when his hand touched my body, he whipped it back as if he had just touched a hot stove.

"He does have substance," Jobar said, looking at his own hand as if it had somehow betrayed him.

Now there was a chorus of demons declaring it was impossible for an Izbo to have substance among demons. None of them seemed threatening, just disbelieving and curious, so I let them come up one by one and touch me.

Word quickly spread and demons from far and wide joined the group to do the impossible, and touch the Izbo that had substance in the demon world.

As it was such a wonder to all of them, I had to assume that none of them had ever encountered, or even heard of a Taz, although that seemed like a farfetched idea. I kept waiting for a demon to say I was a Taz, but it never happened.

During the next fifteen minutes or so, I had to have been touched by at least two hundred demons, but not one tried to hurt me or even speak to me. Multitudes of arms just continued to reach out towards me from all directions, and many fingers at a time touched me, from my legs to my head.

Even though I never felt threatened, it was actually a very unnerving experience. After a while, I couldn't take it anymore. I held up my hands and asked everyone to back up and give me some space.

All the demons took a couple of steps back as I asked and then just stared at me in silence, even Mateo.

After an uncomfortable moment of silence, I concluded that they must be waiting for me to speak and explain myself. I wasn't sure how to do that without potentially causing problems and conflicts, so I began by asking them some questions.

"How many of you are Original Demons?" I asked, but nobody responded. I wasn't sure if that was because they didn't want to answer, or because there were no Original Demons among them, which I found unlikely.

Half expecting to be met again by either silence or a great number of raised hands, I asked, "How many of you Metastasis Demons?"

Once again, not one demon reacted, so I assumed they were just being indifferent and uncooperative.

Though I expected just more stone-cold silence, I figured to include the last category of demons just to be thorough.

"How many of you are Purgatory Demons?"

Slowly, hesitantly, a hand went up, then another, and another, and another. I looked around me, to all sides, and as far as I could see, every single demon had their hand raised.

"How is it possible that this entire town is filled only with Purgatory Demons?" I asked quietly, more to myself than aloud, as I didn't really expect an answer.

To my surprise Jobar the pirate stepped forward. "Lord Lucifer designated St. Augustine as our prison.

"Many Purgatory Demons, from all parts of the demon world, who are not making any progress at all to becoming Metastasis Demons are confined here, and in other city prisons in the 1st Dimension. We must either Metastasize and prove we are worthy to be demons by hurting Izbos, or run out our five hundred year clock and be dispatched to die a real death of our soul in the Demon Torture Games; but only after hundreds of excruciating deaths and revivals of our half-demon, half-human body."

"But you are not half-human," I pointed out. "You are 100% demon."

"We are now," Jobar admitted, "but every year that we remain Purgatory Demons, and do no evil to Izbos, our souls gain more light. If we continue to gain light for the entire five hundred years, we will no longer have enough darkness in our souls to be fully demon. That is when Lord Lucifer makes us die the final death in the Torture Games."

Jobar looked around and swept his arm to include all of the demons in the crowd. "Lord Lucifer has actually done us a great service. St. Augustine is a very nice prison. It certainly is no hell."

"All these demons, every single one that lives in this beautiful little town, we all are happily counting down the five hundred years to our demise. That is when we will be free to no longer be demons. We may be truly dead with no eternity of either heaven or hell, but we will be free of the curse of being demons. We may become nothing. But at least in being non-existent we will no longer be demons."

I was very surprised by what Jobar was saying. I remembered the husband and wife Purgatory Demons I had observed in the demon school, and how hard they were working to learn how to inhabit humans and become Metastasis Demons. The demons in St, Augustine, if Jobar could be believed, all seemed to be going in the other direction, to *not* be demons.

It was all somewhat confusing and I asked Jobar to give me some more clarity. "My understanding is that all of you once were human. How did you become demons, especially if that is not what you wanted?"

Jobar looked down at the ground and shuffled his feet a bit before answering. "All of us, when we were Izbos, committed unspeakable atrocities against other Izbos, not just once, but many times. There is no sugar coating it. We were the slime of the Earth.

"Each time, our soul lost some light. When we died, our soul could no longer manifest as an Izbo soul. We had lost so much light we could only be demons.

"At first, for most of us, it seemed great. Our punishment for our crimes was to be able to live forever doing even worse crimes without penalty, without judgment, because we were surrounded by millions of demons even more evil than we were.

"Problem was, we weren't evil enough in the demon world. Many of us had been soldiers. We were brainwashed by our superiors and our religions to hate the enemy, to not even think of them as human, so we killed them without remorse, and in most cases, with cruel happiness."

He pointed to my erstwhile guide. "Mateo, is a good example. He is getting close to his 500 years and freedom. Tell him what you did to become a demon, Mateo."

Mateo looked down and swayed nervously back and forth a bit on his feet before finally speaking. "I was among the first settlers of St. Augustine. We arrived in 1565. French Protestants had landed just north of here the year before and had established a fort.

"The king of Spain sent General Don Pedro Menendez de Aviles here to destroy the French and establish St. Augustine as a bulwark to further French Protestant incursions.

"We arrived on thirty ships carrying over twenty-six hundred men, women, and children. My wife and ten-year-old son were among the passengers.

"During the long journey across the ocean, a great deal of time was spent by the military leaders and the padres inciting us to hatred against the French; not because they were French, but because they were Protestants, which we were told were the minions of Satan and had to be exterminated from the land, lest they lead more people, including the indigenous natives, into a false religion.

"Not long after our arrival, the General ordered the

soldiers, of which I was one, to march north to attack the French fort at the mouth of the St. Johns River. We marched through a hurricane, but only lost a couple of men in the floodwaters.

"When we reached the fort, the surprise was total. The last thing they expected was an armed force coming through a hurricane. When we attacked, most of the men tried to flee because we considerably outnumbered them. As it turned out, a large group of them had left the day before in a couple of ships to go and attack us at St, Augustine.

We caught over one hundred men at the fort and killed them without mercy, usually with a stab in the stomach so they would die slowly and painfully, along with several slicing wounds all around their bodies to attract ants and insects to torture them with a thousand bites.

"There were women and children too, and some of them were killed if they fought against us, but most were taken to become servants.

"Some of the men we nailed up on trees so their suffering would be long, and they would take days to die. There they would remain until they turned into skeletons to be warning signs to the French and Indians not to mess with the Spanish.

"After destroying the fort, we hurried back to St. Augustine to defend against the French ships heading south.

"The French had very bad luck that week. A few days after we returned, a group of Frenchmen were discovered across the southern inlet of the St. Augustine barrier island. Apparently, their ship had run aground in the hurricane and they were making their way north to return to their fort.

"They had no boat to cross the inlet and General Menendez ordered a boat across to parlay with them. The officer of the boat revealed enough details to convince the French that we had captured and destroyed their fort. He offered to take them prisoners and even provided food to them to lull them into trusting us.

"The French agreed to become prisoners and many looked forward to being reunited with their wives and children. As we only had a small boat, we could only take six Frenchmen at a time across the inlet.

"After they landed on the island, we made them walk out of sight around a large sand dune. We bound and gagged them, then stabbed them numerous times until they were dead.

"One thrust through the heart would have killed them quickly and mercifully, but they were Protestants, hated minions of Satan, so of course we wanted their deaths to be painful and agonizing. With relish we stabbed them everywhere except the heart, all the while calling them vile enemies of God and the Virgin Mary, not worthy of a dog's death.

"We killed the entire party of survivors in lots of six, and there was triumphant elation in our hearts to be able to be servants of God by killing the heretic Protestants.

"Unbelievably, a few days later, the campfires of another group of French shipwreck survivors were spotted in the very same location across the inlet. This group included the Admiral of the French fleet. We used the same ruse with them and killed them all in the same manner. In total, we killed over three hundred Frenchmen with that ploy.

"That time of slaughters at the fort and with the castaways was the beginning of the end for me. All love left my heart. For the rest of my life, I was cruel to my wife, my son, and my other children born in St, Augustine.

"I had been a pious Catholic, but I turned into a terrible man that beat his wife when she wasn't obedient, raped female prisoners and native women, had no time for my children, and took joy in killing anyone my church or military leaders said was an enemy.

"By the time I died I fully expected to go to hell, and I wish I had gone to that mythical place. Finding myself no longer human and now a demon was a worse punishment.

"I tried to be eviler; to become more fully demon, but something inside me changed. I never felt remorse in my life for the evil I did, but I felt it in my afterlife. I knew it was too late to make amends, but I vowed to not continue on the path of wanton evil.

"I'm still a wretched soul. I told you I have inhabited an Izbo. But I think I am not evil enough to still be gaining darkness to my soul and falling further into the demonic abyss. In less than a hundred years, I will finally be killed in the Torture Games and I am so looking forward to the peace that true death will bring."

He stopped and looked at me in silence for a minute. "That is my story. Now, what is yours? How can you be an Izbo and also have tangible substance among demons?"

CHAPTER
Thirty—One

This was uncharted territory for me. I had to keep reminding myself to be cautious, that being deceitful was as natural to demons as breathing was to me. How much to tell them? How much to withhold? Were they just playing me for a fool?

My natural inclination was to believe them as they seemed so sincere. However, my limited Taz experiences told me that demons were universally evil and could not be trusted. Somehow I needed to find a way to walk a line between those two points of view and tell the St. Augustine demons something without giving away everything.

I decided to start with the elephant in the room to see if anyone had ever heard of an elephant.

"How many of you are familiar with a Taz?" I was greeted by a sea of blank stares.

"Is that some type of Izbo mixed drink?" one of the demons in the crowd with a sharp-pointed hat asked.

"No," I assured him, a Taz is not a drink. It is a type of human."

More blank stares.

"There is more than one type of Izbo?" another demon with a tall conical hat asked dubiously. "Oh!" he proclaimed wisely, "you must be talking about an Izbo race, like Asian, or African, but I have never heard of it so it must be a sub-category, right?"

"Not exactly," I replied hesitantly, but you are on the right track."

Obviously and shockingly, none of the St. Augustine demons that were present that night had even heard of a Taz.

"I am a Taz," I admitted, "and like Mr. Conical over there correctly assumed," I said pointing to the demon with the pointy hat, "a Taz is a variation of the normal human, but we are not a race. In fact, any human race can be a Taz."

"What makes you different?" a demoness dressed like an Egyptian goddess asked.

I pointed to myself. "Well, the obvious one is I can see you, and talk to you like a psychic human, but I can also touch you and you can touch me."

An unshaven, disheveled demon that looked like the murderer he probably had been in life interjected. "So we could kill you physically?"

"Hopefully, none of you will try," I said with a laugh trying to deflect the question. A smattering of demons laughed with me, but many did not, and that made me a bit nervous.

I decided to move on and not answer the question by

getting them interested in something more unique.

"I can also physically travel to the 2nd Dimension."

Once again I was met with silence, but this time they were a bit dumbstruck, with mouths agape in disbelief.

Jobar stepped forward and peered at me closely, like he was seeing some kind of alien for the first time.

"No Izbo can travel to the 2nd dimension, except the apparition of a psychic Izbo. You should not tell us lies. We have been truthful with you. Most of us have never even been to the 2nd Dimension. It is a cherished dream because at least we would have a semblance of physical substance there. But not you; not Izbos."

I thought of telling him about all the mythical creatures I had encountered in the 2nd Dimension, but realized a psychic human would have been able to see all of those beings and creatures as well.

Then I decided on the one sure, irrefutable way to prove to them that a Taz was a different kind of human than they had previously encountered. I'm not sure why that seemed important to me, but it did.

"How about if I take you there Jobar; right now?"

"Now you are just taunting me," Jobar said sadly. That is something a demon would do. I told you, we are in prison. If we could go to the 2nd Dimension and have a semblance of a body, we would all be there already.

"Maybe you are just a different type of demon that can masquerade as an Izbo and have come to torment us."

"No, no, I assured him. "I am a human. And I can take you to the 2nd Dimension. This is not a prison for me. If you hold my hand, we will be as one for the blink."

I reached out my hand. "Hold my hand and we can go right now."

Very hesitantly Jobar took my hand. Immediately, I closed my eyes and willed us to the leialli meadow. When I opened my eyes I was there, but Jobar was not! I looked all around the meadow for him, but he was nowhere to be seen!

Yikes! What an idiot I was! How stupid could I be to bring a demon to the place where demons had already caused such misery? And now he was loose somewhere on this world and I had no idea where!

My first thought was to call out to Qadir for help, but I knew I would be raked over the coals for my stupidity. I decided to blink back to where the demons were gathered in St, Augustine to get some of them to tell me more about Jobar. If I knew his proclivities, I might be able to figure out where he had gone on Sx.

I also held out a faint hope that maybe he really was somehow imprisoned in St. Augustine and had not been able to travel with me on the blink to the 2nd Dimension.

I immediately blinked back to St. Augustine, to the spot on St. George Street I had departed from. To my immense relief, Jobar was standing right where I had left him.

"I don't know where you vanished to," he said. "But as you can see, it was without me.

"You have not proven that you can travel to the 2nd Dimension. But I have proven to you that we are in prison and that there is no escape from here for us. Either we become evil enough to become a full-fledged demon, or we remain a Purgatory Demon for 500 years and then die in peace.

"Whatever you are, we choose peace. Visit us all that you wish, but no more lies about being some different kind of human that can physically go to the 2nd Dimension." With that statement, all the demons turned away and began to walk off into the night.

"Wait!" I called out. "How do you explain that I have physical substance in the demon world?"

But none of the demons seemed to care about me anymore. Even Mateo had continued to walk away.

Reluctantly, I decided I had accomplished all I was going to that night and willed myself back to my boat, a bit frustrated that things had not gone better with the St. Augustine demons on our first meeting.

When I opened my eyes I didn't see the forecastle of my boat and my sleeping physical body as I expected. Instead, the evil face of Hamerac was staring at me.

"Welcome back to my humble abode Trevallion."

"Dammit!" I wasn't a person that tended to cuss, but being once again summoned to Hamerac's lair against my will, no normal expletive seemed adequate.

I immediately used every mental convolution I could muster to call my Dragon Sword, but to absolutely no avail.

Hamerac just sat on his big throne looking at me amused.

"By the grimaces on your face, you must be trying to call your Dragon Sword. I told you before, this is my home and the place in the universe of my greatest power. Correspondingly, it is the place of least power for you, or any other Taz.

"So why don't you stop your useless efforts. I will not take much of your precious time."

I did stop trying to call Fury, not because Hamerac had told me to, but because it was obviously futile.

"What do you want Hamerac?" I asked curtly. The tone of my voice was angry, but inside I felt worried and defenseless standing before an upper-level demon in the place, as he pointed out, of his greatest power.

"I want to begin our partnership," Hamerac said smugly.

"I have no intention of partnering with you in anything," I spat out resolutely.

"You have so much to learn young Taz. You should be thankful I am willing to teach you, and even help you to be a better Taz. With my assistance, you shall certainly become infamous in the demon world."

"No thanks," I replied brusquely. "I prefer to learn all I need from the other Taz, whom I trust!" I said with emphasis. "Just send me back home and don't summon me again."

"Ah trust," Hamerac waxed philosophically, "such a fragile belief. As you have such trust in the other Taz, I am sure they have already enlightened you about how every time you banish a demon with your Dragon Sword, it sucks away some of your own life essence."

"Not likely," I replied confidently. "If that was true, I'm sure I would have heard about it by now. Stop trying to bait me and just send me home. I want nothing to do with you."

"Very well, I will return you to your pitiful little sailboat and the pathetic excuses for demons in St.

Augustine."

"Wait!" I called out. "How do you know about my sailboat and my meeting with the demons in St. Augustine, which just happened?"

Hamerac smiled his scary wicked grin. "Crystal Ball, remember? I see everything. How else do you think I was able to make you appear here? You must not be as bright as I assumed, as I explained this to you thoroughly at our last meeting."

The ramifications of that hit me hard, and I'm sure my face went a little ashen. If Hamerac could see everything I did, how could I have any secrets or ever find a way to banish him? He would know my every plan before I executed it, my every spell or enchantment as I crafted it.

Even worse, if he knew about my sailboat, he knew about Skye who lived on the boat with me. He might be able to incite inhabited humans to harm her, or attack me, sink my boat, or who knows what other mischief or catastrophe?

"Don't worry," Hamerac said calmly. "I sense your thoughts and I am not going to hurt your girlfriend or sink your boat. I need you, and as they say in your land, I have bigger fish to fry."

Yikes! "You can see me in your crystal ball and read my mind?"

"Of course," Hamerac acknowledged nonchalantly. "It makes negotiations and battles so much easier when there are no surprises."

"Hardly fair, I can't read your mind!" I objected loudly, disturbed by this new reality.

"Obviously," Hamerac replied as if I was a dimwit.

"How successful of a demon would I be if I played fair?

"Enough with the theatrics," he said tersely. "I promised to only keep you here briefly and I occasionally keep my promises when it serves my interests. You are lucky, as this is one of those times.

"Has your inept mentor educated you yet on the Nexus?"

"I thought you saw and heard everything I do. Shouldn't you already know the answer to that question?" I asked suspiciously.

Hamerac began to tap his fingers in running succession on the wide arm of his throne chair. "You vex my patience, Taz junior. Do you think I have nothing better to do with my time than to continuously stare into the crystal ball to follow you around? Do you, or do you not, know of the Nexus?"

"I do," I confirmed.

Hamerac nodded and handed me a slip of paper. "Good, there will be a Nexus from the 3rd Dimension that will be opening up at these coordinates in the 1st Dimension, in approximately fifteen hours. As you cannot take this paper with you, memorize the coordinates.

"A horde of well over a thousand demons will be coming through the Nexus. These are particularly vicious demons from the Gosli Horde. That horde has been patiently waiting for the next Nexus to the 1st Dimension to open.

"Every one of them has experience inhabiting Izbos. And every one of them has, in times past, been banished to Oblivion by various Taz that predate any of you

350

currently living by hundreds of years.

"Having recently returned from an extended stay in Oblivion, these demons will be ravenous to inhabit Izbos again and because of their past experience, they will be able to do so easily.

"But they will not be targeting the usual down in their luck nameless Izbos. I have learned that they plan to only inhabit politicians, celebrities, and powerful business leaders, so they can have greater influence on the Izbo world and bring it to a heightened state of conflict and war."

"I looked at Hamerac with abject suspicion. "I don't believe a word you are saying. Why would you tell me this? Even if it was true, I know you would not have brought me here and told me this unless there was some benefit to you. And if it benefits you, then it can't be good for me or any other human."

"You so misunderstand me," Hamerac said irritated. "Obviously I am telling you this because I hope to reap a benefit, but my gain does not need to be your loss, or humanities.

"Keep your mouth shut and your ears open and I will explain it all to you. After my explanation, you can act upon the intelligence I am providing, or not. In either case, you will be free to return to wherever you wish to go in the 1st dimension."

"Alright," I agreed reluctantly, "I'll listen."

"First you need to understand that the only beings that can willfully transit with substance to and from the 3rd Dimension are very high upper-level demons and Taz.

"None of the demons that have returned from Oblivion to the Gosli Horde have the ability to transit dimensions by thought. They are all lower-level and mid-level demons and can only pass to the 1st or 2nd Dimension when a Nexus opens.

"They have been amassing their numbers as more and more of them are returning from Oblivion. Now they are ready and are prepared to rush through in mass to your Earth when the Nexus opens.

"Obviously you and your fellow Taz will not want such a scourge coming to the 1st Dimension, let alone your own homeworld. In this, our paths intersect because I do not want them going there either.

"There is great competition in the demon world among hordes to out evil one another. Whatever terrible things we do to Izbos, we do far worse to each other.

"Ruthless savagery against other hordes, when successful, is one of the key attributes of gaining greater knowledge and power that is useful for advancing to a higher demon level.

"The gift of more knowledge and power is bestowed by Lord Lucifer on any demon or demon horde that exhibits pure evil. Whether the evil is against Izbos or other demons is irrelevant.

"Because treachery and betrayal is to be expected, we gather into hordes that vow fidelity to the members of the horde. This offers some level of protection against assaults and maleficence from other hordes. It also allows us to mount offenses against them to decimate their numbers.

"And that is the purpose of our meeting today. I

would like you to go to the other Taz and alert them to the catastrophe that will be unleashed on your Earth in less than a day, unless they act. They will know what to do from there."

Demons are so slippery. I was sure Hamerac was providing a little truth in hopes of ensnaring me and the other Taz in a greater lie. However, on the chance that what he said might be true, I couldn't just ignore it and would need to alert the other Taz.

"Why are you telling this to me? Why not contact one of the other more experienced Taz? I think you are just taking advantage of my ignorance and inexperience in the ways of demons and Taz."

Hamerac shook his head in disavowal. "None of the other Taz would even deign to listen to me. Nor would I be able to compel them to come here as I did you.

"On that subject, I have no doubt that one of the first things you will do when you meet with the other Taz is to learn how to block my summons. Hereafter I expect my ability to do that to you will be nullified. As you will see however, my forewarning will be accurate.

"In the future, when I have something I feel will be helpful to both you and your world and also serve my own purposes, I will call out to you telepathically. In light of the accuracy and value of the information I can share, I hope you will be wise enough to heed my invitation.

"Goodbye Trevallion, until we meet again."

In a flash, without any control on my part, I vanished from Hamerac's presence and found myself once again back on my boat.

My first thought was to urgently call out to Qadir, and

I didn't hesitate a moment!

CHAPTER
Thirty—Two

I expected Qadir to tell me to meet him somewhere, but instead he popped onto my sailboat within a couple of minutes after I called him telepathically. Luckily he appeared in the main salon, as I was in the forecastle bedroom where there really was little room for another Taz body.

Before Qadir's arrival, I had been reflecting upon how night traveling used to be so uncomplicated and carefree while I slept and dreamed. My Night Self was 100% insubstantial in all situations; it could go anywhere and be unharmed by anything.

Now my Night Self was no more. It had been supplanted by my Taz body which was now the traveler when my Earth body slept. In the 1st Dimension on Earth, my Taz body was invisible and without substance to any people, just as my Night Self had been. But unlike my Night Self, the Taz body could only pass through living organic substances that didn't have too much mass; so people and small animals yes, elephants no. More importantly, my Taz body had physical substance when it came in contact with demons in the 1st or any dimension, and could be physically injured by them.

My Taz body also had physical limitations in the 1st Dimension that had not constrained my Night Self. Where my Night Self could float through the air, my Taz body was weighted down by gravity and had to walk around on the ground like anyone else.

Thankfully my Taz body could still avoid walking when necessary by blinking in an instant anywhere on Earth, or into any other Dimension. Unfortunately, while Taz were invisible to normal humans, solid non-organic objects in any dimension were still solid to the Taz body; no passing through walls like my Night Self had done. Now I had to walk through the door like everyone else, even when I was in the 1st Dimension.

I laughed a little to myself thinking about opening doors in the 1st Dimension with my Taz body. That and moving other tangible objects was likely where a lot of ghost stories came from.

My momentary reflection was interrupted by Qadir. "This is most disturbing," he fussed. "You should not have met again with that foul upper-level demon, Hamerac. It's a miracle you are still alive. I suppose we are going to have to check you all over again for a hex."

"It wasn't really up to me," I pointed out. "Hamerac summoned me without warning and there was nothing I could do about it.

"Or was there?" I asked with a tiny bit of suspicion.

Qadir lifted his eyebrows off to the side and raised

his eyes as if contemplating his answer. "Well, actually there is. We just haven't progressed to it yet. After all, you have only very recently become a Taz. I can't teach you everything in just a handful of days."

I decided to let that somewhat evasive answer pass for the moment and relayed all that Hamerac had told me about the imminent arrival of over a thousand inhabiting capable demons through a Nexus. More ominously, according to Hamerac, these demons were not looking for the typical physical thrill of inhabitation. Instead, they were committed to dwelling inside influential people so they could use them to cause greater damage in the human world.

Qadir was quite disturbed by what I told him and decided we should immediately call a Taz council to decide how to proceed.

He fished into his bottomless vest pocket and pulled out a small glass vial about the length and width of a little finger. Its opening was sealed with a tight-fitting cork, which Qadir struggled a bit to wiggle free.

He poured what appeared to be a tiny, shiny red jelly bean onto my open palm. "Chew that and swallow it," he directed. It will allow your Earth Self to go about its day independent of your Taz Self for the next 72 hours."

"Well that's handy," I said cheerfully. "I could use a few more of those," I added. "Care to share?"

"I just did share," Qadir said with a bit of irritation. "I gave you one of only three that I had. Magick of that caliber is not easy to obtain in the 1st Dimension, so you will need to be satisfied with only one for now.

"Let us go," he said reaching out his arm.

I rested my hand on his forearm, "where to?"

"Table Mountain," he said firmly, and then we blinked away.

When I opened my eyes we were in a narrow, natural passageway that seemed to be a crack in the bedrock, just barely large enough for a single person at a time to squeeze through. The crack continued up quite far above me and seemed to pinch down to just a few inches in the higher regions. But it must have opened up above to the surface because the only illumination came from the little bit of daylight that seeped in from above.

"Where are we?" I asked in a hushed tone that seemed to be appropriate when transiting a dark fracture in bedrock.

"This is the entrance to Nkosi's lair on Table Mountain near Cape Town, South Africa," Qadir answered.

"For defense, he has his hideaway spelled so only he can transit in or out. Anyone else, including other Taz, can only enter through this narrow, winding passageway. That feature gives him plenty of time to decide whether to allow visitors to pass, or destroy them before they ever arrive in his sanctuary."

"Why did we come here?" I wondered aloud.

Qadir answered while continuing to move forward through the tight passageway. "Nkosi's place is the most central to all of the other locations where Taz live on Earth. And it is the safest. Hence this is where we meet when we all need to get together in the 1st Dimension."

It took at least five minutes for us to transit the entrance passage to Nkosi's lair. As we passed into a large spacious room carved out of the solid bedrock, Nkosi was standing there to greet us.

"Welcome to my humble abode," he said spreading his arms wide.

The other Taz referred to Nkosi's home as a Lair, and looking around I understood why. It appeared in many places to be a rough rock natural cavern, with a ceiling at least fifty feet off the floor. In other places, it had obviously been expanded by Nkosi as could be seen by rooms with perfect 90-degree corners and relatively smooth walls.

The cavern was fairly brightly lit, but I could not see any electric lights or other sources of direct illumination. This was so curious I had to ask Nkosi about it. "Where does the light come from?"

Nkosi smiled broadly at my question. "It comes from a Jozrym."

I just looked at him blankly, as I had never heard of a Jozrym.

"Sorry for my ignorance," I apologized. "I don't know what that is.

"It is a marvelous device for capturing and storing ambient energy, and then time releasing it as light. The Davos of Dosparage invented it on Sx for the Akara to use in their underground mines.

I was startled by his answer. "I thought we could not bring items from the 2nd Dimension into the 1st."

"Mostly that is true," Nkosi acknowledged, "but I did not bring a Jozrym, as it is purely a mechanical, non-magickal device. I merely memorized its construction, and built one of my own."

My mind immediately leapt to the more worldly

possibilities of such a wonderful invention. "You could be a billionaire if you marketed a device like that!"

"Yes, probably," Nkosi admitted, "but that would be both unethical and unwise. Unethical because it was invented by a davos named Jozrym, not by me; and unwise, as we Taz need to keep a low profile.

"Our privacy and the secrecy of our work is essential to our mission. If I start revealing 2nd Dimension technologies I may gain money, but I would no longer have privacy or likely any freedom. Corporations would hound me for more inventions and governments would demand to know where the technology came from, as it obviously would not have come from me.

"After all, how could I explain how someone with no engineering background produced a revolutionary technology?

"To be a successful Taz, and maintain your sanity as well, you must zealously separate your normal life from your Taz activities, knowledge, and abilities. Cloak who you are as a Taz by being as unnoticeable and nondescript as possible in your normal life.

"The people of the 1st Dimension are not ready to know the truth about the universe, or the true threat from the great number of demons that walk among them, influencing and inhabiting them."

I was fascinated by what Nkosi had to share, but Qadir interrupted us. "Gentlemen, let us forego the chit chat and get down to the urgent business that brought us here."

Nkosi nodded to Qadir, "Yes of course. Why are you here my brother?"

"For the very cause you just elucidated," Qadir expounded, "that, being the threat of demons inhabiting humans. In this case, very crafty midlevel demons, in a very great number, inhabiting powerful and influential people."

In those few words Qadir gained Nkosi's undivided attention, and he quickly went on to fully describe my encounter with Hamerac and his warning.

After hearing Qadir's explanation, Nkosi agreed that a joint meeting of all the Taz was urgently needed. He reached into his shirt and withdrew his Vazaron, the beacon for calling all of the Taz to come as quickly as possible. Where Qadir's Vazaron had a large green emerald at its center, I noticed that Nkosi's had a shiny jet black stone.

Within ten minutes the other four Taz had arrived, including Aurora, whom I had never met. She was slim and of average height, with a very pleasant shade of red hair that fell in undulating waves down to the middle of her back. I estimated her age to be around late forties, but reminded myself that I was never very accurate when guessing women's ages.

She greeted me with a welcoming hug. "I have heard about you Trevallion; our latest member who called his Dragon Sword without even knowing what it was."

"I'm still very ignorant of most things involving the Taz or demons," I admitted. "But I'm doing my best to learn as much as I can as fast as I can."

Once again Qadir interrupted a conversation I was hoping to continue.

"Brothers and sisters, thank you for coming. The

matter before us is urgent indeed, and we must be unanimous in our course of action, as it will require all of us to execute it."

Qadir proceeded to detail my meeting with Hamerac as he had for Nkosi before the other Taz had arrived.w

After he concluded, he looked around the room at the other Taz. "Well, what do you think? What are we dealing with here? Is this a legitimate threat, or some type of trap? Or, was it just another opportunity for Hamerac to put a hex or a spell on Trevallion?"

Marguese stepped up. "I believe this is a real threat. Just yesterday I was quietly following a group of five demons in Lisbon to see what they were up to. I overheard them talking about the Gosli coming. I have never heard of a horde of demons named Gosli, and was not even sure they were talking about demons. But considering Trevallion was told the same name by the demon Hamerac, that would seem to be more than a coincidence."

"I don't agree," Genavieve said adamantly. "Hamerac is a 12th level demon, which means he is a cunning expert in guile. He could have set this all up"

She looked at Marguese. "You think you were following the demons in Lisbon undetected. What if the entire time Hamerac was watching you?

"You weren't in your protected home, but out in the open in a major city. Once he located you, he easily could have been following your every move and telepathically ordered the demons to mention Gosli when he knew you were close enough to be listening. Then you would corroborate with what he told Trevallion, and a great big trap could be set to gather and kill all of the Taz in one fell swoop."

Most of the other Taz nodded in agreement. What Genavieve said made sense.

Nkosi held up his hand and everyone focused their attention on him. "Like all of you, my domain is magickally protected from the spying eyes, ears, or intrusions of demons."

"But unlike all of you, I have devoted my life as a Taz to bringing the magick of the 2nd Dimension here into the 1st." Obviously, it is only possible in a precious few places upon the Earth, where there is a sufficient natural emission of the special energies magick requires.

"My lair inside Table Mountain is one of those rare locations, even more so than the similar places on Earth each of you chose as a home domain.

Nkosi pointed at me. "Even if Trevallion had been hexed and intended by Hamerac to be an unwilling spy, that hex would not just be nullified. Here in my domain, it would be automatically countered and expelled.

"I reveal this to you so you will have no doubt that whatever we speak of and plan here will be unknown to any demon, even Lucifer himself.

"As far as planning goes, I think we need to proceed as if both the possibilities that have been brought up are true."

"I agree," Jenji concurred. "The threat of a horde of demons coming through a Nexus, imminently, within hours, with the specific intent and ability to inhabit influential people, is too great to not prepare as if it is a true threat.

"But neither can we discount that this scenario, causing us to all gather together in one place, by a Nexus, is ripe for treachery and some type of ambush. So that too we must take into account and be prepared to counter."

Qadir being the eldest seemed to be in charge of the meeting by common unspoken consent. After Jenji's statement everyone looked at him to see what he would say.

"Jenji is correct," he affirmed. "We must plan and be prepared for both possibilities.

"Let's look at the tactical points that must be considered for each, and then determine our plan of action."

Everyone nodded their heads in assent and Qadir continued.

"If this is not a trap, but a real threat, how will we stop a horde of a thousand demons from coming through a Nexus opening?"

Marguese, ever the willing warrior interjected. "When the Nexus first opens, it will be small. Only one demon at a time will be able to pass through until the Nexus grows larger. It will be a simple matter to stand here in the 1st Dimension and dispatch them with a strangulation hold the second their head sticks through the Nexus, before the rest of their body has even had a chance to follow.

"The demons on the other side in the 3rd Dimension will see that the demons trying to pass through are being banished before they ever get fully into the 1st Dimension. Just seeing that occur to one demon after another, trying to pass through may strike enough fear into the others that they abandon the entire plan."

Aurora brought her hands together, then split them

rapidly apart. "No, that is not a sustainable plan. As you said, the Nexus opening will widen. Soon there will be two demons that can come through at the same time, then three, then four. If the opening widens as much as some I have seen, it could become big enough for twenty demons to come through at the same time, and we are only seven.

"We are all lightning fast with our Dragon Swords in the 2nd and 3rd Dimensions where the sword itself is magick. Regrettably, in the 1st Dimension we have no Dragon Swords. We have nothing but our bare hands to banish demons, one at a time by strangulation, which is not instant like the touch of a Dragon Sword. And we must remember that the demons are not coming through to battle us. They are coming to inhabit people of prominence.

"The very second their foot or any other part of their body makes a phased connection to the ground, the demons will transit away. It will happen so quickly, many of them will be gone and free in the 1st Dimension even before we have a chance to banish them."

Qadir interjected, "Those are good points. Though we have the power to strangle banish demons one at a time here in the 1st Dimension, we would be completely overrun and ineffective with a large horde coming through a Nexus all at once.

"We need a plan for banishing them on the other side, in the 3rd Dimension before they ever pass through the Nexus, and where we can use our Dragon Swords."

Marguese tapped his index finger on his upturned palm for emphasis. "Being in the 3rd dimension is a problem of greater magnitude. That is the demon domain. Luring us there could be a trap the demon Hamerac may be setting for us.

"Instead of having to fight a thousand demons of the Gosli Horde, if it is a trap we could be facing an overwhelming number. A number so great that no amount of Dragon Sword magickal fighting mastery, or instant spells, would be able to overcome. We could all perish. What a coup that would be for Hamerac."

Nkosi held up a small double terminated quartz crystal that was optically clear. "This is an invisibility amulet I enchanted in the 2nd Dimension. There is not enough magickal energy here in the 1st Dimension to invoke it, even in my own lair.

"However, when the Nexus begins to form, before it has actually opened enough to let any demons through, I can transit to the other side in the 3rd Dimension and invoke the invisibility amulet the instant I arrive. This will allow me to see if there really is a demon horde preparing to come through the Nexus, and if they are numerically as great as the demon Hamerac described to Trevallion. And most importantly, to see if it is just a big trap to corner and kill us all.

"Except," Aurora interjected, "if no Gosli Horde is coming, if that was just a lie of Hamerac's, and there is no ambush waiting to strike either, why would Hamerac have told Trevallion about the Nexus opening? Maybe all of it is untrue. Maybe there is no Gosli horde and there will not be a Nexus opening.

"If neither of those scenarios is real, Hamerac would not have set that table just to hear his own voice or play a big joke on the Taz. What would be an alternative reason that an upper-level demon would want us to have the coordinates and time when a Nexus will be opening, with a warning dire enough to gather us all to that location?"

Nobody had any ideas or hypothesis, or could answer Aurora's question.

Qadir furrowed his brow and held his hand to his chin, obviously deep in thought. "This is an inscrutable dilemma and I am not hearing any good solutions. We are at the epitome of: *damned if we do, and damned if we don't.*"

"I have an idea," I spoke up. Everyone looked at me with somewhat critical faces, as if I was speaking out of turn and too inexperienced to venture a comment. But they remained quiet and let me have my say anyway.

"I'm sure this is too simple to work, as I've only seen a few things since I've been a Taz, so those are the only techniques I am aware of." Everyone remained quiet listening to me, so I continued presenting my idea.

"When I was recently with Genavieve, she used a little quartz pebble that Nkosi had enchanted to shoot out and embed a Summoning Bur into about a hundred demons. My understanding is, she can now summon those demons at any time to wherever she is. She threatened to summon them to the point of her Dragon Sword in the 2nd Dimension and banish them to Oblivion if she found out they bothered any humans again.

"We could do the same thing with the Gosli Horde if they exist, and put Summoning Burs in them when they are all congregated in the 3rd Dimension waiting for the Nexus to open. Then it wouldn't matter how many escaped into the 1st Dimension, as we could summon them at our leisure and deal with them on Sx where our magick is strong."

Everyone was silent for a few moments just looking at me. I couldn't tell by their impassive faces if they thought I was an idiot for my suggestion, or were contemplating whether it might have merit.

Nkosi was diplomatic and gave my suggestion some credence while also downplaying its potential.

"I think that is an excellent suggestion. Regrettably, it comes with significant limitations," he noted.

"The concept would in fact be effective. However, I only have three Summoning Burs prepared and each one has a capacity of fifty burs. So at most, we would be able to imbed a bur in only one hundred and fifty demons.

"Fifty burs is actually the maximum number. The enchanted stone Genavieve had that Trevallion was talking about also only had fifty burs. Because the sparks flew out so fast, all of the demons probably thought they had been penetrated by a bur, but such was not the case."

"I still have one you gave me previously," Aurora quipped.

"As do I," added Marguese.

Nobody else seemed to have one.

Qadir summarized, "Five burs will account for only one-quarter of the demons. "He looked over to Nkosi. "How quickly can you craft more?"

Nkosi shook his head negatively before he even spoke. "It is impossible to craft more in the few hours we have remaining before the Nexus begins opening.

"The process takes several days, as the enchantment

must cure and mature inside the stone. And the specialized magickal energy needed to imbue into the stone, is only available in the 2nd Dimension. I cannot craft such magick here in the 1st."

"Nevertheless, being able to implant a bur in a quarter of the demon horde will still be a powerful weapon," Qadir said with some enthusiasm.

I raised my hand with a question; a little hesitant to once again be injecting myself into matters I knew so little about. "Isn't there something we can do to either not allow the Nexus to open, or to shut it quickly, before any demons come through?"

"Would that it was so," Qadir sighed. "However, the Nexuses that form and connect the dimensions when the disparate energy separating them thins and mixes, is a natural process that exudes far more inexorable power than anything we could counter. In past generations, the Taz have tried to exert control over Nexuses, and with numbers greater than the seven of us.

"It was futile. Neither Taz, demons, nor any other creature can exert the slightest influence on a Nexus, except perhaps Level 13 demons in a small way. Our saving grace is that the Nexuses tend to only be open for mere minutes before they disappear to never return at that location. So there are a limited number of demons that are able to pass through.

"The demon advantage over us, is that the higher-level ones have learned to be aware in advance of where and when a Nexus will be opening."

"I'm still confused," I confessed. "If Nexuses between dimensions have been opening since the beginning

DEMON HUNTER

of time and demons have been coming through them for millennia, resulting in tens of millions of demons currently on Earth, and I suppose other places in the 1st Dimension, why are we so worried about this lot of a thousand coming through? It seems like a drop in the bucket compared to the millions that are already here."

Genavieve looked at me with some impatience, as if this was not the time to be asking questions that to everyone else had obvious answers, but she answered nevertheless.

"If Hamerac is to be believed, the demons planning on coming through the Nexus are not ordinary demons. They have several distinguishing aspects that make them far more dangerous to the people of Earth than demons typically would be.

"They are all demons that have previously inhabited people, so they have the skills to do it again. For a demon to physically inhabit a human body by harmonizing with the human's energy is not easy. But once they have done it, it becomes easier to do it again because they have a greater understanding of what they need to do to accomplish the merger.

"These demons do not plan on inhabiting the usual human victims - those who are in a weakened state in their life because of mental or emotional traumas. In those typical inhabitations it is sad and destructive for the victim, and sometimes those in a close circle of friends and family that may also be hurt by their negative actions. But the circle does not widen and the collateral damage to others beyond the victim is minimal.

"However, according to Hamerac, the Gosli Horde

is determined to inhabit people of high position and influence and they have honed their skills to accomplish it.

"These types of people are not usually distressed by the same level of emotional and or mental duress as a typical victim. It takes a far higher level of expertise and determination for a demon to inhabit a person of that caliber. But when they are successful, the rewards are far greater for the demon.

"In addition to the usual sought after perk of being able to experience physical pleasures, they can also cause a much wider level of damage in the world and to a far greater number of humans because of the sway and power their inhabited victims have in the human world.

"Can you imagine the damage that could be done if the leader of a major country was inhabited by a demon? Even more so if multiple leaders from adversarial countries were inhabited? War would be the inevitable result. And this is not hypothetical. It has happened several times in history with terrible consequences.

"But the aftermath of the wars of the past would pale to the potential destruction in our era of nuclear weapons. Demon-controlled political or military leaders of major countries could result in the annihilation of the human race and most other life on the planet Earth.

"None of us should underestimate the danger of this horde of demons. If they are real, if they have the ability and intent that Hamerac has said, then this is one of the gravest threats to the human race the Taz have ever faced and we cannot fail to stop it."

CHAPTER
Thirty-Three

Everyone looked somber as they pondered Genavieve's words. After what seemed an interminably long silence, Nkosi spoke up addressing Qadir.

"You are the most experienced Taz, my brother. What should our plan be?"

Qadir took a big breath and let it out slowly, standing up straight and confident.

"All of the points that have been brought up have merit. But I think we need to concentrate all of our efforts, both offense and defense, in the 3rd Dimension. There is simply too little we can quickly do to banish demons once they have escaped the 3rd Dimension and have arrived here on Earth. It is in the 3rd Dimension where we have our Dragon Swords and powerful magick that we will be able to do the most good, even though that is also the place of most danger to us.

"Nkosi, begin as you stated by reconnoitering the

situation in the 3rd Dimension using your invisibility amulet before the Nexus opens wide enough for a demon to come through."

"I will," Nkosi confirmed, "but then what?"

Qadir continued outlining the plan of battle. "Assuming there is a massing horde awaiting the opening of the Nexus in the 3rd Dimension, remain there unseen until the first demon tries to pass through the Nexus. Then call your Dragon Sword and begin slicing, dicing, and banishing demons as fast as your sword will twirl.

"With your invisibility, you will have the greatest tactical advantage of all of us. You don't happen to have any more of those amulets do you?" Qadir asked wistfully.

"Sadly no," Nkosi answered. "The magick can only be contained inside a natural quartz crystal of exact size, quality, and crystal structure. They are extremely rare. Nor will the invisibility last long with the amulet that I have, as there is only so much magick that can be packed into as small of a container as a crystal."

"No matter," Qadir assured him. "Once we are in the 3rd Dimension, all of us except Trevallion will have magick of our own that we can employ."

He looked over to me sympathetically, "Sorry Trevallion, you have not been a Taz long enough to master any worthwhile magick. You will just have to stick to using your Dragon Sword. Let it do all the fighting. You just hold on for the ride."

His words were disappointing and deflating, but they were true. I nodded my head silently in understanding. I was feeling a little sorry for myself when I answered,

"Where would you like me to stand so my Dragon Sword can fight?"

Qadir cracked a smile at my self-depreciating humor.

"Just transit over to the 3rd Dimension when you see the first demon trying to come through the Nexus. Call your Dragon Sword immediately upon your arrival in the other dimension. Though it will weave an admirable defense, you are still the master that decides where it should orient for offense."

He looked around at the other Taz. "The same is true for all of us. We need to transit to a spot in the 3rd Dimension just beyond the Nexus as soon as we see the first demon trying to come through.

"Now here is phase two," he continued. "There are five Summoning Burs; Marguese and Aurora already have one. As they were enchanted by Nkosi, he of course should have one as well. Trevallion doesn't know how to use one yet and I have other magick I plan on employing. The remaining two therefore should go to Genavieve and Jenji."

Nkosi excused himself for a moment and disappeared into a grotto with a heavy wooden arched door some paces off to the right. He returned momentarily and handed both Genavieve and Jenji one of the small quartz stones he had enchanted.

Qadir continued outlining his plan. "Using your Dragon Sword and any magick you choose to employ, do your best to banish as many demons as possible and prevent them from entering the Nexus.

"Spread out in a circle far enough so everyone has room to fight, but stay close enough that even when the

Nexus widens there will be no space for a demon to slip through our defensive line. This way we will be able to defend all sides of the Nexus and each other's backs."

I felt like a dunce, but Qadir's last battle direction was completely confusing to me and I had to ask for further clarity. "What do you mean by, *all sides*, and we will have *each other's backs*? I thought we would all be standing in a line in the 3rd Dimension facing the demon horde with our backs against the dimensional barrier to prevent the demons from passing through the opening the Nexus creates leading to the 1st Dimension."

"Your confusion is quite understandable," Qadir acknowledged. "You must be thinking of a Nexus like a hole in a wall or some nebulous energy curtain that separates the dimensions."

"That's kind of what I was picturing," I admitted. "Some variation of an opening: a doorway or a tunnel through the dimensional barrier."

Qadir continued to patiently explain the reality to lift the fog of my ignorance. "Well you see the thing is Trevallion; there is no wall-like dimensional barrier. As you and I spoke about previously, dimensions are different energies occupying separate energy bands in nearby space.

"It is like oil and water in a sealed bottle. They are both inside the bottle, but at different locations within the space due to their dissimilar natures. If the bottle is rotated, the oil and water can change positions and locations within the bottle, but they are both still inside the bottle. If the bottle is vigorously shaken, then for a short time the oil and water will mix. But they will soon separate again and once again establish their different energetic levels and locations within the space of the bottle.

"A Nexus is like oil and water in a bottle of the universe being vigorously shaken. For a time it allows the elements of each to freely pass through and mingle with the other, but it is only a brief momentary abnormality.

"This is actually a difficult concept to explain," he said a bit flustered. "It's best to just experience it."

Despite what he just said, Qadir couldn't help himself from continuing to try to explain it to me further.

"The Nexus is a very rare phenomenon that temporarily warps the normal energy lines permeating space that usually separate one dimension from another.

"It always occurs in a spherical shape like a globe. It starts no bigger than a small handball and rapidly increases in size until it is typically as big as one of those Volkswagen Beetle Bug cars, but sometimes larger.

"When a Nexus materializes, it allows the energies from one dimension to harmoniously blend and pass into another dimension, where normally they would be like oil and water and not mix.

"It is critical to remember that unlike a door or a tunnel, the Nexus can be entered from any point of the 360-degree sphere, including from the top or bottom of the sphere.

"Most often Nexuses occur at ground level as they seem to be affected by gravity. However, and this is interesting, the Nexus may occur at ground level in one dimension, but its alternate materialization in the other dimension may be somewhere up in the sky, rather than at ground level.

"Sadly, this results in the death of any human that walks through a Nexus in the 1st Dimension at ground level, only to end up falling to their death from a great height in the 2nd or 3rd Dimension at times when the Nexus occurs high up in the air.

"Because a Nexus is spherical in shape and can be entered from any direction, we need to hope it will be at ground level. Standing in a circle, we can prevent demons from passing into it. They will most likely be charging from all points of the compass simultaneously, so we must defend against those incursions from every direction. Is it more clear now?"

"I think so," I said hesitantly. "As you said, I'm sure it will be crystal clear the moment I see the Nexus."

Qadir started to speak again but I drew his ire a bit by interrupting and asking another question.

"Why don't the demons just circumvent us and blink into the Nexus?"

"First of all, the correct word is transiting, not blinking." Qadir corrected me with some exasperation at having to give another explanation of something that was a mystery to me, but obvious to everyone else.

"Secondly, inhabiting a human is difficult, but transiting to another dimension is a feat that is simply beyond the capabilities of any demons other than 13's and a handful of 12's.

"Lower-level demons tend to not be very good at transiting anywhere with accuracy. Mid-level demons are usually very good at transiting from one spot to another inside a dimension, but are virtually incapable of successfully transiting into the weird, warped, energy of a Nexus.

"If a lower or mid-level demon attempted to transit into a Nexus, the disparate energy would scramble their transiting essence and they would more likely end up in the ground. There they would be forever entombed and unable to escape if the ground was bedrock. It would be a far worse fate than Oblivion."

Qadir looked at me sternly. "Please hold any more questions Trevallion. Currently, you know too little about Taz, demons, magick, or Nexuses and we do not have the luxury to explain them further, as the time for this Nexus to open is almost upon us."

I silently nodded my head in agreement to not ask any more questions and hoped I would actually be able to restrain myself.

Seeing my silence and promise to not interrupt anymore, Qadir concluded his battle plan.

"This plan is simple, but it should be effective. We will form the circle around the Nexus in the 3rd Dimension and dispatch as many demons as possible using our Dragon Swords and any personal magick we wish to employ before they can pass through the Nexus.

"At the point that anyone feels they are being overrun and can no longer prevent the demons they are facing from reaching the Nexus, invoke the Summoning Bur amulet. That will allow us to summon any demons that escaped through the Nexus to Earth and banish them from somewhere in the 2nd Dimension after the main battle, but soon enough that they will not have had time to inhabit any humans.

"When the dust has settled and the battle is done, we hopefully will have banished the entire horde, or put burs on any demons that escaped through the Nexus."

Qadir paused reflectively for a moment, then began speaking after letting out a deep sigh.

"We like to believe that we will accomplish this without any losses or injuries, but we all know the reality: fighting this many demons in their own dimension where they are the most powerful, we may not all come out of this uninjured, or even alive.

"If that is the case for me, let me say now that it has been the honor of my life to know each and every one of you. I am truly humbled to have been able to be counted among you, to see you so willing, so often, even now, to offer your lives for the sake of a world that knows you not, and wouldn't believe in you even if it was revealed.

"I know each of you have a home in the 2nd Dimension, some on Sx and some on Oaswan. For lesser people, it would be easy to turn their back on the 1st Dimension and the mess that is our homeworld of Earth, and just live their lives out in the 2nd Dimension where they have a beautiful world, plus magick, and esteem from all the people and denizens of that world, but you are not lesser people.

"Though the people of our home planet know you not, you are the greatest, most selfless of all. I just want you all to know that I know who you are; you amaze me; you humble me; and I am so grateful for every minute I have ever had to spend with each of you."

Qadir's deep words from his heart brought tears to the eyes of most of us.

"Dear Qadir, we all feel the same," Genavieve said lovingly. "But shush such talk. It is as if you expect to die in this battle. I'm sure we will all live to fight another day."

Qadir forced a smile. "May it be as you say Genavieve."

Qadir regained some composure and added a few points to his conclusion. "If any of us get too injured to continue the fight, transit to Veldalei. When the battle is concluded, whether we succeed or fail, let us all rendezvous at Veldalei to heal our wounds and plan our next actions if necessary."

I know I had promised to remain silent and not ask any more questions, but this was such a vital point, I could not restrain myself.

"Where is Veldalei? How can I blink, excuse me, transit, to a place I do not know?

"A legitimate question," Qadir acknowledged.

Nkosi silently and mysteriously left the room and went back to the grotto he had gone into to retrieve the Summoning Bur amulets. When he returned he placed a fairly non-descript brownish-red rock, about the size of a robin's egg, into my hand.

"That is a rock from Veldalei. When you are ready to transit there, just hold the rock in your hand and squeeze hard. You will immediately travel to the place the rock came from, even if you do not know where it is."

"Thanks Nkosi," I said with a big smile as I placed the rock in my jeans pocket. "That's pretty handy. Is this a magickally enchanted rock?"

Nkosi let out a little laugh. "No, it is just a rock. But it is one of the helpful quirks of a Taz's transiting ability that you can use stones native to a particular area in the 2nd or 3rd Dimensions to convey yourself to that location while you are holding a piece of the land from that place in your hand, either a rock or even a handful of dirt. It is even possible with woods from certain trees or flowers, if they are so rare that they are only found in one small area."

"How can that work?" I asked with curiosity, "if there is no enchantment?"

Nkosi chuckled again. "Well it doesn't work inter-dimensionally, but inside the 2nd or 3rd Dimension, *you* are the enchantment Trevallion. You are a Taz. For a Taz, the land is very powerful. We are connected to all life, even the life of the places we walk upon. We protect the land, and it can protect us. Little stones, like that which you can pick up off the ground anywhere, may save your life someday because even powerful conjured magick cannot stop the land from calling to itself. Wherever you are, you are part of the land, and it is part of you."

Qadir clapped his hands together to get everyone's attention. "Brothers and sisters, the time to depart to the Nexus co-ordinates is upon us. The actual time Hamerac said the Nexus will begin opening is still a couple of hours away. However, it is never wise to take anything a demon tells you at face value, so we will go early to the party."

We were all gathered closely in a circle and Qadir took a moment to, one by one, look into everyone's eyes as he spoke.

"Remember, demons cannot tell a full truth. It is their innate nature to reveal only a portion of truth to help them accomplish a more sinister hidden purpose.

"When we arrive at the supposed point of the Nexus, nothing at all may be as the demon Hamerac said. Or, some parts may be true, but only revealed to deflect and divert us from an even more sinister purpose of the demons.

"And let there be no doubt, as grave as we are assuming this incursion of a demon horde may be, there is undoubtedly still something we do not know that is of vital importance. Whether it is a trap to ambush and kill us all, or something equally as devious and perilous, we all need to be on high alert and ready to change tactics at a moment's notice as the situation dictates.

"First we are going to see if there is already an ambush waiting for us here in the 1st Dimension."

Qadir pointed to Marguese. "Brother please go now to the coordinates Hamerac gave to Trevallion. Based on the latitude and longitude, I'm guessing this should be somewhere near the middle of the United States.

"Take care and be cautious. Do not go to the exact coordinates. Aim your arrival for a point at least five thousand feet in the air above the coordinate location and off horizontally by another two thousand feet or so.

"This should ensure you do not materialize inside a mountain or at the bottom of a lake if the coordinates themselves are meant to be like a mousetrap with us as the mice.

"As you are free-falling through the air, remain long enough to get close enough to the ground to determine if there are any obvious threats to us, or to people that live nearby."

Marguese nodded his head in acknowledgment. "I will be back in a moment," he said as he blinked away.

As he promised, within thirty seconds after departing, he returned. "It is safe. The spot we were told the Nexus will open is in a wide meadow, near a forest. It seems to be a fairly uninhabited area. There are big snow-covered mountains within sight, but they are far enough away to be of no concern when transiting to the coordinates. I saw nothing that would indicate a trap, but my time to look was only a few seconds, as I had to transit back before smashing on the ground."

"Excellent!" Qadir said with enthusiasm. "We want to transit together to ensure we all arrive at the location. So please hold hands now everyone. Blank your mind from all thoughts of other places to allow me to bring us to the Nexus coordinates."

As Qadir bid, we all reached out to our right and our left and held the hand of the Taz standing next to us in our little circle. To ensure I didn't think of another place, I looked down and focused on my right foot.

There was a brief flash of darkness and when I saw my foot again just a second later, it was in an entirely different place in the world.

CHAPTER
Thirty — Four

As Marguese had described, we arrived in an open pasture of lush green grass. It was so profuse, I was surprised looking around to not see a herd of cows happily munching the grassland.

Immediately after arriving, Qadir had us spread out to look for any signs of demons or demon inhabited people nearby. After a few minutes, we all came back and reported that we saw nothing out of the ordinary.

Demons of course would have been easy to spot. They would be invisible to most inhabitants in the 1st Dimension, but as tangible as a regular person to the Taz.

Inhabited people were a bigger challenge to discern. Hence, they had the potential to be a greater threat to us during this particular time, when we were wary of attack from any direction and any source.

If a person was inhabited by a low-level demon, their aura would obviously show the disruption. But experienced mid-level demons were much better at influencing a person's actions without giving away their presence in the person's aura.

If we had enough time to observe them, what they said and how they acted, the demon influence would become obvious. But when we first encounter those inhabited by mid-level demons, they could seem like normal, good people at first glance, and their aura would not immediately give away their destructive hidden secret.

As there were no obvious threats at the moment, Qadir had us randomly spread out about fifty feet apart from each other. When the Nexus began to open up, hopefully one of us would see it.

Disappointingly the time Hamerac had given for the Nexus to open came and passed. We patiently waited an hour, then another, and another. It was beginning to look like nothing more than a big demonic joke. Or the opposite, a big lie to get us all in this one spot while the demons were actually doing something terrible and unopposed somewhere else in the world.

Qadir called us all back together and pretty much confirmed that thought. "Well, it looks like we have been hornswoggled," he declared. "Which begs the question, what was Hamerac's real motive of gathering us all here?

If there is no Nexus and we have not been ambushed, it would seem something important is amiss elsewhere."

"Let us think!" Marguese demanded with a bit of anger. "We have almost no power here in the 1st Dimension. So, if there is no Nexus, and we do not have the ability to monitor demon activity in this dimension, whatever awful thing is occurring while we are here, is something that would be obvious to us if we were not here. We need to figure out what that can be and go to it."

Jenji was about to offer a thought, but was interrupted by a tiny little vortex of spinning rainbow light that appeared about three feet off the ground and about one hundred feet to our left.

It was the Nexus beginning to open! We all rushed over to the spot with adrenaline heightened awareness.

It was my first time seeing a Nexus and it was spellbindingly beautiful, unlike anything I had ever seen or imagined before. It was spherical in shape, and seemed to be filled with thousands of pieces of rainbow-colored shards of light that were moving slowly inside the sphere, like they were suspended in water. The shards seemed almost solid as they had definite sharp, angular edges. They were translucent and reflected and emitted multiple colors of light. Certainly otherworldly!

Qadir pointed to the Nexus, which was about a foot in diameter and then looked at Nkosi. "Brother, now is the time to use your invisibility magick and transit through the Nexus to see what is on the other side, before it expands large enough for demons to pass through. If there is a real threat, just remain there and communicate with us telepathically and we will soon follow you to the other side."

Nkosi nodded silently and blinked away. Within seconds he was connecting with us telepathically, but not in the way I was expecting telepathic communication to be. Instead of hearing his voice in my mind, I was seeing what he was seeing with his eyes, and a frightful sight it was!

I wasn't sure what a horde of a thousand onrushing

demons would look like, but the image Nkosi transmitted to our minds seemed to be a lot larger number!

Nkosi quickly looked to his right and then to his left, and along with what he had been seeing in front of him, all I saw in my mind's telepathic vision was demons in a myriad of sizes, races, and a mind-boggling array of clothing choices, rushing toward the Nexus like a cloud of locusts.

"Transit now!" Qadir bellowed.

Instantly all the other Taz vanished and after a moment of hesitation, I followed.

Upon arriving on the other side of the Nexus in the 3rd Dimension, I was horrified into inaction to see that I was alone with an enormous number of demons bearing down upon me, not more than one hundred feet away.

I wasn't even sure I had blinked to the right spot in the 3rd Dimension because I couldn't see the Nexus, or any of the other Taz. I was in a bleak, barren world with a large hot sun and a huge number of angry demons heading right for me!

Suddenly, I was yanked backward by some powerful unseen force. Happily, I soon realized it was a magickal pull of friends as I ended up with Qadir on my left and Genavieve on my right, standing off about fifty feet in either direction. Although I didn't know any magick to use, it was comforting to know that the other Taz did and could use it now that we were in the 3rd Dimension.

"Call your Dragon Sword!" Qadir shouted with frustration tingeing his voice.

I immediately complied and yelled out, "Fury." To my great relief and happiness, Fury appeared with the hilt in my right hand and tip pointing skyward.

"Qadir glanced over at me momentarily and saved me a little face with the other Taz for my inaccurate transit. "Though I admire your bravery standing out there in front of us, our best defense is to stand in the same circle around the Nexus."

I barely had time to nod in agreement because the demons were now just steps away from us. I didn't dare take my eyes off the dozens rushing straight for me, but I assumed a similar scene was taking place behind me and all around our circle in defense of the Nexus.

Just as I raised Fury to take my first slice at a demon, out of the corner of my eye I caught Qadir take something small out of his bottomless vest pocket and throw it on the ground. Immediately, rapidly expanding waves of electric blue goo rolled right through us in all directions of the circle and out into the mass of demons rushing toward us with murderous intent.

As it moved forward it inflated in size and became like an undulating mist. The entire horde of demons, even those far back in the crowd, were soon enveloped in the mist.

Then a marvelous reaction occurred. All of the demons started moving in slow motion! Even though the blue goo had also passed through all of the Taz, none of us seemed to be affected.

"Charge forward now!" Qadir yelled telepathically, even as he began moving forward and dispatching demons to Oblivion.

"The slow-motion hex will only last for one minute. Count aloud forty-five seconds and dispatch as many demons as you can," he directed. "Then give yourself fifteen seconds to reform the defensive circle around the Nexus."

Without hesitation we all did as he commanded and the slaughter of demons in that short period of time was astounding. The demons were moving very slowly, perhaps one-fourth of the normal walking speed. There was nothing they could do to attack us that wasn't easily avoided. They in turn were helpless before the onslaught of the Dragon Swords. A single slice of Fury would often cut through one and continue in the same motion to banish another.

By the time we all regrouped to form the defensive circle, looking out at the demon horde it was obvious we had banished almost half the horde in less than a minute. Those that remained were still back about a hundred feet as we had cleared out all of the demons closest to us.

For those that might question how so many demons could have been vanquished so quickly, remember a Dragon Sword merely needs to touch a demon to banish them. The instant their body is touched, they vaporize. It happens so quickly, there is not even a moment of resistance to the momentum of the sword. Once it has touched the demon, they are gone and the sword is instantly just slicing through the air as if the demon had never even been there. This effect, plus the fact they were charging us bunched tightly together, made it possible for us to banish so many in less than a minute.

I excitedly looked over at Qadir. "Another one of those and we will have finished this horde," I said gushing with optimism.

Qadir continued to look steadfastly forward at the remaining oncoming demons as he answered me telepathically. "As you will learn Trevallion, the more powerful the magick, the more difficult and time-consuming it is to prepare. There will be only one of those amulets today."

The remaining demons approached us much more cautiously after seeing so many of their horde banished. They were walking toward us now instead of running.

I was so focused on the physical aspects of our confrontation, I momentarily forgot that we were in the demon dimension and they had magick here! My memory was soon jarred to reality when I saw a cloud of hundreds of fist-size rocks suddenly come flying through the air from every direction.

The rain of missiles was almost upon us. I crouched down and held up my left arm and crossed it with the flat of my Dragon Sword to offer the meager protection it could.

From the other side of our circle I heard Marguese shout out "Iozoa!" At first I thought it was some Portuguese expletive, swearing at our situation. I soon realized otherwise when I saw all the rocks were hitting an invisible shield above us. Ah magick, so wonderful. I really needed to learn some.

More amazingly, the rocks were not just being repelled, they were turning around and zooming back to the senders and were quickly raining down upon the demon horde to howls of pain and anger.

Most of the demons did not stick around to be pelted, but blinked back away until the rain of rocks had passed.

They then regrouped into their former positions and continued their slow, cautious approach toward us.

Next, the demons built a large fire in the middle of their group. I'm not sure if it was a normal fire made with combustible materials like wood, or a magickal fire. I suspected the latter, as I didn't see any of the demons adding wood or other burnable materials to the bonfire.

I was waiting for the demons to somehow launch the fire at us, but it never happened. I heard Jenji utter a few magickal words, "Kalai, Kazorq, Mateek," and suddenly the fire snuffed out and nothing the demons could do would reignite it. Wow! They were angry about that and their howls of hate were a crescendo of sound, even from the distance that they were still away from us.

The demons must have decided to give up on magick because from where they stood encircling us about 100 yards away, they suddenly charged from every direction, each swinging their deadly weapon of choice from swords, to battle axes, to spiked maces.

Several spears were sent flying toward us, but after a few magickal words from Nkosi, they fell harmlessly to the ground before they ever reached us.

When the onrushing mass of demons was only about fifty feet from our defensive line, all of the ones at the front of the horde suddenly fell to the ground helplessly flailing their arms and legs, and screaming out in fear or anger, I wasn't sure which.

All the demons behind them immediately pulled up like they had come to the edge of a precipice. Some of them were pushed over the invisible line by the surging mass still coming behind them that hadn't yet realized the frontline had abruptly stopped, and they started helplessly flailing about as well.

I was quite perplexed as to what was happening. Genavieve must have sensed my confusion. "It is all an illusion," she explained. "The demons think we are suddenly surrounded by a bottomless chasm and they see and feel as if they are endlessly falling. When they try to transit out of the chasm, they are unable. Actually, they could easily escape, but in their mind they cannot, and what the mind believes becomes their reality.

"If I can maintain the illusion long enough the Nexus will close and disappear and the demon threat will end."

Wow! More powerful magick. I wasn't learning how to do any of it, but I was certainly being awed by what I was witnessing.

However, Genavieve's hope was not to be. The demons that had successfully stopped before falling into the illusionary chasm got smart and started blinking across it. They did this suddenly in mass and in a few short strides they were upon us and there was no more room for magick in the confusion of Taz and demon bodies enmeshed in frenzied battle.

I felt woefully unprepared to fight even one demon, much less a constant stream of enraged monsters coming at me from all sides. But with firm resolve I did as Qadir had directed. I just held on tightly to my Dragon Sword and it did the rest. If I looked at a particular demon, they would be dispatched by the sword within a breath; all the while it automatically sensed any danger and deflected it.

I almost got cocky as I saw that no matter what a demon tried to do, split me with an axe, stab me with a sword, impale me with a spear, or bash my brains out with a mace, my Dragon Sword countered. To anyone observing, it would seem like I was the greatest swordsman that had ever lived. In reality, I was just holding on to the magickal Dragon Sword for the ride.

And then it all came crashing down. I heard Jenji cry out in pain behind me. Somehow the demons had broken through her defense. Marguese was beside her and telepathically yelled out to us, "Jenji lost her sword and was injured before she could call it back. She released her burs but has fled to Veldalei. We are only six!"

Within moments of Marguese's dire alarm, we lost another Taz. Genavieve and I had combined forces and were standing at angles to one another to both guard each other's backs and still protect the Nexus, while engaging wave after wave of demons.

Suddenly Genavieve just froze, literally right in the middle of her movement. "I have been hexed!" she yelled out telepathically and then she too vanished, I hoped in a transit to Veldalei. But in any case, because she was frozen, she had not been able to release her Summoning Burs.

The ranks of the demon horde were getting thinner, but so were we. More and more demon magick started being thrown at us and it soon became obvious that the higher level, more experienced and powerful demons had held back, while the less experienced and more expendable had been used to wear us down.

With only five of us remaining and with hundreds of demons still raging toward us and around us, we had to spread further apart to defend the Nexus, which by this time had grown as big as a Volkswagen Beetle as Qadir had foretold.

Then to my horror, I heard a gunshot and immediately I heard Nkosi yell out in pain. I saw Summoning Burs flash out and into demons so I knew it was his last act before he either died or transited to Veldalei.

In quick succession there was another gunshot and I saw Marguese fall off to my right where Genavieve had been. More Summoning Burs flew out and embedded into demons and Marguese also vanished.

With only three of us left, we were too far apart to completely defend the Nexus, and demons started to charge past us, or blink behind us to race through the Nexus into the 1st Dimension of our Earth.

I suddenly felt the rising fury inside of me like I had experienced the day of the demon attack on the leialli, and I waded into the demons around me with a berserk rage, swinging my sword with focused abandon; no longer just holding on but meting justice for my fallen comrades by my own guiding direction.

Aurora was now to my right and Qadir to my left. Demons were pouring into the Nexus behind us. Aurora released her Summoning Bur as there was nothing else we could do to stop them, as the ones in front of us were obviously more interested in killing us than getting through the Nexus.

And there was still the demon with the gun. I spied him up on a little ridge off to my left, aiming what appeared to be a rifle. How unfair was that! We were fighting with swords and he brought a gun!

I was so reminded of the old saying not to bring a knife to a gunfight and wondered how he had even been able to bring a rifle from the 1st Dimension to the 3rd, or figure out how to manufacture one in this dimension. I realized if it was the latter then we were really in trouble because bullets sped faster than most magick could react. A maniacal horde of demons with guns was a terrible thought!

Qadir had also spotted the gun-toting demon. To my dismay, I saw him stick his Dragon Sword into the ground and begin moving his hands as he cast a spell to nullify the shooter.

But before he finished the incantation I heard Aurora scream. A quick glance her way and I saw blood flying into the air and she too vanished.

With satisfaction, I looked up on the ridge just as that demon was banished by Qadir's spell. I looked over at Qadir to acknowledge his feat only to disbelievingly witness his death.

While he was casting his spell and his sword had been embedded in the ground he was defenseless, and the demons around him had not been standing idly by to see what would happen.

To my horror and tremendous grief, because there was nothing I could do to prevent it, a demon with a battle axe came up behind Qadir and brought his axe down in a mighty blow to split Qadir's skull. He sensed it coming and moved to his left to avoid it, but he wasn't quick enough. The axe scrapped down the right side of his head cutting off his ear and continuing down through his collar bone and into his body.

He immediately spit up bright red blood and looked at me with his dying gaze. He feebly lifted his right index finger and pointing it at me uttered some words aloud I could not hear, and then he vanished. I was really frenzied in my rage now and went to swing my Dragon Sword with tremendous vindictiveness at the nearest demon only to find I could not move it out of its position pointing up toward the sky!

I tried to take a step to my right, and then to my left, but found that I could only move a little, but not as far as a step. I tried willing myself back to the 1st Dimension, to the pasture where we encountered the Nexus, but I could not blink away from the 3rd Dimension!

Seeing my immobility and inability to blink, several demons around me got evil smirks on their faces and charged at me together, vying to see who would be the first to kill me.

I was prepared for the end, but to my surprise, all the blows of their deadly weapons were as naught. Qadir's last act must have been to put some type of invisible force field around me.

One demon after another came up and tried to kill me with various weapons, but to no avail. However, I got a plunge of fear in my stomach when I saw one of the demons come up with the rifle dropped by the demon Qadir had banished. He brought it up to my face and pushed it until the tip of the muzzle came right up against the invisible force field, about a foot away.

I was staring right into the muzzle when he pulled the trigger; there was a bright fiery flash, but it was not the end for me. The force field held and the bullet just ricocheted into the demons gathered around. The idiot demon tried again and several more times with the same results until he ran out of bullets. Several demons were shot by the stray ricochets, but the shooter didn't seem to care.

To my confused surprise, all of the demons suddenly turned away from me and faced the other direction. I soon saw why.

Another group of demons was rushing toward them and they angrily left me and moved to do battle with the new group, which was obviously a different horde coming to use the Nexus as well.

From my lonely vantage point encased inside an invisible field I could not leave by foot or blinking, I watched with a little happiness, a great and terrible battle between demon hordes.

At first, I thought it would be over quickly as the horde that had attacked the Taz still numbered in the hundreds, while the horde rushing to battle them couldn't have been more than fifty, and probably less than that.

But the battle did not go as I expected to the horde with greater numbers. In just a few minutes their numbers had been reduced to less than a couple of dozen, and it seemed to have all been done by magick, as the demons from the other horde had no weapons I could see. The second horde had also suffered losses, but disproportionately less than the first.

The remaining demons from the first horde obviously defeated, blinked away before they could be banished by the demons from the second horde.

About two dozen demons from the second horde remained and they all came up and surrounded me. Their silence, and the fact that they didn't attack me, but just stared at me, was unnerving. And then I saw why.

The demons right in front of me parted and Hamerac confidently strode through them to confront me.

"Ah Trevallion, so nice to see you again. Thank you for bringing the Taz to so effectively thin the ranks of the Gosli Horde so we could conquer them. Their numbers were too great for us to do it alone, thus proving that demons and Taz can effectively work together for a common good, as I proposed to you in our previous meetings. A pity so many of the Taz were lost in the battle. Are you the only survivor?"

I didn't answer Hamerac, but just fumed at him in silence with the angriest scowl I could muster.

Hamerac came up and tapped on my invisible force field with his index finger. "Very effective," he said in admiration. "I was watching when Qadir cast a spell to envelop you in this, very powerful magick. I am impressed. He was certainly one of the greatest Taz I have encountered in the last couple of thousand years.

"But you cannot transit out, can you? Nothing can come in, but neither can you go out.

"Let's see if we can move you, as that would open up some possibilities."

Hamerac directed two of the burliest demons to hold on to the surface of the force field and see if they could move it and me; to my consternation they could! They lifted me and my force field right off the ground.

Hamerac walked around me in a circle eyeing the force field up and down. "As you didn't fall out the bottom when the field was lifted up, it obviously extends below you as well as to your sides and I'm sure above you as well. I suppose we could just bury you in the ground to suffer a gasping death as you run out of air. But you are in such a dramatic pose, holding your sword with its tip pointing skyward, that I think it will be more satisfying to take you back to my domain as a trophy to display."

At least I could frustrate his desire to demean me as a trophy. I released my hold on the Dragon Sword, letting the hilt drop to the floor of the force field, and lowered my hand down to my side.

Hamerac was obviously disappointed. "Why did you have to do that? You were in such an excellent pose for a trophy. Now you just look like a captive."

Oh well," Hamerac said with some resignation. "Do be careful not to hurt yourself with the tip of your sword pointing up, I wouldn't want blood smeared all over the force field impeding everyone's view of my trophy."

Hamerac looked up at all of the demons standing in a circle around us. "Twenty-three of you remain. All of you go now, before the Nexus closes. You each have the list of Izbos to inhabit. The most senior of you takes the number one on the list; with number two going to the next most senior, until you have inhabited the top twenty-three Izbos on the list. Go now!"

Without another word, the demons quickly walked into the Nexus and onto my Earth. I feared that for all of the problems we experienced from political, to social or even natural disasters, the scourge that was coming with those twenty-three demons would be worse than anyone had experienced in their lifetime, and there was nothing we could do to stop it.

"This was your plan all along wasn't it?" I asked Hamerac, my voice dripping with disgust and disdain.

"Of course!" Hamerac admitted proudly. "A classic demonic misdirection, and it worked perfectly!

"Actually, more perfectly than you realize I'm sure, my young Taz. You see, those were not just ordinary demons from my horde that just passed through to your world. They are all high-level demons, levels 10 and 11. They are all vastly experienced at inhabiting Izbos and influencing them to do their will.

"The pitiful Gosli Horde that you Taz almost vanquished were all just low and intermediate-level demons. There was not even one upper-level demon among them who was present today.

"They were merely pawns in a bigger game than they knew. All they wanted to do was to get into the 1st Dimension and get physical with any Izbo they could find.

"I was the one that casually mentioned to some of their leaders that this Nexus would be opening. I explained that my horde was too deeply involved in another project, and they could have the Nexus if they wished, for a price.

"I was hoping some of those upper-level leaders would have been here today to be vanquished. Nevertheless, they paid very handsomely for the information, giving them the time and place of the Nexus opening. And some of their horde did get through so the survivors really have nothing to complain about.

"And today, thanks to you, I have taken the first step of conquering your world. My horde has over ten thousand demons. Those that passed through today were just some of my upper-level leaders.

"What I told you in our earlier meeting was true. The invading horde is targeting the movers and shakers of your world; your political leaders, your religious leaders, your social influencers. Of course, the horde I was speaking of was not the pathetic Gosli, it is us!

"And now it's time to come back to my home, your home away from home if you will. I'm hoping you will last at least four, maybe even five days, as the living trophy of one of my greatest victories in the last thousand years.

"I will try to figure out a way to get food and water to you, so maybe you can last much longer," he added hopefully.

"Please try to stay alive as long as you can," he asked sincerely, as if he wanted me to do him a favor and not die too quickly.

But I barely heard him. My mind had drifted elsewhere away from Hamerac's banal banter. Like echoes in a distant canyon, I heard him calling out to me, but his voice sounded like nothing more than a faint and fading din.

I was remembering the words of Nkosi when he handed me the stone from Veldalei. "Even magick cannot stop the land from calling to itself. And wherever you are, you are part of the land and it is part of you."

With hope in my heart, I gently held the flat part of the blade near the tip of my Dragon Sword. With my other hand, I reached into my jeans pocket until I found the little pebble from Veldalei that Nkosi had given me.

I smiled at Hamerac and that seemed to confuse and perturb him greatly. Then I squeezed. With all the power I had in my hand, I squeezed the stone.

CHAPTER
Thirty—Five

When I opened my eyes, it was to both beauty and horror. Veldalei was the most beautiful place I had ever seen or imagined. The air was fresh and fragrant with a mixture of faint floral scents, and I saw flowers growing profusely in many places and varieties, surrounded by lush greenery from trees, to shrubs, to grasses.

It was like a day early in the summer when the air temperature is perfectly comfortable under a pleasant midday sun; neither too hot nor too cool.

Not far from where I stood, a gorgeous waterfall of several hundred feet fell down a steep moss and vegetation-covered cliff. The water turned into a river which meandered through the land nearby.

The musical sounds of several types of birds came from multiple directions and I would have thought I was in paradise if it was not tragically marred by the sight of all of my fellow Taz, strewn randomly about the area in various states of injury, disorientation and heartbreak.

Off to my right, about twenty yards away, I saw Genavieve kneeling down next to the prone body of Qadir lying on his back and I rushed over to them. I almost vomited looking down at Qadir. The right side of his bloodied skull was exposed, as most of the skin had peeled off when the battle axe had sliced down through his ear and deeply through his shoulder into his broken ribs and lung. I didn't need to ask Genavieve if he was dead, as it was obvious that he was.

She was holding her hands together in her lap and crying with abandon, saying Qadir's name softly over and over. I put my hand gently on her shoulder, "Are you alright?" I asked in almost a whisper.

Genavieve nodded her head and answered in a grieved, hushed voice. "Physically, I am fine. The hex could not follow me here to the 2nd Dimension, but emotionally, I am destroyed," she sobbed again in grief.

I looked around at our wounded comrades. Jenji was slowly making her way toward us. Nkosi was sitting up against a fallen log. He gave a weak wave when he saw me looking at him, but must have been too wounded to get up and join us.

Marguese was not far off lying on his back and not moving. I called out to him, "Marguese, what is your condition?" He did not answer or move, but I knew he was still alive because I could see his chest going up and down as he labored to breathe.

I saw Aurora the furthest away from us down by the river. She was hunched over sitting on a rock. I knew she too must be gravely wounded, but at least she was still alive.

Genavieve looked up at me with profound, deep sadness in her eyes. "You and I are the only ones not physically injured Trevallion. And poor Qadir is dead. Never could I have imagined a tragedy of this magnitude. What are we to do? I need to go home to my husband and children, but I can't leave my brothers and sisters like this. This cannot be how the Taz end."

I gazed at the tall mountain peak looming majestically above scattered low clouds in the distance. I felt somehow disassociated from my body and my own voice as I answered Genavieve while continuing to keep my eyes steadfastly upon the mountain. And from somewhere beyond my own mind, the thoughts and feelings of great Taz from the past seemed to channel through me and I knew what I had to do.

"This is not the end dear sister. Stay strong. We are here for a greater purpose than our own lives, and there are many whom we have helped that will help us now. This is not the end of the Taz, but it will be the beginning of the end for many demons in the near future," I vowed with resolute certainty.

I took her hand in mine and looked at her with compassion. "I will return shortly and I will come back with help." Before she could respond I blinked away.

When I opened my eyes again I was in the leialli meadow near the Hiratol Davos village. I intended to ask the leialli to come to Veldalei to help heal the wounded Taz. And though it seemed futile, I held out hope that somehow they could bring Qadir back.

To my great disappointment, looking in every

direction I saw not even one leialli. I slapped my forehead with the palm of my hand berating myself for my stupidity. Of course the leialli couldn't always stay in the same meadow as they would soon run out of grass to graze.

Hoping they might still be nearby and close enough to come to our aid, I called out telepathically to the two leialli that had made the greatest impression on me: Little Toot and Dorsavel.

I waited for a response, but none came. I tried again. "Little Toot, Dorsavel, this is Trevallion the Taz. I need your help."

Thankfully, after a few seconds of silence, I heard a telepathic response. "Dorsavel here."

I took a sweeping look around the area. "I am at the meadow where we met," I said trying to keep my telepathic thoughts simple enough to be clear. "Can you and the herd come here quickly?"

"Yes," Dorsavel replied simply, without asking why.

I wasn't sure how long it would be before the leialli arrived so I sat down on the soft meadow grass to wait. I had started my telepathic thought by asking if the leialli could come *soon,* but changed it to *quickly.* Though both words were subject to interpretation as to how long of time they indicated, I hoped *quickly* conveyed more telepathic urgency than *soon.*

Thankfully, I did not have to wait long. After only about five minutes, I saw the herd emerging from the forest at the edge of the meadow, running at a full gallop.

When they arrived with labored breathing from their run, they were confused at first.

"Where is the danger," Dorsavel asked. "Did we run for no purpose?" His telepathic question was still able to convey some irritation.

"No danger here," I assured him, "but a very great purpose."

The herd that had come with Dorsavel included twelve adult leialli and three foals, of which Little Toot was one.

Little Toot came over and rubbed up against my body affectionately. I gave him a couple of pats, but then spoke in my mind to all of the leialli. Time for friendly fraternizing would have to come later.

As simply as I could telepathically, I explained what had happened, and how I needed as many leialli to come that would be necessary to heal four seriously injured Taz.

I saved my most hopeful request for last when I told them about Qadir's death, hoping beyond hope, that they could restore his life with their healing magick.

I was deeply disappointed by Dorsavel's answers.

"We would help if we could, but we cannot.

"We cannot travel by magick. We must use our feet to go from one place to another. The land you call Veldalei is far away. It would take the strongest leialli three days to arrive, and another three days back. It is not safe for the herd to be gone that long."

If that was not a great enough letdown, Dorsavel added another. "We cannot heal the dead. When they are dead, they are gone."

I held my head down for a few seconds absorbing my disappointment in all Dorsavel had said. But suddenly I was buoyed up by an energy and thought that didn't seem my own, but inspiration and optimism that arrived from somewhere beyond.

"I can take you there!" I said both telepathically and out loud in my excitement.

"No," Dorsavel firmly replied. "We do not travel by magick."

This couldn't be the deal breaker I told myself. The leialli were my last hope. Apparently the leialli heard me because they all started to blow musical sounds out of their horns.

Dorsavel looked at me. "Some say they will try, but only one until you prove they will return."

"Yes!" I exclaimed in joy. "Who will come?"

A muscular golden leialli with streaks of white stepped forward. I remembered his name was Esjar.

"I went up to him and embraced his neck, laying my head against it. "Thank you Esjar. Thank you."

Esjar nodded his head down once in acknowledgment and blew a little musical note out of his horn. He turned to face the herd. "If I do not return, remember I love you, and it is for the love of the Taz and their love for us that I go now."

Esjar nudged me gently with his head. "Let us go."

I nodded my head in acknowledgment and held on tightly to Esjar's neck. Then I closed my eyes and willed myself back to the meadow at Veldalei.

When I opened my eyes again, we were there. At least I was. I glanced quickly at Esjar and looked up and down his body. Given the leialli reluctance to travel by magick, I wanted to make sure he had also made the blink, and that all of him had arrived. I was very happy to see he seemed to be in one piece.

I pointed to Marguese who was the nearest Taz to the point where we had arrived. He was still lying in the same position on his back and unmoving. I hoped he was still alive. "Please hurry and help him Esjar. I will return to the meadow and bring another leialli from the herd."

"No," Esjar said firmly. "I must return before I can heal. That was the word of Dorsavel."

"Of course," I agreed. I didn't want to waste another moment so I held on to Esjar's neck again and willed us back to the leialli meadow. We arrived as fast as thought.

The herd was startled to see us back so quickly, as it had probably not been more than fifteen seconds since we had left.

Dorsavel cocked his head a bit as he looked at Esjar, I suppose to see if he had returned in the same condition as he had departed.

"You are well?" I heard him ask Esjar telepathically.

"I am," Esjar answered. "The magick is safe. The injuries to the Taz appear grave. Many must come to heal them. For our safety, all of the herd should come."

"The grass is very green there," he added.

Dorsavel tooted an agreeable sound through his horn, which I took to be an affirmation. In a hurry to proceed, I once more held on to Esjar's neck and willed us back to the spot in the meadow at Veldalei where we had left Marguese.

Upon arriving I let go of Esjar and pointed at Marguese. "Work the magick of your love upon my friend, I will return for the others."

Esjar nodded once and took a few steps over to Marguese and gently placed the tip of his horn on his chest. Immediately, a bright white and golden light began to radiate out from the tip of his horn.

I looked around quickly and saw Genavieve trying to get my attention. I waved at her and yelled out, "I will return with more leialli." Then I blinked back to the leialli meadow.

I did not linger even for a second to explain my actions to Genavieve because I had a particular plan in motion and it depended upon me getting all of the leialli back to Veldalei with the greatest of haste.

Arriving back with the herd I didn't waste any time with further explanations or formalities. "Who is next?" I asked hurriedly and held up my arm for one of them to come up to it. A mare named Fosa, whom I assumed was mated to Esjar stepped up.

We arrived at the same spot I had with Esjar, and Fosa quickly stepped over to Marguese and added her horn to his chest, doubling the white and golden light radiating from the tips of the two horns touching his body.

One after another I returned for the leialli. Some were very hesitant to travel by magick, while others were enthusiastic about having the experience, but they all came. I blinked the entire herd of six mated pairs plus three foals, including Little Toot, one by one to Veldalei in about ten minutes.

Despite just having a marvelous new magickal experience and arriving at a most beautiful and lush green land, none of the leialli were distracted. Immediately, upon setting hoof in Veldalei, they located the nearest injured Taz and went directly to them.

I walked over to Genavieve who was still kneeling next to Qadir's body. Seeing him like that, dead, bloodied, and mangled, was still almost more than I could bear.

"You brought the leialli," Genavieve said in soft amazement. "They will be our salvation, but how did you ever get them to agree to travel by magick? I have never heard of such a miracle. I did not even know it was possible."

"They agreed to try," I explained. "Once they saw one succeed, they all wanted to come to help the Taz."

"I am so grateful to them," Genavieve said quietly through tears, "and to you Trevallion. I would never have thought to try to transit leialli here to heal the wounded. None of us would. I guess it took someone new, who didn't yet know what couldn't be done, to show us that it could."

I took a big breath and let out a big sigh filled with my hopes and prayers. "It is wonderful that the leialli have been able to come and help heal our wounded brothers and sisters, but I am hoping for a bigger miracle here today."

I pointed at Qadir's body. "I want them to heal Qadir; to bring him back to life."

"Oh dear Trevallion," Genavieve said with motherly affection. "After so short a time, you already loved him like a father, didn't you?"

I gritted my teeth trying not to cry and nodded my head, as I knew if I tried to speak, the tears would flow.

Genavieve shook her head negatively. "I wish it was possible, but I know it is not. His injuries were fatal. His body grows cold and his soul spirit is no longer in his destroyed tabernacle of flesh."

"The leialli told me the same thing," I acknowledged. "But the principle is the same as blinking the leialli here. Just because something has never been done before, does not mean it cannot be done."

Genavieve looked at me with empathetic care in her eyes, trying to be supportive. "If you wish, they can try. I just don't want you to be disappointed and have more pain."

I put my hand on her shoulder and looked steadfastly into her eyes. "Succeed or fail, my greatest pain and sorrow would be to have to live the rest of my life without having tried."

The moment to test my faith came sooner than I expected. With the magickal power of the entire herd of leialli at work, Genavieve and I were delighted to soon see all of the other Taz coming over to us one by one, after they had been completely restored to health and vigor by the loving healing magick of the leialli.

The leialli followed, and Taz and leialli mingled together, surrounding the body of our dear brother Qadir.

Telepathically, I opened my thoughts to all present, leialli and Taz, to hear my words, but as I was pointing to Qadir, I spoke to Dorsavel.

"This is Qadir. The last time you saw him he was wielding his Dragon Sword to defend your herd from the demons. Now he has been felled by a demon.

"I know you have told me that you cannot bring the dead back. My sister Taz told me the same thing, and maybe that is the reality, but maybe it is not.

"All I ask you to do is try, to let all of your love flow from your heart to his; to let your magick expand to its limits and beyond, to unite as one, all of you, to combine your magick and create a miracle, even though one such as this has never been done.

"Will you do this please?"

Dorsavel nodded his head a few times, his long beautiful mane shaking with his movements.

The leialli all moved forward to form a circle around Qadir's body and all the Taz stepped back to give them room. Every single leialli joined the circle, even the three foals.

Almost in unison they all bowed their heads and touched the tips of their horns to Qadir's body. A brilliant gold and white light burst forth that was so bright, it completely enveloped the leialli, and those of us watching ended up having to shield our eyes and look away.

The leialli continued working their healing magick, united as one for about fifteen minutes. Then I saw one of the mares falter and step out of the circle. She was quickly followed by another. Then the entire herd stepped back and they all looked haggard and exhausted.

Dorsavel came over to me. "We have done our best. We need a day of rest and good grazing to recover. His body is healed, but he is still dead because his spirit soul is not there. I am sorry."

I gently stroked Dorsavel's neck. "I understand. Thank you so much for all that you and your herd have done. I will never forget, and will always be your grateful brother."

All the Taz had gathered around Qadir. The magick the leialli had accomplished was truly miraculous. Qadir's body looked as strong and healthy as it had ever been. His ear and hair that had been scraped away by the vicious slice of the axe were back; his massive wound through his collarbone, ribs and lung was completely gone, as if it had never been. There was not even a scar.

I knelt down and put my hand on Qadir's bare chest. His skin was warm to the touch and no longer had the chill of death upon it. Everything looked so normal, except he wasn't breathing, his eyes weren't open, and he wasn't moving.

I looked up at my brother and sister Taz. "How do we get his soul back?"

Many of them shook their heads negatively. "We cannot do it," Nkosi said with regret.

"I think the next life is better than this one," Marguese added. "Once someone has done their best in this life and have departed, they don't look back. They paid their dues in this life so they can enjoy the next with much less to worry about, including demons."

"How do you know that?" I asked, still undeterred in finding a way back for Qadir.

Marguese shrugged his shoulders. "It is what everyone says. We face challenges and work hard in this life so we can have a much easier life for the eternity to come. "It makes sense. Otherwise, life would be a lot of trouble, pain and misery for nothing.

"And we know demons fell from something greater. They admit it themselves. We look to go back to that paradise where we all began after this life. That is where Qadir is now. He would not want to come back to the evil of this world, even if he could."

"I think you might be wrong Marguese," I said with conviction. "I think Qadir would come back if there was a way for him to do it. Just like the leialli healed with the magick of their love, I think we can bring him back with our love, or at least open the path for him, if he wants to take it.

"Love is the greatest magick of all, and it is the one magick that works in every dimension, even in whatever one Qadir has gone to now that is beyond those we know. Will you try with me brother?"

I looked at the other Taz. "Will you all try with me?"

Everyone nodded their heads and we gathered in a circle around Qadir's body holding hands with one another, alternating male and female in the circle.

As this was uncharted territory for everyone, no one objected to me, the least experienced, being the spokesperson.

"I don't know any magickal incantations, spells or enchantments to call back the dead to life, but I know the love I feel in my heart for Qadir. It's the same love I feel for each of you, even though we have barely met. We are Taz. That is a bond unlike any other. Let us call upon it now."

I was being guided to say and act by an unseen force of light welling up inside of me but coming from somewhere far beyond. My words were not my words. My actions were not thought of by me. I was following what was being said, as if it was someone else saying it, and it was.

"Let us reach down and with our hands still joined, with the tips of our hands still touching and connecting, but with our palms on the body of Qadir.

"As one, think of the love for this dear brother. Feel that love pouring out of our hearts. Have faith that as we will it, so it will be."

"Let us say his name aloud over and over."

And so we did. We knelt down and placed our palms on his body while staying connected with our thumb and index fingers, and we began to speak aloud as one. "Qadir, Qadir, Qadir," over and over we said his name.

While we were knelt down calling for our fallen brother to return, the leialli came up behind us. They inserted their horns between our bodies and once again touched them to Qadir.

Immediately the golden while light began to radiate. We had to close our eyes to not be blinded, but we continued to call his name from the depths of the love and faith in our hearts, "Qadir, Qadir, Qadir."

Then there was movement! It was very slight but we all felt it. Buoyed with great hope that our efforts were truly working we continued saying Qadir's name with great passion and the leialli somehow brought forth even greater love because the blinding light radiating from their horns became even more intense.

Suddenly, Qadir's body jerked and then jerked again. The leialli backed away, We stopped saying Qadir's name and looked down at his serene face with great expectations and hope. And then it happened, the miracle of miracles! Qadir opened his sparkling brown eyes and we saw the happy smile of our living brother Qadir!

While we were still kneeling, Qadir leaped up! "Now that was an astounding experience!" he exclaimed joyously.

He energetically went around giving everyone firm, warm embraces and profuse thanks, including each and every one of the leialli.

"When he got to me, I had a lot of tears of joy in my eyes as he embraced me with a hug and kind words. "Thank you for believing in the impossible Trevallion, and helping all of us to remember that impossibles become possible as love, faith, and unfailing determination make it so.

"Having a little magick helps too," Qadir added with a wry smile and a twinkle in his eyes.

EPILOGUE

It would have been nice to have been able to spend a few more days together with the other Taz at Veldalei, just relaxing, recovering and getting to know everyone more, but it was not to be. My Earth Self was in great need of being renewed, as its soul split autopilot mode was already past expiration.

As happy as Genavieve was to see Qadir alive and well, she was anxious to get back to her family in France.

Marguese was already looking for the next demons to battle and we seemed to have a shortage of them at Veldalei. No worries, he said he knew where plenty of trouble makers were in Lisbon.

Jenji also had a family that I didn't yet know much about that she wanted to return to back on Earth.

Nkosi actually decided to stick around a bit as there were some unknown magickal plants he had noticed while he had been sitting up against a log wounded and immobilized, and he wanted to examine them to determine their magickal properties.

Aurora was very anxious to return to Sedona. She said she needed to be meditating in the serenity of the red hills to get back to a place of peace after all the trauma she had recently experienced.

Qadir didn't seem in a hurry to get back to Earth and didn't seem to have a need to be reunited with his 1st Dimensional body as often as the rest of us. He said he was going to return to his home at Corsalain for a while.

I invited the other Taz to help me bring the leialli to their meadow by the davos village, but when we approached the herd and offered to blink them home, Dorsavel wondered if we would mind if they made the extensive, lush, green meadows of Veldalei their new home.

That was a surprise, but a very pleasant one. Qadir explained that Veldalei was our sanctuary as well, and we would be honored to share it with the leialli herd and have them call it home.

An unspoken side benefit was it would be nice to know that in the future if we were wounded, we could return to Veldalei and the healing power of the leialli would be nearby.

Before we parted and went our separate ways, Qadir called us all together.

"I have a couple more things to say before everyone goes off to wherever they are going," Qadir said as he motioned for us to join him in a tight circle.

"First, let me say that I am most grateful and humbled that your love and faith convinced my soul essence to return to this body. Yet, at some point in the future, maybe tomorrow, maybe ten years from now, I will die again, from either natural or demon causes. When that happens, please do not recall me once more to life.

"Being a physically active Taz is not a task for an old man whose body is naturally suffering the decline of time. The leialli healed my wounds, but they didn't turn back the clock and make me any younger.

"I took on Trevallion as an apprentice for the express purpose of training him to take my place and be numbered among you so I can retire. My body is no longer up to the task of being a robust, physically capable

Taz. As time continues to tick on, I will be more of a liability to you than an asset in active confrontations, such as the one we just experienced.

"I have spent decades gradually increasing the time the part of my soul that is in my Taz body can be separated from the part of my soul that is in my 1st Dimension body. At this point, even if my 1st Dimension body dies from old age, my Taz body in the 2nd Dimension will live on for some months and perhaps much longer if both halves of my soul end up reuniting in my Taz body, which I suspect is possible.

"Therefore, I intend to go into semi-retirement at my home in Corsalain. I will still be available to offer advice to any of you in the future and will be happy to craft any spells you need within my capabilities, to help you fight and banish demons, but my days of physically fighting demons need to come to a close. Our next campaign will be the last that I will physically participate in."

Everyone nodded in understanding. Qadir would surely be missed, but the justification he presented for his need to retire was true and we all knew it, so there were no objections to his announcement.

Before anyone could make any comments, Qadir continued speaking. "We need to talk about what comes next. We cannot just go back to the way things used to be. There is much you do not know that occurred after the battle with the demons that will necessitate a change in our focus and strategy. One of the greatest challenges that have ever faced the Taz of any generation is now before us."

Everyone looked at him both confused, with no idea

what he was talking about, and also expectantly, looking forward to finding out.

Qadir explained, "After I was killed during the demon fight, because my Earth body still lived, the conscious spirit of my soul was able to linger at the scene, and I heard and witnessed a most ominous encounter between Trevallion and the demon Hamerac.

"My last act before I died was to encase Trevallion in a Wazdon Bubble."

There were a few gasps from the Taz at that revelation. I guess there were ramifications to a Wazdon Bubble that I was unaware of, whether good or bad I didn't know. Although I had to admit that being unable to escape, and being threatened with being buried alive with the Wazdon Bubble as my coffin, as Hamerac had said, did fall into the bad category.

Qadir lifted his palms contritely. "I know, I know, there are a lot of risks using that magick. But with my death, Trevallion would have been alone to battle against the remaining demons. There were too many, especially for one as inexperienced as him. His demise would have inevitably followed mine if I hadn't protected him in a Wazdon Bubble."

Despite Qadir's explanation for why he had to use that magick, there was still a lot of concern etched on everyone's face.

"Not to worry," Qadir assured them. "The Wazdon was spelled to dissipate after a day, so Trevallion would not have remained encased within it until he died as others have been.

"I had no idea that Hamerac would show up after the

fact. But he did, and what he said and what occurred, changes everything."

Qadir started to explain further, but as dire as his words were, everyone seemed to be momentarily focused on my entombment in the Wazdon Bubble.

"How did you escape a Wazdon?" Jenji asked staring at me a bit incredulously. "Even if it was spelled to dissipate after a day, that time had not yet elapsed."

Nkosi also seemed perplexed. "It should not have even been possible," he added.

I pulled the little pebble from Veldalei out of my pants pocket and held it up for everyone to see.

"You provided the solution Nkosi, with this little rock from Veldalei you gave me back in South Africa. I just remembered your words that the land calling to itself was stronger than conjured magick.

"It worked exactly as you said it would. I arrived here because of the power of that stone to be drawn to its motherland was greater than the magickal force of the Wazdon Bubble to contain me.

"Even being locked momentarily in the Wazdon Bubble was a blessing as it allowed both me and Qadir to hear the nefarious plan of Hamerac.

"And because I escaped from the Wazdon Bubble I was able to bring the leialli here to heal everyone."

I held the stone from Veldalei up high, and then brought it down and gave it a kiss. "Everything good happened because of this blessed little rock. Thank you for giving it to me Nkosi. I will always treasure it."

Nkosi had a baffled look on his face. "I didn't know it could do that," he said with surprise. "Transiting from one place to another using a stone is simple, primitive natural magick that can defeat more complex magick because it draws its power from the mass of the whole planet.

"However, defeating a Wazdon Bubble...there is no magick primitive or complex that should have been able to do that, that I am aware of. This will require further study to unlock the mystery."

Qadir interrupted Nkosi, "And that will have to wait for another time my brother. As I said, what my spirit overheard and witnessed after my death, needs to become the number one priority of all of us."

"What is it?" Aurora asked with a little impatience as if Qadir wasn't getting to the details quickly enough.

Qadir calmly smiled at Aurora and continued his account. "After my body died, my spirit lingered on the scene until Trevallion escaped from the Wazdon. While he was still in the Wazdon a few dozen demons from Hamerac's Horde suddenly arrived; obviously unexpected and unwanted by the demons of the Gosli Horde that we had been fighting to prevent access to the Nexus.

"Hamerac's Horde got into a most peculiar battle with the Gosli Horde. I thought at first that it would be a quick end to the interlopers as they were outnumbered four to one and had not arrived with any weapons I could see.

"To my great surprise, Hamerac's Horde quickly decimated the Gosli Horde and they did it completely with magick!

"Even more startling, they did not lop off limbs as I expected in a typical demon on demon fray. Instead, they banished their opponents! In all my years as a Taz, I have only seen that occur once before. It is something only the highest level demons can do to another demon. In just a couple of minutes, the entire remnant of the Gosli Horde was either banished or had frantically transited away to escape.

"These were powerful demons! As I overheard Hamerac soon tell Trevallion, they were all 10th and 11th level, and I am most sad to say that these twenty-three, worst of the worst, passed through the Nexus to Earth!"

Qadir's announcement brought forth more expressions of shock from everyone.

"Twenty-three 10ths and 11ths?" Aurora repeated in a tone of dismay bordering on disbelief.

"There are probably not more than a dozen demons of that high of a level already on the whole planet, and they are scattered among several hordes so they do not work together.

"To have almost twice that number come through all from one horde, all at the same time, is ominous. There certainly must be some great mischief afoot."

"I'm afraid it is more than mischief Aurora," Qadir said gravely.

"Hamerac boasted of his plan to Trevallion, never imagining his scheme would be revealed because Trevallion would escape the Wazdon, or that my invisible spirit was listening in. And terribly insidious that plot is. Hamerac revealed that those upper level demons are his vanguard in a plan to dominate and control all of the people of Earth."

Marguese let out a little chuckle. "Let's not get too melodramatic. I think Hamerac is biting off more than he can chew. Twenty-three demons, even upper levels, are certainly formidable, but they will have little impact on a world with many billions of people.

"Without doubt millions of demons can cause great misery to tens of millions of people. However, even if Hamerac's demons are the advanced leaders of a bunch of lower-level demons that are going to follow them to Earth, they along with all other demons of every horde, are still vastly outnumbered by the billions of people on Earth that are unaffected by demon machinations.

"Personally, I look forward to having more upper-level demons around to banish. They will be an invigorating challenge compared to the insipid lower-level scum we normally have to obliterate. That lot practically rolls over and plays dead just hearing a Taz is coming for them."

Qadir seemed unmoved by Marguese's view. "Normally your assessment of the demons to humans risk ratio would be correct," Qadir agreed. "But not in this case.

"According to Hamerac, these very high-level demons are specifically targeting politicians, celebrities, and religious leaders to inhabit. They will use their power and influence to lead the people that follow and look up to them down darker paths, making them easy prey for the lower-level demons of their horde.

"More ominous, they will use these people of power to start wars and conflicts that will tear the human race asunder. In a world of nuclear weapons, and diseases with no cure that can be weaponized and quickly spread around the world, I believe that Hamerac's ultimate goal is to extinguish a great deal of human life on Earth and enslave to demons those that survive.

"And once accomplished, they will have the template to do it over and over again on the many other Earth-like planets filled with humans in the 1st Dimension.

"Our Earth must be the place that we make a stand, and completely defeat and banish these upper-level monsters of Hamerac's Horde; not just for our beautiful homeworld, but for the untold trillions of humans on other worlds too.

"It seems too great of a task," Jenji mourned. "We are only seven, and we have no idea the identities of the twenty-three demons, where they are, or who they are targeting. It seems like we are trying to defeat the wind."

Qadir nodded in understanding. "No doubt it will be a challenge, but the presence and actions of demons of that high of a level will soon be known and talked about by lower-level demons wherever the upper level demons are active.

"I have no doubt that in fairly short order, from listening in on the conversations of lower-level demons, we will know who the upper-level invaders are, what they are up to, and where to find them. However, they will be too powerful to strangle banish. We will have to work with three Taz together to contain the demon and their inhabited human host in a Crystal Matrix so the demon can be banished without killing the host."

Nkosi, put his head down shaking it gently side to side. "And what if we are too late and the demon host falls so far down the dark path that they become demon-like themselves, on the abysmal path to becoming Metastasis Demons and start the slaughter of innocents? It has happened before. It could happen again."

Qadir put his hand on Nkosi's shoulder in empathy. "When a human becomes like a demon, we have to be strong enough in our heart and mind to treat them as such, just as we would any other of the foul creatures of hell that seek to hurt humans.

"There are many great burdens we have to carry brother. Let us not shirk from them or dwell on the ways we might fail or falter. In this case, let us simply vow to do our utmost to find and banish these upper-level demons quickly before any of their wicked seeds bear fruit. In the end, all we can do, is all we can do."

Genavieve raised her index finger in a forceful movement. "I believe there is more we can do. There is more we must do. We may be only seven, but as Qadir said, the evil we stop on Earth prevents it from spreading to other worlds.

"So let us call upon the Taz on some other planets in the 1st Dimension to come to our aid, because ultimately our fight is their fight, either now or later, if we fail to stop the threat on our Earth. And what of the Guardian Lazarus? Would this not be a fight where our stewardships of protection would overlap?"

Qadir's face beamed as he smiled at Genavieve. "That indeed is a plan dear sister, and a worthy one it is. This is too big of a threat to not call in some reinforcements.

"I will take care of this and contact the Taz on other worlds and Lazarus as well. In the meantime, all of you go home or wherever you wish, to get some well-deserved rest and time with your families. I will call you when I have solidified some help and we are ready to go out demon hunting."

"Yeah! Marguese yelled out. "Now you're talking my language!"

With those parting words we all took turns embracing everyone farewell, and one by one in quick succession all the Taz blinked away except for me, Qadir and Nkosi.

Qadir put his hand on my shoulder with fatherly affection. "You need to go Trevallion. Go give your full consciousness to your soul on Earth; it has already been separated too long. I will see to it that your Taz body has a deep, comfortable sleep at my home in Corsalain until you return.

"When can I come back for more training?" I asked expectantly.

Qadir cracked a slight smile. "I'm afraid all your training from this point, at least until we banish the 23 Hamerac demons, will need to be on-the-job training. This is a threat so enormous that we will not have the luxury of a time set aside for training.

"After everyone has had a few days with their families to recuperate, we will need to dive into eliminating these very dangerous demons with an intense, unwavering focus. All other projects are off the table, for all of us, until we've ended this threat to our world and others."

"I understand," I said solemnly, holding his gaze.

I gave both Qadir and Nkosi another hug. "Until we meet again in a few days then," I said with some reluctance to be parting.

"Until then," both Qadir and Nkosi replied in unison.

My last image was of those two great Taz standing side by side as I blinked back to fully unite with my Earth body and Qadir sent my Taz body to repose at Corsalain. The rest and respite would be so brief, and the ferocious battle for the soul of humanity so daunting.

AUTHOR'S NOTE

I hope you were both entertained and enlightened by reading my account of my early days as a Taz. It was challenging writing this book, as there was also a lot of opposition among many of the other Taz to making knowledge about our activities public, as this had been kept secret for thousands of years by every Taz before me.

I never would have considered breaking that continuous line of secrecy if it wasn't for my other major calling in life, to share the teachings of *Celestine Light*, and the assurances from an angel I hold most dear, that revealing some of the secrets of the unseen world was the right action to take.

Around the turn of the last century, I was called to *revelate* the **Oracles of Celestine Light**. This was akin to time travel, where my consciousness was transported back 2,000 years to the time of Yeshua of Nazareth. I was able to see the tiniest details, hear and understand every word that was spoken, even if it was in a language I was unfamiliar with, and smell all the interesting and novel aromas wafting through the air.

My sacred task was to record the fullness of the life and teachings of Yeshua of Nazareth; and what a full and amazing life it was! The Oracles is over 800 pages in length, and would have been twice that size if the book dimensions and fonts used were of standard sizes. Yet, there were still precious events that I heard and witnessed that I was constrained by Yeshua not to write until some years following the publication of the Oracles.

After the *Oracles of Celestine Light* was first published in 2010, I was blessed by continuing to receive clear and detailed telepathic communication with Yeshua's wife Miriam (Miriam of Magdala), who had become the *Angel of the Covenant* near the end of her sojourn in mortality. I am still fortunate to be able to speak with her regularly today. It was due to Miriam's prompting that I first contemplated revealing the Taz and the mysteries of other dimensions and the unseen world.

Miriam reminded me that as I heard Yeshua himself speak, and was recorded in the *Oracles*, this was the generation for all the secrets of the past to come into the light.

"That which has been lost is given again in fullness, for my teachings bring joy and that which I ask does not burden but enlightens, for it is the Gospel of love, of life, and of light.

"Verily, I say unto you: This generation shall not pass away until all that has been hidden is brought again into the light, for it is the epoch for the fulfillment of promise.

"Unto this generation has my Father and Mother saved the greatest spirits of Heaven to come forth upon the world, and to them will be given the plentitude of truth, both that which was lost and that which is new."

Oracles of Celestine Light, Nexus 1:20-22

Those verses from the *Oracles* really impacted me. Despite the disagreement of some of my brother and sister Taz, I realized that the story of the Taz and the truth of the unseen world that surrounds all of us, needed to be revealed.

In the process of writing *Demon Hunter*, I felt there were questions readers might ask that really had no way to be answered in the narrative of the book, as neither I nor any of my Taz brothers and sisters clearly knew the answers. So I asked Miriam, the *Angel of the Covenant*, if she would answer them from her timeless and complete understanding.

Embrosewyn (E): There are several things relating to Taz that none of my brother and sister Taz have been able to fully explain. Will you answer my questions about Taz?

Miriam (M): Of course.

E: The first question is how do Taz have the abilities that we do? Not the learned abilities like magick, but the innate abilities like being able to easily travel through dimensions and to see and have physical contact with demons in any dimension?

M: I'm sure that you already know that like all male Alamars (humans) you were created in the image of our Heavenly Father, even as all female Alamars were designed from the template of our Heavenly Mother.

All Alamars have the potential to be much, much more than they can imagine in the physical life they now live. As each and every Alamar is born from the template of our Heavenly Parents, they all have within them the genetic code to wield a myriad of powerful psychic abilities and even manifest as a Taz.

There is nothing different in your genetic code than there is in any other Alamars when it comes to being able to manifest as a Taz. What sets you apart from the billions of other Alamars on the Earth is you actually succeeded in unlocking the hidden Celestine energy within you that allows your Taz abilities to manifest.

E: So my friends could become Taz as well?

M: If they unlock and expand the energy within that is related to manifesting as a Taz. It was the hope of the Elohim (Heavenly Father & Heavenly Mother) when they created Alamars in their image, that at any one time there would be millions of Taz on the Earth to counter the millions of demons that would someday be there. Alas, very few are those that have been able to make the leap from the mundane to the extraordinary.

E: I would love to be able to have my close friends share my experiences as a Taz. What can I do to help others to discover and fulfill their potential?

M: You can teach the principles of how to discover and use a myriad of psychic abilities, but there is nothing you can do to teach or aid unleashing the Taz within others. Once someone has manifested as a Taz they can be taught how to use their abilities even as you were, but they must make the initial evolution solely by themselves.

E: How do they do that? How did I do it? It does not seem to me that I did anything. My transition to a Taz just happened on its own.

M: No, your transformation from the man that you were to the Taz that you became did not *just happen on its own*. Every one of your life experiences, your good choices, the knowledge you gained on a myriad of subjects and ever questing to know more, the respectful and helpful way you treated other people, your love of and connection to the Earth and all of the animals upon it, and your steadfast efforts to discover and magnify your psychic abilities, were some of the important steps that brought you to the point that the metamorphosis of your physical and spiritual body occurred.

It may have seemed spontaneous to you, but there were thousands of little actions and personal improvements you took over the years that led to the point that the greater you could no longer be contained within your physical body.

E: That's humbling, but I know there are countless numbers of people who have done far more to improve themselves in both psychic and personal areas than I have. Why did they not evolve into Taz?

M: Many would have if they were also completely open in their heart and mind to discovering the mysteries of the unseen worlds, and willing to be unselfish stewards of their gifts and use them in the service of others.

Beyond that, there is one critical ingredient that most people never encounter and that is their catalyst. This is usually a Soul Mate or very strong Twin Flame that will come into their life, and because of the synchronicity of the two souls, will cause all of their energy centers to spin and expand in perfect harmony. The unified expansion is the final key to releasing the Taz within, if all the prerequisites I spoke of earlier have also been met.

E: My wife Sumara was certainly the catalyst you describe. It was amazing when we first met how expanded I felt. It was like nothing I had ever experienced before. Everything about me, from my brainpower to my love and emotional empathy for others, was tremendously enhanced. Yet I changed into a Taz some years before I ever met my wife. How was that possible?

M: You had two Twin Flame relationships in earlier years that stimulated your hidden gifts enough that your Taz abilities were able to manifest even before you met your true Soul Mate and catalyst. This still was only able to occur because you had so diligently worked to expand your psychic abilities and were so open to discovering the unknown. Nevertheless, you did not gain the fullness of your Taz abilities until you had a relationship with your catalyst.

E: How did the Taz begin? Who and when was the first Taz?

M: The first Alamars to evolve into their potential as a Taz were Adam and Eve from the Garden of Eden and most of the other Edenites that survived the journey to establish a new home in Kamoya. After eleven generations had passed from the days of Eden, the prophet Enoch organized the first school to train new Taz that had blossomed into their higher potential.

In the early days of Alamars upon the Earth, a large percentage of the people became Taz as they found their catalyst, their Soul Mate, and reached a maturity of their body and sufficient wisdom and knowledge in their years. Sadly, as the Alamars progressed through history, less and less of them evolved into their Taz potential, even as more and more demons over the millennium began to travel to Earth from the 3rd Dimension and sow their discord upon the blessed lands of this jewel.

Today science and technology have supplanted religions and the higher power that still resides within each person becomes more distant for most people. Machines and devices accomplish tasks from healing, to power and communications that people used to rely on their own knowledge of auric energy, telepathy, and magick to accomplish.

As people have turned from the old ways, few of them remember any longer how to even seek out the power within, let alone call it out. Hence, less and less Taz walk the Earth or the other worlds of the 1st and 2nd dimensions, and the demons hold greater and greater sway over the minds of people and the tragic events in their lives.

E: Can you explain the different types of demons and why so many people and scriptures from various religions refer to them as *fallen angels*?

M: I believe you answered the types of demons well in your book, therefore I will comment on angels as there is certainly confusion on that score.

As you know angels are not some strange being created by God as they are often depicted in religions and the entertainment media. That would totally be outside the bounds of Eternal Progression, as how would these peculiar beings progress? If there were such beings that were forever doomed to only be servants of God and never masters of their own lives, never capable of enjoying and progressing in a physical life, marrying, and having children, they would probably have justification to rebel.

I am an angel. I have special powers given to me by Elohim enabling me to fulfill my stewardship as the *Angel of the Covenant.* Before I was called to this sacred calling, I lived a mortal, physical life as did all angels that have ever existed.

My stewardship is an office, like a mayor or governor. This is true for all angels. Being called to be an angel by Elohim is a great blessing, but no one is an angel forever. That would be a life that was damned, not one that could progress. Before me, there was a different person that had previously lived a physical mortal life that filled the office of the Angel of the Covenant.

As you know, there was a rebellion in the premortal Celestine Realms, led by Lucifer. He was a premortal spirit of high responsibility. Scriptures of multiple religions call the rebels *fallen angels,* which is fine, as that is the easiest way to refer to them as there is no other term, but that is actually a misnomer and was not the case.

No true angel has ever, or would ever, rebel against Elohim. Premortal spirits did, but that is because even those that were high in the premortal world, were still not far in their Eternal Progression, as none had ever lived a physical life. They erred due in part to their ignorance of the bigger picture.

True angels have lived full lives, both in the premortal

world and in a 1st Dimension physical body. They have a more complete understanding of the challenges and rewards of life and why Elohim has organized everything as it is for the blessing and ultimate benefit of everyone.

It is like when you were a teenager and you thought many actions of your parents were wrong and that you knew better. But after some years passed and you too became a parent and had to deal with the challenges that entails, you had a greater perspective and greater appreciation for your parents and the choices they made.

All of those that followed Lucifer departed from the Premortal Celestine Worlds when they lost so much soul essence energy by their actions that they could no longer dwell there. As they were all premortal spirits, none had ever had a physical body. They devolved even further due to the loss of energy from their soul essence.

Most, including Lucifer, devolved into demons. They can exist with full tangible substance only in the 3rd Dimension. They have partial tangible substance in the magickal realm of the 2nd Dimension, and no tangible substance perceptible to Alamars in the non-magickal realm of the 1st Dimension where your Earth is located.

Some poor souls were so maniacal in their rebellion that they lost even more soul essence energy than demons and devolved to become even lower creatures, such as Raval, and have almost no tangible substance in any realm.

Heavenly Mother promised all of those who had been cast out of the higher realms, that because of the Eternal Progression Plan of Salvation, there was a way back for any of them that repented and once again walked in the light. But few are those among the Original Demons that have ever taken that blessed opportunity.

In the days of Noah, there was a very small group of high premortal spirits that used the powers given to them by Elohim as leaders, to come down to Earth as fully formed adults in physical bodies. They allowed their joy of a physical body to turn to lust and then perversion. They fell from from being among the highest children of Elohim down into the lowest. Though their numbers were small, their destructive actions in the lives of normal mortals was horrendous.

To save the Alamars of Earth, Elohim had to eventually intervene. It is only those few that were forever banished to be demons, and never again be able to have physical bodies, never again be able to have the possibility of forgiveness or Eternal Progression.

These few are the only ones that are almost always referred to as *fallen angels*, even in Celestine Realms, in recognition of the depth of their fall from the highest light to the lowest darkness. Elohim also cursed them to never even have the full abilities of demons, so Lucifer and the higher-level demons would always be able to rule over and subjugate them.

E: What do you recommend as the best way to deal with Metastasis Demons that have devolved into demons due to their wickedness, but are still in human form here in the 1st Dimension? I'm thinking in particular of people like the serial killer Ted Bundy who murdered my High School friend Georgann Hawkins and several other young women in 1974. This was before I had become a Taz. However, because it was so personal to me, as my very sweet friend was a victim, if I had been a Taz then I would have been relentless in tracking down her killer.

But then what? Even if I had been a Taz, though Bundy had become a Metastasis Demon in his energy and actions, he was still in a human form. How am I supposed to act in those situations? I can't banish him because though the man had literally become a demon, at that point he was still a human; I can't kill him because I would be a murderer; I can't turn him in to the police because I would have no evidence, and if I did find physical evidence through the abilities of my Taz form, there would be no way I could explain how I obtained that evidence.

M: I believe the way the Taz have always dealt with troublesome Metastasis Demons is effective and appropriate. I'm not sure what more you expect I could add to that protocol. As the devolving Metastasis do not fully become demons until the physical Alamar body dies, all you can do is what the Taz have always done while the Metastasis still lives in a physical body: use magick to thwart them, dreams to haunt them, and anonymous threats to hurt them or reveal their secrets if they do not cease. Once they physically die and become full demons, quickly banishing them to

Oblivion becomes a very long prison sentence for their crimes.

You say you cannot go to the police, but I'm not sure why you feel that way. As you know, giving the police anonymous tips revealing the killers has been very effective at stopping their sprees of death in the past with many of them.

As the Taz can travel in the first Dimension, invisible to all the inhabitants, it would seem that is always a valuable ability to thwart evil, whether it is from Metastasis demons or merely evil humans. Unseen to all human eyes, find the root of the evil, reveal it anonymously to the Alamar authorities, and then let them deal with the perpetrators. The Taz can mete out further justice to Metastasis Demons by banishing them to Oblivion once they pass from a mortal life.

E: Why are the worlds of the 1st Dimension so lacking in magickal energy, while worlds in the 2nd and 3rd Dimensions have it in abundance?

M: There are two parts to that answer. The root is, why did Elohim create the dimensions so differently, rather than more similar? Each dimension was created specifically to have worlds tailored to the type of inhabitants that would dwell upon them.

1st Dimension worlds were created for Alamars (humans) and other races and creatures that have a great deal of physical emphasis in their persona. Whether it is an Alamar, a tiger, or an alien race you may never have encountered, if their homeworld is in the 1st Dimension, being able to do physical feats with their bodies is important. More ancient races have evolved to become more mentally powerful, but that was not the case when their race was young.

Due to the predominant physical nature of the 1st Dimension, magickal energy was only given to be present in very small amounts, as it is an entirely different way of being and acting than the physical mode.

Worlds in the 2nd Dimension have inhabitants that for the most part are not physically imposing, glash and dragons excepted of course. Magickal energy was given in abundance to this dimension to allow the inhabitants to develop strength in an entirely different way than the physically imbued inhabitants of the 1st Dimension.

The 3rd Dimension is the realm of the demons that were cast out of the premortal life. It too is imbued with powerful magickal energies, but for an entirely different reason than the worlds of the 2nd Dimension. Though demons make good use of the magickal energy available to them, the primary purpose of allowing the 3rd Dimension to have magickal energy is to ensure that when Taz or angelic representatives of Elohim pay a visit to the demons of the 3rd Dimension, that they will have the full force of magickal energies available to thwart and counter demons as needed.

On the whole, demons are also extremely vicious and physically destructive to one another. Without magickal energy available to aid their healing, the immortal lives of most of them would be nothing more than endless rounds of painful, dismemberment, death, and extremely slow regrowth and renewal. Though they are demons, they still have the opportunity to become better than they are and closer to the light.

Though magick can aid their evil actions, it can also ensure they have enough quality of life that some will still aspire and strive to be a force for good in a domain of evil.

Now to the second part of the answer, which is to explain how it is possible for worlds of one dimension to be full of magickal energy that makes events and actions possible that are nothing more than fantasy in the 1st Dimension. This all comes down to the minerals that compose the planets of these dimensions.

On Earth and on many other worlds in the 1st Dimension, you will find a natural non-magickal mineral called magnetite. In earlier days this was called lodestone on your Earth. It is a naturally magnetic mineral. You cannot see the magnetic force, but it is present and it is has the power to attract iron. The magnetic force radiates out from the magnetite continuously and never diminishes.

Similarly, in the dimensions that have magick in abundance, they have minerals that radiate out magickal energies that then are available for the residents of those planets to use. These minerals are either not found at all on 1st Dimension worlds or are very rare.

For instance, in the first dimension the non-magickal mineral feldspar is very common on the surface, but the mineral Laganatz, which radiates magickal energy in the same way magnetite radiates magnetic energy, is not present at all. On the planet Sx, where your Taz twin spends much time, Laganatz comprises around 15% of the surface minerals. The worlds of the 2nd Dimension derive their magickal energies from the predominance of the magickal minerals of which they are composed.

E: In the *Oracles*, there is a single verse that speaks about the Earth attaining its *crystal resonance*. Can you please explain the meaning of this?

"Yeshua smiled at Miriam, a soft smile of deep love and contentment, and said unto her, "You know this is the end of the beginning?" She nodded her head silently and then replied in a soft voice, "Yes, my Lord, the third step of the twelve you have said must transpire before man and earth are transformed into the crystal resonance of Celestine Light and the earth rises to its glory."
Oracles of Celestine light, Vivus 100: 70-71

M: It is easy to see many problems and challenges facing the world and certainly there is no denying there are many. Less noticed or touted are the many good people in the world of all faiths, all races, and all creeds. Despite the obstacles they face personally and in their communities and countries, they strive every day to be a good person and to follow the Golden Rule to *do good unto others as you would have them do unto you.* These are all Children of Light. Though it may not always be obvious, their numbers are growing not shrinking.

As the light grows, the darkness must recede. Darkness can only overshadow light if light chooses to be muted and not be seen. As the light in the hearts and minds of more and more people in the world begins to shine, the darkness must retreat, hide and diminish. In a room of light there can be no darkness.

As more and more people in the world embrace the best side of themselves, as more stand up for what is right and fair and just, not just for themselves but for everyone, even people they will never know, the light of the world will grow brighter and the darkness in the world will recede.

There will come a time when the darkness, which the demons glorify in, will become so threatened with extinction that in a last gasp to prevail, there will be hideous battles waged in many forms across the planet between the forces of light and the forces of darkness. This will envelop all of the people of the world. At this time of greatest peril, for the very soul and existence of all humanity on Earth, there will be a great rising of the light in the hearts and minds of many who will recognize that they are Children of Light, and that a world of light is one in which they wish to live, and for their children to live, and all the generations to come. Where previously to protect themselves, they would have just stayed silent and done nothing as the darkness grew, they will now stand and declare that they will be silent and do nothing no more.

When that moment comes in mass across the planet, the demons will be completely driven off the Earth. There will not be one remaining. And Elohim will bless the Earth and all of its people that choose to live their lives in the light. Forevermore the Earth will be protected from the opening of Nexuses. Never again will a demon travel by that means to Earth. From that moment, the ambiance of the Earth will be like the purity of a crystal and the vast majority of Earth's people will be motivated by higher ideals and nobler pursuits.

E: Thank you Miriam. Namaste

M: Namaste Embrosewyn

APPENDIX A

How To Help Alleviate Demon Problems

Though demon human interaction is not common, most people in the world have likely encountered multiple individuals under the influence of demons from time to time. With millions of demons existing on our planet Earth, it is fairly impossible to go through life without occasionally noticing or having to interact with someone under a demon's influence, in one way or another.

Unfortunately, there are a lot of myths and misconceptions regarding demon influence on people. Throughout history, some unfortunate individuals have been killed because they were thought to be inhabited by demons. Witches were burned at the stake and non-conforming people were tortured during the Inquisition by those who assumed that by killing the person or subjecting them to violent torture, they were getting rid of the demon. The sad fact is, the people instigating the torture or killing were more likely influenced by demons than the people that were killed.

Even if the person that was tortured or murdered by the mob was inhabited by a demon, which was unlikely, injuring or killing the person would not kill the demon. As demons are immortal, they would simply leave the dead host and seek out a new one.

Even more misguided is when individuals supposedly inhabited by demons are physically injured or accidentally killed by the violent techniques used by those who have not been properly trained in their attempt to exorcise a real or imagined demon from a person's body. This is especially sad when death by overzealous exorcism happens to a child, which unfortunately has occurred, even recently, as news reports have attested.

A quick search of the Internet will reveal several accounts of individuals that have been killed by the exorcism process used by supposed professionals. One particularly grievous case has a detailed and descriptive account of the misguided efforts involving a woman named Joan Vollmer from a small town in Australia. It is well worth reading this article to see how absolutely ignorant and idiotic actions are sometimes taken to exorcise real or imagined demons out of people. In many cases, the exorcism victims were simply having health issues and needed professional medical or psychiatric help. They can be greatly hurt and even killed by the misguided efforts of their friends and family.

The Difference Between Demon Influence and Demon Inhabiting

At any given time, approximately 1 out of every 25 people around the world are being regularly influenced by a demon to take actions that are destructive to their mind, body, or relationships, and often all three.

However, people take self-destructive actions all on their own as well, so it should not automatically be assumed that someone self-destructing is only doing so because of demon influence. Demons are certainly a possibility to look at as a cause, but that is less likely than the individual who simply made a bad choice for some other reason.

Demons would be happy to be the cause of everyone's

woes if they could. But with a world population of over 7 billion and demon numbers on Earth limited to a few million, there are simply not enough demons to be affecting every human that is in a downward spiral.

Nevertheless, demons can multitask, and a single demon is most often making concerted efforts to negatively influence many people at a time. They will typically have 3 to 5 people that they are working to debase at any given time. It is also not uncommon for multiple demons to be working in concert to negatively influence a human. A good example of this was in Chapter Two of this book

A person can be exposed to demon influence, both while they are awake and while they are asleep. Being targeted simply means a demon is trying to influence an individual to take self-destructive actions in their life. It does not mean the demon is being successful, and in many cases they will not be.

If someone has been targeted by a demon, the demon will usually spend one to two hours each day while the person is awake trying to inject unhelpful thoughts and feelings into their mind and heart, which the person may act upon, or use their will power and higher character values to resist. Unreasonable anger, unjustified jealous rages, spontaneous anxiety or depression that was not caused by a chemical/nutritional imbalance or other external causes, are just a few of the many types of negative energies demons throw at someone when they are trying to influence them.

Demons seeking to negatively influence people will typically also spend a couple of hours each night contributing to horror dreams or other disturbing dreams while the individual sleeps in an effort to disrupt their auric equilibrium.

Everyone is more vulnerable while they sleep and dream as their conscious mind is not present to act as a protective, rational barrier. Because of the absence of conscious protection, we can be influenced to take actions in dreams that we would never contemplate doing if we were awake.

Demon influence does not in any way involve any part of the demon's persona or energy actually physically being inside of the person. It's more akin to having someone that does not have your best interest at heart whispering in your ear, trying to convince you to hurt yourself.

However, when a person is inhabited, the demon has succeeded in getting their aura and some level of consciousness to physically merge with the aura and mind of the human individual. In essence, the demon is inside the human's body.

It is important to note that only one human can be inhabited by one demon at a time. One demon cannot inhabit multiple individuals at the same time and one human cannot be inhabited by multiple demons simultaneously. There is a commonly held belief that one person can be inhabited (possessed) by multiple demons and this is simply not accurate. Even the multiple personality effect can be instigated by a single demon.

About 1 out of every 30,000 people is inhabited by a demon. For a demon to adjust and match their aura close enough to an individual human in order to inhabit them is actually very tricky. Relatively few lower-level demons are successful. It is a skill that most often is only perfected by mid to upper-level demons.

A demon inhabited person will have the demon with them continuously with no respite. The demon will be able to see out of the person's eyes, hear out of their ears, and much to the demon's delight physically feel anything the human feels. However, they cannot command the human to take actions against their will. They have incessant influence, but they do not control the body or mind.

Nevertheless, the demon influence upon an inhabited human is pervasive and they are often successful at swaying the individual to do what they wish, as wrong or depraved as it may be, as it also becomes the desire of the human once their auric energy field has been infected by the demon's energy.

How to Identify Someone Under Demon Influence

A single demon can negatively influence multiple individuals, all on the same day. The good news is, unlike an inhabitation that is 24/7, a demon can only influence someone when they are physically adjacent to them, within five feet at most. Due to that limitation, as both the demon and the individual move around throughout the day, and the demon has multiple people they are working to influence, any one person will only be exposed to demon persuasions from time to time, even if the demon is targeting them.

An exception to the distance restraint limiting the number of individuals that can be negatively influenced, are venues where people sit close together in one spot in large groups for extended periods of time, such as concerts, movie theatres, and sporting events.

If the event is one that will be discombobulating the spectator's aura, such as horror movies at a theater, or Heavy Metal concerts, it becomes a Happy Hunting Ground. Many demons will congregate there as they can remain with very little movement within the location and work to negatively influence a larger than normal number of people in quick succession that are within five feet of them.

While most depictions of demons in various media are very inaccurate, one that is visually helpful is the image of a little devil sitting on someone's shoulder whispering in their ear and encouraging them to behave badly. Demons are invisible to all of our normal senses and most have no ability to physically touch people or organic objects. However, they often excel at touching people's minds with thoughts that lead them down self-destructive and relationship destroying paths.

It is helpful to remember that demons have no physically perceptible bodies in the 1st Dimension in which we live, and they are extremely envious of the physical bodies of tangible substance and physical sensations that we have.

Using their ability to sow thoughts in weakened minds, demons revel in convincing us to abuse and debase our bodies in any way. Addiction to drugs, alcohol, or tobacco; unprotected casual sex; overeating; undereating; lack of exercise; anything and everything that will make our bodies sicker and weaker, with our lives being ruined as much as possible, these are the destructive goals of demon influencers.

Someone being influenced by demons will most often noticeably change their habits from good ones to bad ones in a short period of time.

- Perhaps they were only light social drinkers, but they began drinking more often and with stronger drinks.

- Perhaps they never smoked and suddenly began.

- Perhaps they never used drugs or only a little marijuana from time to time, and then start taking harder drugs and indulging with increasing frequency.

- Perhaps they never indulged in sexual relations outside a monogamous, committed relationship, and then began having sexual relations with people they barely knew and never saw again.

- Perhaps they had been a diligent honor student for all of their life and unexpectedly and unexplainably their grades began to plummet.

- Perhaps they were always friendly and social and then without obvious reason became withdrawn and unsocial.

- Another intriguing tell is, people heavily influenced by a demon often and suddenly become extremely fanatical about something. It can be anything from a smothering, overwhelming affection for another person, to a fitness fanatic, to a religious zealot, to a political firebrand.

All of the above and similar unexplained detrimental changes in behavior can often be attributed to the influence of a demon. However, this is not always the case. It should not automatically be assumed if someone begins exhibiting any of these signs that they are inhabited by a demon. There are many other life traumas and physical ailments that can cause similar changes.

However, if after looking for other sources in life that might have motivated someone to drastically and detrimentally alter their normal balanced behavior, and finding none, then the likelihood that the source is demonic increases.

Sadly, people get in ruinous ruts that become a challenge to escape. Once a demon has firmly entrenched someone in a bad habit, they lessen the amount of time they endeavor to put thoughts in their minds during the day or inflict poisonous dreams on them while they sleep. At that point, the demon is satisfied with their nefarious work, as once deep in the rut, most individuals will continue on being their own worst enemy without any further push needed by the demon.

Mild to medium mental health issues can arise from individuals being influenced by demons. That does not mean that everyone with mental health issues is being bothered by a demon, as many of those problems have other sources, nor does it mean that everyone being influenced by a demon will exhibit mental health problems.

How to Alleviate or Prevent Demon Influence

The good news is, it is usually fairly easy to avoid or get rid of demon influence by taking actions that will discourage and drive them away. Demons are lazy. They like instant gratification. They will not waste their time trying to influence someone that is not showing quick susceptibility to their wiles, nor will they even attempt to bother someone that is in an environment that repulses them, as there is far easier, more enjoyable prey elsewhere.

There are certain things that demons hate to be around. Simply surrounding yourself and others you are concerned about with these items and ambiance will drive away and keep away demons seeking to instill negative influence. They will quickly go elsewhere to seek out less troublesome victims.

If you are endeavoring to create a demon-free space around yourself or to protect someone else from demon influence, you can successfully do so by creating an ambiance in your surroundings that is repugnant to them. These methods are equally effective at repelling demons if you feel one is already present.

Here Are Some Of The Things That Demons Hate:

Religious Settings: Demons do not like anything to do with organized religion, especially if it is with a group of believers gathered together. It doesn't matter what the religion is: Christian, Jewish, Muslim, Buddhist, Hindu, or any other. As long as the religion teaches and encourages its members to be a non-violent, loving individual and supports them by word and deed to be so, the beneficial effect to repel demons is equally effective.

Entertainment Choices: Books, movies, television shows, and other forms of entertainment that depict or involve violent, perverted, or hurtful acts against humans or animals are tools demons love to exploit. Those types of subjects discombobulate the normal balance of the human aura making it easier for demons to interject further disruptive thoughts and feelings.

Simply being more selective about entertainment choices and choosing those that entertain without depicting the dark side of humanity, can be very effective at not presenting an opening for demonic influence.

Music: Music is fascinating as the selection listened to can either open the door to demon influence or lock it shut, completely keeping demons away. Demons HATE harmonious music of any genre, or songs with catchy rhythms and positive lyrics. The key to music is how does it make you feel? If the music uplifts you, expands your spirit, and even makes you feel euphoric, you have a very effective shield against demons whenever that music is playing.

Aromas: Similar to music, certain aromas have the ability to lift us to a higher state of happiness. Whether it is the fragrance of a favorite essential oil or perfume, or the aroma of a beloved food cooking in the kitchen, wonderful scents balance and strengthen our aura and the energy centers of our body, effectively shielding us from any kind of demon intrusion.

Which Essential Oil Or Fragrance Works Best As A Demon Shield?

The fragrance that lifts you the highest in your spirits and mood is the one. It really is not about the fragrance itself. The only power in the fragrance is its ability to transport you mentally and emotionally to a happier place. It is that energy balance in your aura that makes you impervious to the wiles of demons.

Crystals: Minerals and various crystals can be very effective protectors from demon influence when they are magickally enchanted for that purpose. Rutilated Quartz works especially well to hold that type of enchantment. The gems and crystals can be in various forms from the raw natural form, to artistic shaping, such as spheres or carvings, to jewelry, which is handy as it can be worn easily and always by you.

Most unenchanted crystals, minerals, and gemstone jewelry have little power to dissuade demons, as to them they are just unsubstantial 1st Dimension rocks. The exception is if you have a crystal in one form or another, from a large cluster to a vibrant sphere that you have placed in a central location that is often viewed and that buoys your spirit every time you gaze upon it. Similar to music and aromas, anything that helps balance your energy centers and specifically expands the energy centers of your heart and mind to higher more joyous levels, is a wonderful demon shield.

Symbols & Sigils: Like crystals, minerals and gemstone jewelry, symbols and sigils, especially if they are made into jewelry, can be enchanted to repel demons and can be very effective against low-level demons when the items are easily visible. However, their enchanted power is muted and diminished if they are hidden under clothing or in books or other places.

Prominently displayed religious symbols such as the Christian cross, or the Jewish Star of David, if you believe in the light and virtues they represent, can be helpful when dealing with low-level demons, but will have no effect on mid to upper-level demons. Jewelry incorporating religious symbols can be useful, but only if the person feels a connection to the religion in their heart.

However, religious symbols and jewelry can be enhanced by enchantments to make them effective shields against mid and upper-level demons as well.

How to Identify Someone Inhabited by a Demon

A person that is inhabited will exhibit many of the same symptoms as someone that is just being influenced, plus additional and more severe effects. One notable difference is an individual that is inhabited will often cause a wider field of human misery and destruction than just upon themselves.

Someone merely being influenced by a demon takes destructive action that primarily hurts them, with only limited pain and suffering to a small circle of people closest to them that they interact with frequently.

An individual inhabited by a demon is prodded much more incessantly to cause problems with whomever they are with, and wherever they are. The demon will purposely incite the inhabited human to have arguments and confrontations with as many family members and friends as possible. They will cause disruptions and problems at work with coworkers, bosses, and even take actions to sabotage the business.

Another common indicator is they will tell lies to hurt and destroy other people's relationships. For instance, they may tell someone in confidence that they saw their husband/wife/partner cheating on them. Of course, that lie will be refuted when the person is confronted, but the relationship damage will be done and trust may be in doubt thereafter.

A variant of that commonly seen is to seduce a friend's husband or wife, and then gloat about their unfaithfulness and spread it around as gossip with other friends and family.

On a larger scale, demons try to inhabit people of influence, from supervisors at businesses, to managers, politicians, actors, and any person who because of their position, has a greater control or influence over other people. The inhabited person then becomes a weapon to manipulate and use to make the lives of other people as miserable as possible. Their actions often create a domino effect, where something hurtful is done directly to one person, and the repercussions then negatively affect other people.

A good example would be someone being fired and blacklisted from their job, and the husband and wife then getting into arguments at home over finances, and perhaps even leading to losing their home because they can no longer make the mortgage payment.

Many of the signs of demon inhabitation can mirror symptoms of schizophrenia. One notable difference is that mental illness is normally a gradual process that evolves over many months or years, whereas someone who becomes demon inhabited will usually show the symptoms in a very short period of time. They will go from being normal to acting very abnormal, often in just a couple of weeks, or sometimes even days.

Here are some of the symptoms to look for in a person that has become demon inhabited. An inhabited person may have only one or two of these symptoms, or many of them. When they are inhabited, rather than just having an occasional bad day, the symptoms will be persistent over time.

- Crazed fears and paranoia without a true cause; fearing people or institutions are out to get them.

- Careless and frequent sexual promiscuity.

- Begin or increase using mind and mood altering drugs.

- Very critical of other people and often wanting to do harm to others in some way.

- Major changes in the way they choose to dress and/or adorn themselves, often with an "*I don't care what I look like*" attitude.

- Start neglecting regular bathing and personal hygiene and grooming.

- Hallucinations or delusions not induced by drugs.

- Loss of interest in work, relationships, and daily chores or responsibilities.

- Withdrawal from social activities

- Lack of passion or emotional response.

- Inappropriate responses such as laughing at something that is not funny or crying at something that is actually happy or funny.

- Disrespectful and rude to people that are normally given polite respect such as teachers, parents, clergy, and other leaders. This can extend into social situations such as intentionally going into a "no smoking" area while smoking a cigarette or cigar and purposefully blowing smoke in people's face.

- Unreasonable irritability or overly sensitive reactions on a very regular basis, beyond just having a bad day.

- Very frequent nervousness and/or anxiety without any real cause.

- Hyper infatuation with a person they know or just see from a distance, particularly if that person would normally be considered undesirable due to their appearance or proclivities.

- Out of character becoming overly verbose and just rambling on and on.

- Talking incessantly to themselves or to an imaginary person or something inanimate like a tree or a building; often punctuated by loud outbursts. They may also speak both parts of the conversation where they pose a question to the imaginary person and then speak aloud the answer.

- On the other end of the speaking spectrum, they may trail off their sentences without finishing the thought and be unable to go back and recall what they were talking about.

- It is also common for them to interject topics that have nothing to do with the conversation. Being demon inhabited messes up the brain, creating regular problems with speech and coherently expressing thoughts.

- Memory may slip away, even for recent events and activities.

- Drug and alcohol abuse is common and is especially notable if the person previously did not have those addictions.

Please note that every person with mental illness is not inhabited by a demon and most are not. Nor does every inhabitation by a demon cause mental illness, although most inhabited people will exhibit some signs of it.

People merely under demon influence tend to be mostly self-destructive. Of course their negative actions can also cause relationship rifts, as well as troubles at work or with friends, but those are lesser side effects of the main effects on the individual. However, with a person that is demon inhabited, instigating them to create headaches, heartaches and schisms with other people is one of the main goals of the demon.

When A Demon Inhabits A Human They Usually Seek Three Objectives:

1. Because the demon inhabiting a person can see, hear, smell, taste, and feel everything the human does, and these are sensations the demon can usually not experience, the demon revels in these physical

sensations and they will seek to have them often and more gluttonously, with particular attention to both food and sex.

2. However, they do inject some moderation into the inhabited person's thoughts because they want their physical body to last as long as possible so they can enjoy the physical pleasures for the maximum amount of time. This compares to a demon influencing a human where they simply want to lead them as quickly as possible down the most physically, mentally, and emotionally self-destructive paths.

3. A person inhabited by a demon will consciously seek to cause rifts and disruptions with other people. Through both obvious and subtle means, they will seek to hurt other individuals and groups in as wide of a circle as possible. These actions will usually take place in all aspects of their lives, from close relationships to just acquaintances, which include co-workers in work settings.

How to Help Someone Inhabited by a Demon

Driving a demon out of an inhabited human body is not an easy task. It is beyond the capabilities of someone not trained in that skill, unless it is a fairly low-level demon being expunged. Unfortunately, many of the people that might be called upon for assistance, both clergy and purported professionals in the field, often use techniques that actually do nothing to drive away the demon, and may end up being quite harmful to the inhabited person.

Whether an untrained person can drive or exorcise a

demon from an inhabited human body will depend, to a large degree, upon what level of demon they are dealing with, and there is no way that can really be known by anyone other than an expert demon hunter.

There are thirteen levels of demons. The 12th and 13th levels do not bother themselves with inhabiting - they send their minions to do their bidding. About 30% of all inhabitations are by lower level demons, Level 4 or below. About 65% are by mid-level demons in levels 5-9. The remaining 5% or less would be upper-level demons in the 10-11 range, and they will only inhabit individuals with a potential because of their position in life, to inflict a range of ills on a large number of people.

If someone is inhabited by a lower-level demon, the demon can often be driven out by a combination of actions that are extremely irritating to them. The person inhabited will most often also be irritated by the same actions, so someone close to them will need to ensure that the proper actions are taken to help them. With lower-level demons, the actions listed below can be taken in a less focused manner. However, if someone is inhabited by a mid-level or upper-level demon, professional assistance will be required.

Before You Take Any Demon Purging Action

Before actions are taken to expunge a demon that is suspected of inhabiting someone, it is wise to have them checked out by a psychiatrist (not a psychologist). Mental health issues are often signs of demons. However, sometimes they are simply mental health challenges that need to be dealt with in ordinary ways by medical professionals.

Appendix A

Besides being a mental health specialist, psychiatrists are also medical doctors. They can assess a wide range of physical, chemical, hormonal, and mental issues that could be causing the symptoms someone is exhibiting.

Psychiatrists can prescribe medications to alleviate chemical and hormonal imbalances. They can also recommend diet changes and other therapies that could completely eliminate the symptoms if they are caused by internal issues that have nothing to do with demons.

On the other hand, if the psychiatrist recommends a treatment course and it has no effect, then a demon inhabitation is the more likely cause of the troubles.

In both cases, whether someone is seeing a psychiatrist or attempting to purge the demon on their own, the following actions are very useful and effective at convincing lower-level demons to depart and find a more hospitable host.

- Remove from the home and workplace, easy access to any sources of negative media, from books to videos, to games to movies or TV shows that have any form of violence or disrespect to humans or animals.

- Replace the removed items with books, games, shows, etc., that have the opposite energy - one that is uplifting and positive.

- Only play melodious, harmonious music and play it as often as possible. No songs with lyrics unless they are positive and upbeat. Also, even with instrumental and classical music, choose selections that are uplifting and expanding and not deep and foreboding. Demons love discordant,

467

discombobulating music because it keeps the human host's aura out of balance and makes them easy to inhabit. Contrarily they hate harmonious, uplifting music, which tends to balance and expand all of the energy centers and strengthen the aura. Being forced to listen to melodious and harmonious music regularly will often be enough to drive a low-level demon out of the body.

- Very important. Purchase a Tri-field meter to measure EMF's in the home and workplace. The Triple Axis EMF meter is another very popular model. The invisible electromagnetic waves can be very disruptive to the human aura, especially the emotional and mental state. This little device will show you the sources of any electromagnetic radiation coming from electricity, radio fields, or magnetic fields. Once pinpointed, remove them from the inhabited person's area.

- If removing the source of the EMF's is not possible, you can use protective screening materials to limit the EMF's radiating out from the source. While EMF's are discombobulating and destructive to humans, they are like energetic candy to demons. By removing them, you take away some of the demon's motivation for inhabiting the human.

- Whatever the demon inhabited person's religion is, even if they are not active in it at the time, increasing the religion's presence in their home and life will be helpful. Attending church, synagogue, mosque, or other religious places of worship will greatly irritate the demon within, to the point that lower-level demons can be driven away. The technique is effective because the inhabited individual is surrounded by many people of a common faith and their combined auras emanate support for the individual and a desire for evil to not be present.

- Just as being around the auras of positive, supportive people that loathe evil is helpful, the opposite is true as well. Certain negative and unsavory people and places should be avoided as they are aurically supportive of demon influence rather than expulsive.

- If these methods do not succeed and you have been applying them diligently and frequently, then you are likely dealing with a high mid-level demon, or even an upper-level demon. In this case, you will need to seek out professional help. Lay people or clergy should be avoided unless they have a proven and verified track record of success and guarantee completely non-violent methods. The Catholic Church in some cases, and the Church of Celestine Light, are the only two religious groups I am aware of that have clergy that are specially trained to remove demons from inhabited people.

Can Everyone See Demons?

Yes and no. An individual needs a highly developed psychic sense to actually be able to see demons. This sometimes occurs with children, as they often times have more active psychic centers. A lesser psychic ability will allow people to sense, but not see the demons. Everyone has the potential to develop and increase their psychic abilities, but innately, without focused efforts at improving their psychic sense, 99% of the people in the world will not have strong enough natural psychic abilities to see demons. However, if it is something they truly desire, everyone can hone and increase their psychic abilities.

To help in that endeavor I recommend two of my books:

Unleash Your Psychic Powers is a 400+ page manual that provides exercises and background on increasing 17 of the most useful psychic abilities.

Psychic Self Defense is a detailed manual that helps you understand the techniques to use to ward off, not just demons, but all types of negative energies from the unseen world, including ghosts and psychic or magick attacks from humans.

Can Anyone's Night Self Travel to the 2nd Dimension?

Most definitely, and I assure you it will become one of your great pleasures and mind-opening experiences.

You might find my book, *Dreams* helpful as you expand your ability to have vivid, lucid dreams.

As your last conscious thought just before going to sleep, say aloud, "*I want to go to Sx in the 2nd Dimension.*" Repeat that several times aloud, and then lay your head on your pillow and go to sleep. You have just given your Night Self its travelling orders for the night and it will do as you command.

For you to truly experience and remember your Night Self travels to Sx and the 2nd Dimension, you will need to have vivid, lucid dreams. You can have vivid dreams that are extremely detailed and real without simultaneously being lucid dreams.

When you are lucid dreaming, you are in the middle of a vivid dream but you have conscious control in your dream of where you go and what you can do. When you are Night Traveling, you will not have visible or tangible form and none of the people or creatures on the worlds you visit will be able to see or hear you, but you will be able to see and hear everything and everyone, and have complete control of your environment.

In addition to mine, there are a couple of other good books to help you learn how to lucid dream that I recommend:

Dreams (by Embrosewyn Tazkuvel)

Exploring the World of Lucid Dreaming

The Art of Lucid Dreaming: Over 60 Powerful Practices to Help You Wake Up in Your Dreams

If you would like some supplemental help with achieving Lucid Dreaming, this product has been recommended as useful.

Galantamine - 6 mg - Lucid Dreaming, Nootropic, Brain Health - Vegetarian Capsules - Dye-Free

APPENDIX B

CASE STUDIES

During the time before my retirement, when I was still a physically robust, active Taz, I helped many people suffering from demon problems to be rid of their demonic tormentors.

It is strongly discouraged among the Taz to help individual people unless that person is having a negative or detrimental effect on over a hundred other people.

This is especially true in the 1st Dimension of our planet Earth where Taz are much more limited in our capabilities to banish demons because we lack our Dragon Swords and the magick we have available on 2nd Dimension worlds like Sx.

The Taz are totally empathetic with the plight of each individual and wish we could help everyone in need of our special talents. Sadly, it is simply a matter of needing to invest the limited time and energy we have available to banish demons that are affecting the largest number of people; hence we are helping the greatest number of people.

Nevertheless, over the decades of my active life as a Taz I have had many individual people contact me and ask for help, and whenever I could, I did help them. With the advent of the internet and email, it became possible to prescreen people with substantive back and forth communication to determine what exactly their problem was, and what the best course of action would be. Demons were not always the problem.

Oftentimes direct intervention was unnecessary and

situations could be rectified with written advice alone. Thanks to email, I could usually ascertain whether they were actually inhabited by a demon, merely being harassed externally by a demon, or had some other source of their problem that was not demon related, including other denizens of the unseen world such as ghosts, or a more mundane cause such as a chemical/hormonal imbalance, causing depression. Over 50% of the cases were from some cause other than demons.

If it seemed likely from their responses to my questions that a demon was involved, I would ask them for their address and the hours they would be asleep. While they slept I would travel there in my Taz body. Standing outside the home I would summon any demon present to stand before me. This is a special type of summoning only a Taz can do.

If a demon appeared, I would quickly grab him by his throat and strangle banish him. However, that is easier said than done. If the demon had been inhabiting someone, there is only one to two minutes when the summoning will hold them before they are drawn inexorably back into the person's body.

When demons suddenly appear before a Taz, they know they have been summoned to be banished and they will immediately react as quickly as possible to escape. If the Taz does manage to get ahold of the demon's throat, which isn't always successful, the demon will fight furiously to get away before the banishing takes effect.

The subsequent battle is as exhausting as any no-holds-barred physical fight and often takes the Earth body of the Taz a full day to recover afterward because it is so energetically connected to the Taz body.

Thankfully, though the Taz body may be physically injured from the encounter with a demon, the Earth body merely suffers fatigue.

However, this energy-draining effect on the Earth body is one of the reasons the Taz focus on demons that are affecting a large number of humans and not just one individual. The exhausting after-effects of the fight are the same on the Taz and the Earth body, whether it was a demon bothering just one person, or a demon whose actions were affecting many people.

I also often had more demons appear to a summoning than I expected. If the house was a fairly new house that had only had a single-family live in it since it had been built, and stood alone on a piece of property, there would almost always be just a single demon inhabitation, if there was one at all.

However, in many locations, townhomes and row houses share common walls with the residence on either side of them. Apartment houses have that type of proximity even more so. If a Taz arrives outside of a residence and summons a demon, more than one may appear, as they are pulled from multiple adjacent residences.

I have gone to old row houses in Philadelphia, Pennsylvania, and even older tenements in Edinburgh, Scotland, where as many as a half dozen demons appeared when I was only trying to summon one. When two or more demons appear in the 1st Dimension, it is simply not possible for a single Taz to banish any of them. While we are trying to strangle banish one, the others would be slashing, gouging and pounding the Taz to a pulp.

With that background understanding of why Taz cannot come to the rescue of every individual inflicted by demons, I would like to present some snippets of seven cases, including the initial communications sent to me by people who have contacted me for help with supernatural problems, along with a very brief summary of the case.

These are only a small representation of the numerous requests for aid and support I have received over the years. Of course until now, none of the general public has known that I am a Taz. Most of the pleas for help came as a result of people contacting me after reading my book Psychic Self Defense and often involved issues with ghosts, black magick, or psychic attacks. Upon investigation, many of those actually did have demons as their root cause.

I chose examples in this small selection of Case Studies that will give you a good feel for the diversity of quandaries that people sometimes find themselves in. Some had true demon problems, while others had different sources from the unseen world that were plaguing them. And some just had an inner demon of their own creation or actions.

These were often lengthy communications back and forth. The full communication and details of the actions taken to alleviate the problems will require its own book. As *Demon Hunter* is already a large tome, I am just going to present a small portion of the Case Study, including the initial contact and a brief summary of the actions taken to conclude the case, so you can get an idea of the range of situations that can be encountered.

If enough people express an interest in knowing more, I will be happy to publish a dedicated follow-up book that contains many full-length case studies including the full correspondence and details of the actions taken to alleviate the demons or other supernatural problems.

Case Study #1

My first correspondence with this gentleman was in 2016. He expressed a most unusual quandary. He said he was an upper-level demon trapped in a human body and limited by human capabilities. He asked for my help restoring his full demon persona and abilities. This was a lengthy correspondence as I worked through helping him. I'm just including parts of his first emails introducing himself and his predicament, along with some of my comments to him and a summary of the conclusion of this case.

INQUIRER:

"I'm unsure of the current means as I am rather disconnected from my um well soul is the best word. My real name is Abraxas, and I need help freeing my human limits.

"I came to you out of desperation for hardly anyone has ever even heard of my name and what I was in the past... I have reached a dead end, I can feel what I am able to do but I am bound and sealed to this crippled humanly state.

"I want to be freed from his body. Yet a god mightier than I, scattered me power into three hundred and sixty five human proxies for lack of a better word. I hope you have a means to break the binds placed by the arch angels Gabriel, and St Michal.

"The need is dire, please I need help."

EMBROSEWYN'S 1ST REPLY:

"I might be able to help you depending upon who you think you are. I am familiar with the demon Abraxas, known in more ancient times as Abrasas. There are also non-demons, both human and non-human, who have adopted this name over the millennia, some of them doing very noble acts. Tell me a little about yourself and your circumstances and why you have come to me for help rather than look for it elsewhere. As you do not claim a soul and already know your name, you must be seeking some other kind of assistance from me. If you are suffering, and helping you will not hurt any others, or you, I will consider being of assistance."

I asked the gentleman to send me a picture so I could tune into his aura. This always helps me to know something about the state of the individual, but usually is not sufficient to determine if they are inhabited by a demon because the distance separating us is too far.

However, in this case, his picture allowed a strong auric connection and I was actually surprised to see that he was inhabited (possessed) by the demon Abraxas, but it was not a normal inhabitation. Because Abraxas was such a high-level demon, he did not need to fully inhabit the gentleman's body to have a pervading influence upon it. This is something only upper-level demons are capable of achieving. They rarely inhabit humans, unless they are influential people like politicians, religious leaders or celebrities. Even in those cases, they only send a small part of their auric energy for the inhabitation, a skill that has only been mastered by just a few Level 11's, but more commonly with Level 12 and Level 13 demons.

In this situation the demon's auric energy had been with the man for so many years that the gentleman thought he was the demon Abraxas. My first task was to get him to see the reality that he could not personally be the demon Abraxas.

EMBROSEWYN'S 2ND REPLY

"Think of a society of invisible beings dwelling among us. We are visible to them, but they are usually unseen to us. That is the world of demons. They can be in our world, but also reside in an adjacent dimension. It is that dimension that is most interesting. For in their dimension they have a complete society of their kind, including institutions of higher learning. Some demons are very smart, not just because they have millennia of experience, but also because many of them have been going to school for a very long time.

"Because of their knowledge, demons can be very helpful. Some of them, working to someday legitimately have a physical body again, are benign and useful. They can answer a lot of otherwise unanswerable questions. Unfortunately, Abraxas is not one of those.

"Most demons are like Abraxas. They are truculent and out to hurt, not help those who have physical bodies and lives. Because they cannot have a body of their own, they are thrilled to possess someone like you who does. Even more thrilled if they can make you abuse your body, or use your body to hurt other people's bodies. You are like a puppet on a string to them.

"Now for the solution to your problem: First, you need to clearly understand why you are NOT the demon Abraxas, but are merely possessed by his energy. Abraxas is ancient and powerful. While he can keep you as a puppet for his amusement and pleasure simply by connecting a tiny bit of his energy to your auric field, it would be impossible for any human body to contain, let alone retain, the complete energy of Abraxas. That would be equivalent to saying a squirrel could contain the mental and emotional level of a human.

"Nor is there any spell, curse, or means that Abraxas could be, or would allow himself to be, confined inside a human body and unable to exercise his full demonic powers.

"However, as some of his energy does reside in you, of course you sense that you have many powers that you cannot manifest. You are sensing some of Abraxas' abilities, but your human body has no capability of doing them. It never will. Your frustration can only build and never be solved as long as the energy of Abraxas remains with you."

Case Conclusion:

I offered the gentleman an easy solution to his predicament by enchanting a piece of jewelry as simple as a plain silver ring. The enchantment would force out and keep out Abraxas or any other demon. It would be life-changing.

However, after making the offer to solve his problem I never heard back from him. I've seen this type of reaction many times with some people that are inhabited by a demon. Barring this case, which involved an influential person, it almost always is with a person that is unnoticeable in life. Other than their closest family, nobody knows who they are. Many times even their close family members barely interact with them, if at all. They will very likely live and die in complete obscurity, unknown and unremembered. Though their life is unfulfilling and miserable because of the demon inhabitation, they would rather stay as they are because in a warped way of thinking it makes them special.

However, the typical scenario of an obscure person not wanting to give up their demon inhabitation because it made them special was not the case with this unnamed gentleman. He actually was inhabited by a portion of Abraxas' energy, which meant Abraxas had to have some larger more nefarious purpose than a simple inhabitation.

I subsequently presented this case to my brother and sister Taz and much effort over many years was needed by all of us to dismantle the sinister tendrils of the plan of human misery Abraxas had initiated, of which the poor gentleman that contacted me was just a tiny part of. However, from the Taz perspective, his part was a key, as it alerted us to something quite foul that was in motion. Certainly the plan of Abraxas and the actions we took against him would be worthy of recounting in full in a book all its own.

Case Study #2

This was another case that began with a lengthy correspondence, as this lady had multiple issues originating from different sources. Some of her problems were demonic, but she was also enduring psychic and magickal attacks.

INQUIRER:

"I am 33 years old and am a ballet teacher and have always been into yoga and occults. I read your book on Auras in my Kindle and then decided to try your Psychic Defense book, which I found truly superb. In the last week, I read more than 6 books on this subject but yours was the best so far. Then I downloaded all your books for kindle and now I am reading the rest.

"The reason why I wanted to contact you is because I had a very "unique" experience that some people categorize as a psychic attack. I am trying not to draw conclusions, and to be honest I could only find one other reference in a book to a similar case as mine. With the difference being that person was found dead, while (if this is truly an attack) I seem to be very resilient to evil.

"There are some people on the internet who have had similar experiences but these are very few, with almost no explanations to them. Very few websites state clearly that these occur by demons. Why and how, eludes them though. Your book alerted me very much. I knew some of the things you described, I suspected others, but there were several things I did not know or had not ordered that way in my mind.

"A couple of weeks ago while I was wide awake and aware, in the presence of other people with whom I was talking, I suddenly started to feel some sensations at my back and neck. At first I thought they were mosquitoes, then I thought maybe I was bit by spiders, and my third idea was I must be having an allergic reaction to some plant. It was burning but I had to go on with the lesson and no time to check it out.

"After an hour, I returned home and looked in the mirror. I was quite shocked by what I saw. I took timed pictures with my camera and there were many scratches on my back, going to the neck, and even to the lower part of the face. They were burning and sore. The pain was gone only after I did a fire ceremony (havan) after 2 days.

"On the day of the attack I was not feeling well. I skipped my spiritual exercises (mantra, anusthan and stotram chants that I had been doing for 3 weeks) and saw some nightmares as well.

"So I am trying to figure out what that was, why it came, what it wants, whether it was sent by another person and if it was an isolated event. I also worry for my students and other people around me that may be in danger. If you have any suggestions or information on paranormal scratches I'd be very grateful."

Embrosewyn's Reply 1: *(reply after reviewing pictures she sent showing the scratches on her back and neck)*

"Your scratches are most peculiar indeed. I will give you my best insight and recommendations based on your pictures, description, and requests. First, regardless of what is causing the problem, if it is psychic in nature or a threat from any type of unseen being, neither your students nor anyone else nearby should notice any effect whatsoever. There is no danger to them.

"If this is any type of attack from an unseen source, it would be targeting you. Each person's aura is different and for attacks to be successful on a scale as tangible as yours, the attacker would need to know the nuances of your aura very well. In other words, it would need to be a physical person that personally knows you, or an unseen being that frequents your presence often enough to be very familiar with your aura.

"Second, I'm glad you considered normal possibilities such as bug bites and allergies. As those were discounted, please look deeper at the other possibilities and try to isolate the most likely source. Do you have people that are upset with you and are also into the occult? They would need to be pretty knowledgeable to leave physical scratches on your body, but that is a possibility. If not a person, have you been involved in any occult practices, even something as simple as using a Ouija Board that might have opened a door to unseen entities that are staying with you like a shadow and causing this and maybe other disruptions?

"Before I get into specific countermeasures, please give me your thoughts on the questions I have posed. If we can more exactly zero in on the likely source, we can more effectively create a countermeasure."

INQUIRY 2:

"I am very glad to read that people around me would not be affected if it was anything dark.

"Yes, there is a person who is into the occult, who had been tutoring me for a while into very intensive, complex, long, tantric rituals. One day he asked me to do something which was against my idea of karma and involved controlling another person's will. I refused, he got angry, really angry, really abusive and I told him goodbye. Our ways parted last November.

"Recently he had contacted me and apologized to me. For some reason, which I cannot fathom, he was trying to get in touch with me again, but I was keeping some distance from him. On the day that these marks appeared, he had sent me some messages to which I did not reply. Mainly because I felt too tired and distressed to reply. When I left him, he did threaten me. I kicked him out of my Facebook group, which is quite popular and he had gotten really angry. I know he is capable of such things.

"But the truth is that this is only a suspicion, I have no way of really knowing if it is him and I don't like to accuse people without proof. In any case, I blocked all his emails and even deleted all our common friends on Facebook (some of which he was using to get to me). I also got rid of all the ritual items he had sent me. Yantras, malas etc. just to be on the safe side.

"When this happened I was in the middle of a spiritual discipline I was doing for 3 weeks. I had started that discipline because I really felt like my life had reached a very low point. This included daily chanting of Hanuman Chalisa, my own guru mantra, gayatri mantra and maha mrityunjaya mantra. These practices lightened the atmosphere and alleviated a lot of my health issues. I also started to feel happiness again during these chantings. I did some powerful fire rituals after the marks appeared but I have not resumed my spiritual practices. Though I actually should, because my guru mantra would connect me to my normal gurus, who are beyond doubt, souls of the light.

"These tantric rituals were my most recent and

probably the most dangerous practices I have ever done. When I told my yoga acharya about them, and the incident with that person, she told me that "I was rescued before anything too bad happened to me." But many years ago, I was practicing out of body states, mainly because they were happening spontaneously since I was 15 years old. And of course I have been into tarot very intensely, into Indian Astrology (jyotish) very intensely and have tried several things through the years. Some of the people I dated also seemed to have occult powers, more than mine. The possibilities are really many :)).

"The truth is that I have become very suspicious and very jumpy since this happened. I am always alert, and noticing any changes in how my body feels. But nothing else has happened since then. I go almost daily swimming in the sea, diving many times :). I play the piano (for some reason I think this also helps)."

Embrosewyn's Reply & Case Conclusion: "Though we could delve deeper to find the cause, I think a more expedient course to ensure the problem does not return regardless of the source, would be to simply enchant a piece of jewelry that you always wear to protect against curses, and a second piece of jewelry which you always wear to protect from the attacks or attempts at attachment by unseen entities from lowly blobs to demons. Based upon your description and the pictures of your scratches, I recommend enchanting 18 Kt gold jewelry, without any stones. This will hold the most powerful enchantment for your defense."

Case Study #3

This was one of the easier cases to solve as the lady simply needed to send a piece of jewelry that she regularly wore to be enchanted for the specific purposes she needed.

INQUIRER:

"Hello Embrosewyn, I would like to have an enchantment made for me. I have been tortured and tormented by an ex-lover with black magic and even though I have sought help, it has been to little avail.

"I work in sales and my business has suffered terribly, I have been unable to meet any men who find me attractive. In fact, it appears that I am invisible to men. People who I believed were friends have left me and a string of other things.

"I saw on the website that you make enchantments and I would like to have one made for me that will allow me to have my life back. In essence, I am asking for a new beginning in my finances, in my love life, for protection and a new job. Can it be done? Thank you kindly."

Case Study #4

This young man had multiple issues. He didn't really know the source of the problem, but knew he needed help. Upon further investigation, his biggest problem was that he was inhabited by a demon. I went outside his house one night as a Taz, summoned the demon, and strangle banished him. That was very helpful, but was not the end of this young man's challenges as the demon inhabitation had brought in other dark energies that had caused additional problems and still needed to be addressed, even after the demon was gone.

It should be noted here that all of his problems arose because he was dabbling in magick. It is very easy to innocently be led down a dark path when magick is involved. Great care should be exercised by anyone seeking to learn magick, to be absolutely sure the sources you are reading, or the people you are looking to as teachers, are sharing a path of white magick. Otherwise, the door is quickly opened with an invitation for demon inhabitation and a cascade of life-debilitating problems. The following is just a little snippet of this truly fascinating case.

INQUIRER:

"About 6 months ago I was taking a magick course with some advanced magicians. I didn't realize they were dark. They described themselves as grey and they were teaching the magick described in the Tarot so I assumed it lined up with the Golden Dawn tradition in some way.

"I remember channeling this grayish green energy in my room one night, which started talking to me and told me it was a tree spirit of the tree outside my window.

"I was put through a ritual where they had "God" in my room…and told me I had to kill God. I refused but eventually I was forced to kill him through this scenario playing in my head. None of it was my choice. There was like two weeks of this, which they kept me up through the whole time and I didn't get any sleep.

"They kept telling me that I had to be dark and there was no choice, then began shoving the abyss in my body and filling me with darkness…they wanted to fill me up with the power of Lucifer…I could feel them changing things in my brain...I started hearing voices...demons would conjure themselves around me...they began attacking my mind and my thoughts, wiping my mind and my memories. Each time would get deeper and deeper into my psyche and my soul. I was put through mental torture.

"They put this alien thing over my head and it slaughtered my inner child and I could hear it screaming and dying...it reduced me to nothing and I had no thoughts at all.

"They make me vomit at their will and it's terrifying.

"They caused me to have a seizure, which was the worst thing I have ever experienced. I felt trapped in hell for eternity with no way out.

"They have taken away almost all of my memories. I feel empty inside, my mind is empty as I have no thoughts. I just barely know how to function.

"Help me. I don't know what I am dealing with or how to get rid of it."

Case Conclusion: This is still an ongoing case, but I have done as much as I can do. The demon that was the root of the young man's problems has been banished. But some of the ramifications of the inhabitation continue to manifest and will still need to be remedied by follow-up actions. As he still had lingering effects from the demon inhabitation I referred him to a Celestine Light Priestess. She is a healer that works specifically with energy and is very familiar with paranormal sources of problems.

My additional recommendations to wind down his continuing problems included a special herbal tea mixture to help ground and balance him, and to start taking SAM-e regularly to help his moods and brain chemistry balance. Of course to first check with his doctor to ensure it didn't clash with any prescribed drugs he might already be taking.

SAM-e is a prescription drug in Europe, but can be purchased without a prescription in the US in most natural food stores. It works very quickly for a myriad of problems for most people, but the effects are cumulative and increase over time of use.

Beyond getting rid of the demonic source of his problems, recommending the herbal tea, SAM-e, and referring him to a Celestine Light Priestess, this case was closed for me.

Case Study #5

This was an incident where the woman felt she was being negatively affected by a curse. After hearing her description of the symptoms, it sounded highly possible that a magickal curse could be the source. The easiest way to solve her problem was to enchant a piece of jewelry she always wore to counter the curse. She sent me a necklace, which was duly enchanted, and her problem was immediately alleviated once she donned the necklace. I am including part of my response to her as well as her initial inquiry as it explains how a counter curse works.

INQUIRER:

"Please respond. I am suffering from a woman who has placed a curse on me and continues it every time I see her. It results in blinding head pain, inability to speak etc. Can you please help me? Thank you."

EMBROSEWYN'S RESPONSE:

"I am glad you contacted me. First, I assume you have checked to make sure that the affects you are experiencing are not from a medical/health problem. If they are not, then they very well could be from the source you wrote about.

"I can help you and the beneficial effect should be almost immediate as long as the cause is the curse you suspect. This is a situation where a reverse reflection enchantment works very effectively. A piece of jewelry you wear, a ring or a pendant, will be enchanted and you will need to wear it 24/7 until the curse no longer has any power over you. It usually takes about two weeks for the last vestiges of the curse to be removed and neutralized.

"A few points to be aware of: This only works if the cause of your symptoms is truly a curse from any person. The enchantment will cause the curse to no longer effect you. Instead, it will reflect back and affect the curser with the same malady they afflicted on you and often worse!

"However, if the person you assumed cursed you, in fact did not, then nothing will happen to them. If some unknown person cursed you, the enchantment will work just as well on them or any other person and your symptoms will also vanish."

Case Study #6

When this woman contacted me it was obvious she was in a desperate situation. She gave me her address and I went as a Taz the first night after receiving her email to check out the area where she lived. It was a row house back in the eastern United States dating from the early 1900's. This presented several likely sources of her problems.

Whenever there is an older home that has had multiple families and multiple generations living in it, there will always be lingering negative energies. Ghosts are also fairly common if one or more people had died in the home or on the property.

The preponderance of negative energies makes a very hospitable environment for many unsavory denizens of the unseen world, including demons. This problem is exacerbated in old town-homes or tenements where many people live very close to each other; often-times with common walls on all four sides and above and below with other residences.

All those people, in all those tiny residences, had many personal, relationship, employment, and financial strains. Subsequent arguments, fights, and despair, as well as death from disease and old age and the pain and sorrow of the surviving family left behind negative energy imbued in the very walls, floors and ceilings, and even the lingering stagnant air of age, for future residents to encounter.

INQUIRER:

"I hope you can help me. My life has been destroyed in just 6 months and I am in a fog to how it happened. I went from being healthy, happily married with a good job and many friends and having just bought my first house, to being divorced, unemployed, no friends, sick with illnesses that the doctors can't explain, and had to sell almost all my possessions to pay my bills and keep my house. I am so depressed now I stay in bed for most of the day and am having suicidal thoughts because I have lost everything and see no way back to the life I had."

EMBROSEWYN:

Unsurprisingly, I discovered a large number of negative energies and entities. The negative influence was pervasive and emanated from her house, plus all the surrounding ones. It was particularly strong at her home. In older homes, that is usually a sign that multiple deaths occurred there that were not peaceful transitions to the next life.

Due to the negative energy imbued in the numerous adjacent row houses over decades, it would take a major energy and entity cleansing in coordination with all of her neighbors getting rid of the omnipresent bad energy as well. As that was an unlikely scenario, her best course of action would have been to move out of her house. As drastic of a remedy as it was, I recommended that course of action. However, she was unwilling to do it as it was the first home she had purchased and was really all she had remaining in her life. She had already sold most of her possessions to keep paying the mortgage.

As she was unwilling to move out, I took a rare action by asking permission to enter her home in my Taz body at night so I could more closely investigate the sources of negative energy. She agreed and this allowed me to discover exactly what supernatural problems dwelt in her house and figure out what I could do to help her, as well as recommend remedial actions she could take while still remaining in her home.

Surprisingly she was not inhabited by a demon. She did have an angry ghost in her home and was being overwhelmed by a huge amount of lingering negative energy emanating from her house and the surrounding row houses caused by all the negative incidents that had happened there in earlier years with prior residents.

Case Conclusion: Many ghosts are like dogs that just do not want to give up a bone, or a person that forces themselves to stay angry long after the other parties that might have been involved have dismissed the issue and moved on. Although my special talents are focused on dealing with demons, I can also see ghosts and communicate with them telepathically.

In this case, the name of the ghost was Robert and he had grown up in that home. His mother had died while he was young. When his father was in his 60's he became terminally ill. Robert was already planning on inheriting the house with his brother. However, Robert actually ended up dying suddenly before his father. Robert insists his brother poisoned him so he could have the house all to himself. His brother did inherit the house and he quickly sold it and moved away. Robert couldn't get revenge on his brother, but he insisted the house was rightfully his and he was intent upon driving anyone else that lived there away, or at least making them miserable in the house.

The correct way to deal with ghosts is to convince them one way or the other to move on to the next life. However, that is often easier said than done. Once a person dies and reverts to a soul spirit form, they become extremely aware of the next steps in their eternal life. Many ghosts linger as spirits on Earth because they suspect that if they allow themselves to depart, that due to the unrighteous life they had led, the eternity that awaits them is less than desirable. At least that is their perception of a bleak future they imagine for themselves. Likely, it is not as bad of a future as they imagine, but fear of the unknown makes them cling to a nebulous existence in a world that is no longer theirs.

I was unsuccessful in convincing Robert to depart the premises and the planet, so I had to do the next best thing and turn the tables on him. He and other negative energies in the home had been sources of despondency for the living resident. To counter the negative entities and energies in her home I suggested to her that she install tube skylights in every room there was a straight access to the roof, keep the blinds or drapes open all during the day and the rooms she was in, well illuminated with white light (not typical yellow) during the night. I further suggested she only play uplifting music and only watch similar shows at home with no crime dramas or personal heartache or tragedy dramas.

She followed through with my suggestions and later communicated that the effects had been beneficial in all aspects of her life.

Case Study #7

This young woman was 21, happily married, and about ready to graduate from college when she started having bizarre, vivid dreams that disturbed her so greatly that she dropped out of school, left her husband, and moved back in with her parents. For 3 months before she communicated with me as she continued to have the dreams every night while staying at her parent's house, separated from her husband who still visited her on weekends, but had remained at the university to complete his studies.

She gave me the address where her parent's home was located. When I visited that night with my Taz body I was very surprised to see her "family" was a whole group of 29 demons living on her parent's property. The interesting solution to her problem involved several necessary and in some ways peculiar solutions, but that lengthy explanation and a much more complete explanation of this young woman's challenges will need to wait until the next book.

INQUIRER:

"I hope you can help me. About 6 months ago I had a dream that seemed like it was really happening. I never had a dream like that before. In my dream a middle aged man that introduced himself as Guido came and asked me where I had been. He said I was part of his family and they had been looking for me for a long time. I told him he must be mistaken as I had never met him and had a mother, father, siblings and husband that were my family.

"He told me I needed to come with him to meet our other family members and then I would remember. Over the next several nights Guido came every night into my dreams and each night would introduce me to other members of the "family," Robert, Gladys, Sophia, Myrtle, Yves, Hardy and several others. Those were the ones I saw most often.

"Over the next two weeks one or more of the "family" were in my dreams every night. They just did normal life things. Nothing bad or good just normal, other than they were highly and overtly sexual. That part was shocking to me as that is something I have never been exposed to in my family or among my friends. They never stopped telling me I needed to remember I was part of their "family," not part of the family I thought I had.

"I should tell you I have a real family that is very special. We all love and support each other. I love my husband and he loves me. I don't have any kind of problems with any of my mom or dad or brothers or sister and am not looking consciously or unconsciously to replace them.

"By the third week the members of the "family" started getting more and more angry that I couldn't remember them. They started yelling and screaming at me all the time and then physically hurting me in my dreams because I wouldn't do sexual acts with them. It got to the point I was afraid to go to sleep. I had to drop all my classes because I was so fatigued from lack of sleep. I also moved back in with my parents because I was keeping my husband awake all night, either because I was not sleeping or I would wake up screaming from the torture the "family" was putting me through in my dreams.

"Since I moved back to my parents the "family" in my dreams has grown and now includes over a dozen people. I know all their names and personalities. Some are nicer to me than others, but all are mean.

"I went to see a psychiatrist when I got back to my parents and he gave me medication, but it has done nothing to stop the dreams or let me have a good night's rest. Can you help? I want these repeating nightmares to just go away and be able to sleep and return to my husband."

Case Conclusion:

I communicated with this young lady quite a bit and gave her multiple remedies for her situation including a tea formula that would help her sleep through the night without nightmares. Interestingly, the tea worked so well that her nightmares disappeared. But not to be thwarted, she started having vivid daymares, where she would go into an involuntary trance-like state and the people from her dream family started appearing in trance visions during the day.

I finally asked for her address and went to visit her home at night with my Taz body. I summoned any demon present in or around the home and was shocked to see over two dozen appear in front of me, and they were not too happy about it! They immediately knew I was a Taz, but they were unafraid because they quite outnumbered me.

Seeing that many demons also let me know why the young woman had never been inhabited, as that would have let one demon monopolize her torment and their personal pleasure, which would never have been agreeable to all of the others.

We had a wary, but good conversation and I got to meet all the members of the young woman's demon dream family that she had mentioned. They freely admitted to tormenting her for their own pleasure and fun.

I asked why there were so many of them congregated in that place and they pointed out a nearby negative energy vortex emanating out of the ground, which they said was continually invigorating to them. They considered that place their home and added that they had been residing there for over 3,000 years and felt justified in tormenting any Izbo interlopers.

I asked why they were picking upon that particular young woman. They replied that they tormented other Izbos in the neighborhood, but she had always been the one that reacted the most severely. Driving Izbos crazy was one of their favorite pastimes, and this young woman gave them the greatest entertainment of all the Izbos they bothered.

The demoness Sophia volunteered that they had been having fun causing the young woman distress for years. They missed her when she went away to college as none of the other Izbos in the neighborhood were as responsive to their torments. That was why they started with intense intrusions while she lived near the campus, hoping to drive her back home, and their plan had succeeded wonderfully she declared.

They were all quite enthusiastic about their success of tormenting the young woman and had no reservations about sharing the details of their actions with me because they did not fear me as a lone Taz. It was actually a blessing for the moment, as it allowed me to get straight answers from them, which would not have been possible under my normal adversarial relationship with demons.

Gladys also wanted to point out that they were not just hurting her, but they were also helping her. She said the young woman had grown up in a strict home where sex was not discussed and she was very underdeveloped in her awareness of pleasure and was frankly a "prude." They were just trying to open her mind to greater possibilities she explained.

I had to laugh at that as demons cannot feel anything pleasurable from food to sex, even though they like to go through the motions and pretend that they do.

I ended up making a deal with the demons. I promised they could remain there and that neither myself nor any other Taz, would come back and strangle banish them one-by-one, if they in turn, promised to leave the young woman completely alone, as well as the rest of her family and everyone else in the neighborhood. I said jokingly that the home values would all plummet if it was discovered that a mini horde of demons was also living in the neighborhood.

All the demons agreed and sealed their word by swearing it would be so, on the name of *Lord Lucifer*.

I sealed my end of the bargain, by promising to keep my word as they kept theirs and said, "so it will be in the name of Elohim, the god of all, to whom even Lucifer bows and submits." I couldn't resist that last little bit to remind the demons of the reality of the bigger picture.

I have checked back four times in the last years and so far the demons have abided by the terms of our deal as far as I can ascertain. 99% of the time demons are very untrustworthy. However, when they swear on Lucifer's name they tend to keep their agreement meticulously, so there still is a tiny bit of honor, even in them.

Demons, ghosts, aliens, and many different sources of negative energy manifest here in the 1st Dimension of our beautiful planet Earth. Regardless of their source, and often even if they do not have evil intent, they are extremely disruptive to people they come in contact with because their energy is so different and disharmonious.

I look forward to sharing more about this fascinating invisible world that surrounds us in the near future. Until then, please do not be afraid of the invisible world. With the exception of demon inhabitation, you can have far more power over the residents of that world than they can over you.

DEMON HUNTER GLOSSARY

Akara: A race of human-like beings on Sx that live both above and below ground. They are short, stocky and all the men have full beards. They are most noted for their skill at mining and their love for fighting, especially with demons. The nearest equivalent in Earth mythology would be a gnome.

Aurora: A Taz from the Sedona, Arizona area. *"She was slim and of average height, with a very pleasant color of flaming red hair that fell in undulating waves down to the middle of her back. I estimated her age at the time I met her to be around late forties."*

Auvis Flower: A native plant of the planet Sx in the 2nd Dimension. *"The ability of that flower, which is called Auvis by the way, is to induce deep sleep, and is accomplished through a magickal energy it exudes. It has nothing to do with its scent, or its pollen, or touching it, which are all ways noxious plants and flowers might affect you on the 1st Dimension."*

Banish: The primary threat of a Taz to demons is their ability to banish the demon to Oblivion for centuries. Oblivion is an empty spot in the 4th Dimension where the demon will be in utter cold and complete darkness, all alone until the energy of banishment dissipates and they can return to one of the other dimensions through a Nexus.

Baradon: The title of a leader of a Davos Clan. *"Qadir* introduced the davos that invited us as Oshlin, Baradon of the local clan of Hiratol Davos, and advised him that we couldn't stay long as we had pressing business to take care of. By the respectful way Qadir introduced Oshlin, I assumed that a Baradon was some type of head honcho like a mayor or chief."

Barasel: Qadir's Taz mentor. "*Just as I am sharing this knowledge with you, it was shared with me by my Taz mentor, whose name was Barasel. He learned it from his mentor, who learned it from his mentor, and so on back countless generations.*"

Barbaton: A magickal word. "*I started to reply to that cryptic comment but before the words came out of my mouth she waved her hand in front of her and said in a commanding tone, Barbaton. Immediately I awoke wide-eyed and awestruck in my bed and I knew my life would never be the same.*"

Belonzia: A Purgatory Demon and the former wife of Calanstio when they were in physical bodies. (See Calanstio for more info.)

Basilisk: A magickal creature. Though often described in books and movies as a serpent, a Basilisk is actually more like a lizard in appearance. "*The trick is to understand this is a two-part action. As we covered in yesterday's class on transmogrification, you must first spell yourself to have the appearance of a weasel, at least in the mind of the basilisk, as that is the only creature that a basilisk fears.*"

Bilsobe: The name of a leialli foal that I nick-named Little Toot that defended from demons. "*When I knelt down and embraced the young one he surprised me with* *the melodious little musical sound coming out of his horn. I had no idea yet what his real name was but hearing his musical exclamation I couldn't help but affectionately give him a nickname.* **I'll miss you most of all Little Toot, but I'll see you again before the passage of another day.** *In response I heard him in my mind say his name and express his affection,* **Bilsobe, I love you!"**

Calanstio: A Purgatory Demon and former husband of Belonzia when they were in physical bodies. *"He looked keenly at two of the demons sitting next to each other in the center of the group. One was a pleasant-looking man and the other a nice-looking woman. They looked like people it would be easy to have as friends and not demon-like in any way by their appearance."*

"Our inability to grow our demon powers individually is why we lost the capabilities of Metastasis Demons and now must manifest as weak Purgatory Demons, barely able to be demons at all."

Caz Ookata: Magickal words. *"**Caz Ookata**, she said in a commanding voice. This time the nails binding me to the floor ripped out of the wood and flew across the room embedding themselves in the far wall."*

Circle of Protection: A circle formed by Taz or other magickal Adepts to coalesce magick. *"Now we are all within the Circle of Protection, so nothing undesired, material or immaterial, not even words or thoughts, can pass in or out of the circle until we have disbanded it. Only magickal energy that we call and coalesce can enter or leave the circle, so we shall proceed."*

Cobalis: A planet in the 2nd Dimension. *"...walking*

amidst the thousands of vividly colored butterflies in the beautiful forests of Cobalis."

Corsalain: Qadir's home on the planet Sx in the 2nd Dimension. Qadir held out his arm. *"Hold on to my forearm. I will take you to Corsalain so you can begin real training instead of merely discovering your skills by accident while you are jumping out of the fires."*

Crystal Ball: A magickal tool. *"Any upper-level demon has the ability to see and hear anything happening in this dimension that they tune into, as long as they are not magickally blocked. We use an enchanted crystal gazing ball for this purpose."*

Dampening Spell: A magickal spell. *"We also did a Dampening Spell followed by a Circle of Protection Spell. As I'm sure you noticed you were unable to hear the words or see us clearly while we did the spells. Until we have resolved your demon problem we wanted to ensure that a demon could not hear through your ears, or see through your eyes."*

Davos: A human-like being on Sx. They are very beautiful people, usually slight of build. Males are seldom over five feet tall and females rarely over four feet. Their ears come up to points and they were probably the archetype for the Earth myths of elves.

Davos of Dosparage: *"I had never heard of a Jozrym. 'Sorry for my ignorance,' I apologized. 'I don't know what that is.' … 'It is a marvelous device for capturing and storing ambient energy and then time releasing it as light that the Davos of Dosparage invented on Sx for the Gnomes to use in their underground mines."*

Demon Hunter Glossary

Davos of Lartham: *"In the mountain forests of Lartharn dwells a clan of davos known appropriately as the Dragon Clan. They are very famous makers of hand combat weapons. Indisputably, the finest weapons in the in the 2nd and 3rd dimensions are made by the Davos of Lartharn."*

Demon: In the book demons are called by their Earth name. Their actual name on Sx is **Zilkulls**. However, as all of the Taz in Demon Hunter were from Earth we preferred calling them by the name we were familiar with – demons.

Demon Barzas: A demon encountered by me and Genavieve. *"Abruptly, a tall thin demon with an Amish-type black beard held up his hand and yelled out "stop" in a loud voice. He cocked his head slightly and looked at us through snarled lips.*

"You are not psychics, you are Taz. Why are you here? You have no power over us in these numbers in the 1st Dimension. One on one we avoid you, but now we will just ignore you."

Demon Jobar: One of the leaders of the St. Augustine, Florida demons. *"A stocky, swarthy demon with long hair and a bushy beard, dressed like a pirate, including a patch over one eye, stopped us…"*

Demon with Pink Mohawk: *"One head with a pink Mohawk haircut rolled right up to the door I was secreted behind. Looking down at the head with its closed eyes I couldn't tell if it was a demon or demoness."*

Demon, with Spiral Horns: *"The last victor was actually the demon with two spiral horns coming out of his head, only now he just had one and a half. The horns slanted* back at a steep angle from their roots near his forehead and protruded a little past his head in the back."

Demon Yipbid: A demon from St. Augustine, Florida. *"This demon bumped into my back in St. Augustine and discovered I was not just a psychic Izbo without substance."*

Demon Shield: A magickal amulet that creates a protective skin covering over the entire body. *"How come you were not injured by the demon raking its claws against you? I wondered somewhat mystified."*

"Demon shield," Genavieve answered simply. *"Like most of the magick we can use in the 1st Dimension it requires an enchanted amulet made by Nkosi, but it is an absolute essential if you are going to banish demons in this dimension and not get ripped to shreds by their claws in the process. Unfortunately, when they punch you it still hurts. The shield is right against your skin. It's useful to prevent claw rakes, but it does little to limit the impact from a blow of a fist."*

Devotion Spell: A magickal spell. *"...if demons knew your Soul Name they would be able to counter my spell and put a trace on your Soul Essence. I will teach you how to nullify those types of spells and to protect your family with a Devotion Spell..."*

Discovery Stone: An enchanted item to reveal memories like a video recording of the event. *"This is a Discovery Stone. It has been enchanted to create a three-dimensional holographic projection of your memories. Whatever you saw through your eyes and heard through your ears we will be able to observe as if we were present. Once the Discovery Stone has merged with you we will use its* *coalescing words to activate its magick that the truth may be revealed."*

Dorsavel: *"The first leialli I hugged was a large, vivid red and blue streaked male that Little Toot had gone to stand next to. His name was Dorsavel."*

Dragon: In the book dragons are called by their Earth name. Their actual name on Sx is **Zargarz**. However, as all of the Taz in Demon Hunter were from Earth we preferred calling them by the name we were familiar with – dragons.

Dragon Clan: *"In the mountain forests of Lartharn dwells a clan of davos known appropriately as the Dragon Clan. They are very famous makers of hand combat weapons. Indisputably, the finest weapons in the 2nd and 3rd dimensions are made by the Davos of Lartharn."*

Dragon Sword: An enchanted sword made from the inner scales of dragons, just for Taz, through the magickal collaboration of the Adepts from all clans of inhabitants.

Esjar: A leialli stallion. *"Dorsavel looked at me. 'Some say they will try. But only one until you prove they will return.' ... 'Yes!' I exclaimed in joy. 'Who will come?' A muscular golden leialli with streaks of white stepped forward. I remembered his name was Esjar."*

Farvely Davos Clan: *"This is a Yargon,' Ugar said with apparent pride. 'It is a very rare device from my personal collection, fashioned by the Davos of Farvely. I had to torture and kill six of them before I finally persuaded one to make it for me."*

Felaci: Tiny human-like forest beings most commonly

only around a foot tall. They are naturally magickal beings and can create magickal effects, especially with plants, with or without conscious thought, and without the need for spells, enchantments, amulets or any other kind of aids. The nearest equivalent in Earth mythology would be a wood nympth.

Forest of Lartham: *"In the mountain forests of Lartharn dwells a clan of davos known appropriately as the Dragon Clan. They are very famous makers of hand combat weapons."*

Fosa: A mare leialli, the mate of Esjar. *"Arriving back with the herd I didn't waste any time with further explanations or formalities. 'Whose next?' I asked hurriedly and held up my arm for one of them to come up to it. A mare named Fosa whom I assumed was mated to Esjar stepped up."*

Genavieve: A Taz from France. *"Suddenly a bright white light illuminated the room from behind the circle of demons. I thought I must be hallucinating in my pain because I saw a slim, well-formed middle-aged woman with long black hair, in a flowing, floor-length white dress that didn't look anything at all like a demon."*

Gilgore: One of the first demons I encountered as I was transitioning to a Taz. *"A middle-aged man and a younger woman stood on either side of the bed looking down at the hapless lady in distress and laughing hysterically. Both were strangely dressed, or I should say barely dressed. The swarthy barefoot man, whose hairy chest was barely covered by a ridiculous pair of red suspenders pulling up what looked like a lime green speedo swimsuit, yelled out at the woman curled up on the bed."*

Glash: Gigantic and powerful human-like beings on Sx. The males are typically about three times the size of a typical human and the females about 20% smaller than the males. They are known for their limited mental capacities and their preference to eat only meat and only when it is still alive and trying to escape. The nearest equivalent in Earthy mythology is an ogre.

Gold Aura Sparkle: *"Qadir smiled at me and patted me on my shoulder with his palm. 'And I was obviously right to choose you as my protégé. Both Genavieve and I saw the distinct gold sparkle in your aura that only a Taz will have."*

Gosli Horde: *"A horde of well over a thousand demons will be coming through. These are particularly vicious demons from the Gosli Horde."*

Hollavoy Akara Clan: *"Qadir pointed to the old man, 'this is Yzwerb. He is the chieftain of the Hollavoy clan of akara."*

Hiratol Davos: The first davos I met when arriving in the 2nd Dimension. *"Qadir introduced the davos that invited us as Oshlin, Baradon of the local clan of Hiratol Davos."*

Hokrok: A very vicious race of mostly underground dwelling, strictly carnivore, human-like beings. They are typically around half the height of an adult male human, have fairly coarse, grotesque features, and muscular bodies. They are cunning and deceiving by nature and are trained to be thieves and kidnappers. The nearest equivalent in Earth mythology is a troll.

Homerac: A 12th Level demon.

Hweth, Qwargon, Zwasal: A magickal incantation to activate a Discovery Stone. *"The five Taz standing above me formed a circle closely around me. They joined hands intertwining their fingers. In unison, they spoke aloud the words, three times. I assumed these were the words Nkosi has spoken of to activate the enchanted Discovery Stone."*

Iozoa: A magickal word to form an invisible shield. *"From the other side of our circle I heard Marguese shout out 'Iozoa!' At first I thought it was some Portuguese expletive, swearing at our situation. But I soon realized otherwise when I saw all the rocks were hitting an invisible shield above us."*

Jenji: A Taz from China. *"This woman seemed about my age and was obviously East Asian. She was dressed all in white with somewhat baggy pants and a loose-fitting top that contrasted remarkably with her jet-black hair braided in a ponytail that came down to the small of her back. Her straight-cut bangs enhanced her delicate facial features."*

Josrym: A device from Sx that absorbs ambient energy and emits light. *"The cavern was fairly brightly lit, but I could not see any electric lights or other sources of direct illumination. This was so curious I had to ask Nkosi about it. 'Where does the light come from?' Nkosi smiled broadly at my question. 'It comes from a Jozrym.' I just looked at him blankly as I had never heard of a Jozrym. 'Sorry for my ignorance,' I apologized. 'I don't know what that is.' 'It is a marvelous device for capturing and storing ambient energy and then time releasing it as light that the Davos of Dosparage invented on Sx for the Gnomes to use in their underground mines."*

Kalai, Kazorq, Mateek: *"I was waiting for the demons to somehow launch the fire at us, but it never happened. I heard Jenji utter a few magickal words, **Kalai, Kazorq, Mateek**, and suddenly the fire snuffed out and nothing the demons could do would reignite it."*

Kalizia: A Level 4 demoness. *"A shapely blue skin demoness with tightly braided long blonde hair, wearing a pink harem outfit was also a victor but one of her red eyeballs had been gouged out and she was holding it in her hand. Thagin stepped up in front of the blue-skin demoness. 'Kalizia, why are you still holding your eyeball dimwit? The sooner you put it back, the sooner it will heal."*

Lajish: A magickal word to relieve pain. *"The lady in white looked at me intently with vivid, sky-blue eyes. Once more she extended her arms, both of them, and laid her hands on top of my head. **Lajish**, she spoke with firm quietness. As the last sound from that marvelous word escaped her lips all the pain in my body just vanished. I felt renewed, refreshed, and great!"*

Leialli: The word for unicorns on the planet Sx. The Taz in bygone eras had tried to call the leialli unicorns as that was the name we are familiar with on Earth, but the leialli, who are quite intelligent, were greatly offended and insisted on being called *leialli*.

Lercedel: A magickal word used to instantly transport from one location to another. *"Without any movements or magickal tools, Qadir spoke just a single word, **Lercedel**. For a bare second everything went black. The very next moment we were standing in exactly the same position with his arm over my shoulder, but in a beautiful sunny* *location with a deep blue, cloudless sky."*

Little Toot: A baby leialli named Bilsobe that demons tried to abduct that I protected and nick-named Little Toot. *"When I knelt down and embraced the young one he surprised me with the melodious little musical sound coming out of his horn. I had no idea yet what his real name was but hearing his musical exclamation I couldn't help affectionately giving him a nickname. 'I'll miss you most of all Little Toot, but I'll see you again before the passage of another day.' In response, I heard him in my mind say, 'Bilsobe, I love you!"*

Loxadol: *"When what seemed by his stooped posture and long gray hair to be the oldest davos in the clan came to say his goodbye, Qadir pulled him over in my direction. Looking at me Qadir pointed at Loxadol. 'Do remember this fellow Trevallion. Davos are the most ingenious of God's creations and Loxadol is the greatest of them all. Starting with nothing, they can invent marvelous and powerful magickal devices and non-magickal ones as well."*

Marguese: A Taz from Portugal. *"Another Taz materialized among us. He looked to be in his late forties or early fifties, slim and muscular with an olive complexion, dark wavy hair and a mustache. His brow was furrowed and he seemed a bit angry even before he spoke, and definitely after he spoke. This had better be important! I was right in the middle of a great fight with a mini horde that had been tormenting an entire neighborhood near Lisbon. I still had a half dozen to banish and now I will have to track them down all over again!" he declared with frustration."*

Metastasis Demons: Demons that were formerly physical humans but lost so much of their soul essence by the horrendous actions that they took in their lives, which caused them to devolve into demons after they died physically.

Nexus Compass: A complicated, magickal, handheld device used by Level 13 demons to cause a Nexus to expand and give them passage to any place in any dimension they specify on the compass. A Nexus thus opened, will only remain open for about 5 seconds.

Nkosi: A Taz from South Africa. Nkosi specialized in making magickal amulets that would work in the 1st Dimension. *"The first to materialize was a very wise-looking, late middle age, black man. His short-cropped hair was beginning to gray. Qadir turned to look at me and pointed at the new arrival. 'This is Nkosi. He is a proud member of the Xhosa tribe in South Africa and calls Cape Town home when he is not gallivanting somewhere else fulfilling his stewardship as a Taz.'"*

Oaswan: Another pleasant habitable 2nd Dimension planet like Sx, where some of the Taz have a home.

Oblivion: The cold, dark place in the 4th Dimension where demons are banished to. They are there for several centuries before they can return to a normal demon life. Even after the magick of the banishment wears off, the demon can only return if they can find a Nexus during the brief time it is open. During the time they are in Oblivion, they will be in complete darkness, piercing cold, and will not see or be able to communicate with another demon or anyone else. They will be cold, dark, and alone for hundreds of years.

Ookata: A magickal word to invoke directed telekinesis. *"She held out her left arm horizontal from her body with her palm facing down centered above my abdomen. 'Ookata!' she spoke loudly. No sooner had she said the word than all of the Zakcons that had been placed into my orifices popped out of my body and flew up to her hand."*

Oosas: Tiny human-like beings on Sx. They have innate magic from birth and powerful magickal connections to magickal minerals. They are only about 1-2 inches tall and have a pair of wings that flutter extremely rapidly like a hummingbird. The nearest equivalent in Earth mythology is a fairy.

Original Demons: Demons that were formerly premortal spirits and were cast out of the premortal existence for rebelling against God. As they never had the opportunity to have physical bodies, they are condemned to the invisible world. They lost so much of their soul essence when they rebelled that they devolved into demons. They are many thousands of years old.

Oshlin: *"Qadir introduced the davos that invited us as Oshlin, Baradon of the local clan of Hiratol Davos, and advised him that we couldn't stay long as we had pressing business to take care of. By the respectful way Qadir introduced Oshlin I assumed that a Baradon was some type of head honcho like a mayor or chief."*

Paralysis Binding: A magickal spell to paralyze someone so all they can move is their nose to breathe and their eyes to blink.

Purgatory Demons: These are Level 1 Metastasis

Demons that have been gaining light to their soul instead of losing it, hence they can no longer manifest as Metastasis. They have 500 years to gain enough darkness (or lose enough light) to their soul to once again be able to manifest as Metastasis Demons or they are told that they will be tortured and killed by Lucifer.

Purging Pill: *"He fished in his tiny, bottomless vest pocket and pulled out a large gelatin capsule about the size of my thumb. He stepped over to me and instructed me to swallow the giant pill. I gagged just looking at it. 'I can't swallow that!' I protested. 'It's way too big and I don't even have any water to try to help it down.' 'Oh, no worries there,' Qadir assured me. 'It is self-lubricating. Now open up. This will let us know without a doubt whether or not you are hexed or spelled. "If you had been under any type of harmful magick from a demon, within a minute the Purging Pill would have done its job and rid you of your magickal infection. You would have also had a violently upset stomach and would have been puking the demonic infection and a lot of other unpleasantries out of your body."*

Qadir: A Taz from Italy, via Morocco, and Ireland. He was one of the six Taz on the Earth when I was introduced to the demon world. Qadir was able to retire because he trained me as his protégé to take his place. *"A slim elderly man that had apparently been my captor walked around me and stood beside Genavieve. He was of average height, with a short-cropped grey beard and a full head of grey hair that flowed freely down to his shoulders. His dark brown eyes had a twinkle of vitality and I had an immediate sense that this was a man of great experience* *and wisdom. Though he had followed Genavieve's order to release me, it was easy to tell by his head held high confident bearing that he was her equal and not her servant."*

Quorthian Forest: *"Jenji affirmed Genavieve's conclusion. 'I agree, I barely escaped with my life last year when Homerac led a small demon horde in an ambush on me in the Quorthian Forest where I had gone to protect the felaci.'"*

Roxar: *"Qadir reached into his bottomless vest pocket and pulled out three small glass vials. They had a deep green glowing liquid inside and appeared to have both ends of the vial melted shut so there was no stopper.*

"Here are a few Roxars for you and your chief advisors. Next time you have a demon raid just break one of these vials. Upon contact with air, the liquid inside will immediately turn to gas. It is tuned to my aura and will act as a magickal beacon allowing me to quickly blink to your location, even if I am in the Earth Sphere at the time. I will come to your aid as soon as my circumstance will allow, which hopefully will be soon enough."

Scadonz: A demon free for all, no holds barred fight with other demons. *"Therefore, I declare a Scadonz for the prizes. After I say '**go**,' you may begin to attack each other any way you wish. The last four demons remaining in the room will be blessed with one of the four premium skins."*

Summoning Bur: *"Without another word Genavieve slapped her two hands together. It was like a fourth of July sparkler had ignited between her hands. A spray of tiny bits of light burst forth. The sparks all zipped away and* *an individual single spark pierced into the body of every demon."*

Genavieve was only too happy to explain. "Each of you has been embedded with a summoning bur. There is nothing you can do to remove it. You are now marked for the entirety of your eternal existence. If I or any other Taz ever activates your bur, you will be summoned immediately to our presence wherever we are in any dimension."

Summoning Spell: *"It was a magickal summoning spell. It only works on beings and creatures that are not innately magickal. So it will work on an Izbo, a davos, and most higher creatures of this world, but will not work on creatures where magick is part of their physical being such as a leialli or an oosas."*

"One of the essential components of the spell is you must know the name of whoever you are summoning. As lower creatures do not have names, at least not ones we are aware of, we cannot summon them by this spell. However, they can still be summoned by a different type of spell. It is only innately magickal creatures that are entirely immune to summoning spells."

Sx: A planet in the 2nd Dimension where much of the account in the book takes place.

Taz: Humans that develop special psychic and metaphysical abilities usually in their 20's, but sometimes at a later age. Their abilities allow them to see and banish demons and to travel between dimensions. They form a closely bonded secret group that have dedicated themselves to banishing demons, on Earth as well as on other worlds.

Thalgin: A Level 7 Demon professor in demon school. *"A slightly rotund man with a full white beard that tapered to a point, and a long nose with spectacles perched on it, was standing at the head of the class speaking to what seemed to be the students."*

Thomba: A magickal word used by demons. *"Ugar was standing directly in front of me. He waved his hand in the air and said with a guttery growl, 'Thomba!' A glowing, translucent green dial about the size of a fist appeared floating in the air in front of him. He reached out and turned the dial. Immediately I felt terrible pain racing through every nerve in my body. I involuntarily screamed out in agony."*

Truth Stone: *"Qadir fished in a small pocket on the right side of the satiny vest he was wearing and pulled out a small oblong object. It was perfectly clear and looked like a piece of quartz crystal that had been rounded and polished on both ends to be used as a massage tool. Qadir touched me on the top of my hand with the object and it immediately hazed over and turned completely black. 'It would be best if you did not begin our relationship with a lie.' Qadir said solemnly. 'Let's try again. What is your true name?' Whoa! That was a surprise. A portable, magickal lie detector!"*

Ugar: A Level 13 demon. He was beyond frightening. He was the epitome of what many people think of when they picture a demon. *"He peered out at the quaking demons in the class through black abyssal eyes and a deeply furrowed scowl. He was massively muscular and his physique was easily seen, as the only clothing he had on was a ragged pair of pants terminating just below his knees in shredded* *material and leather sandals on his bare feet.*

His chest was absent of clothing but heavily adorned with intricate tattoos and numerous piercings with what appeared to be pieces and carvings of bone.

His skin was dark red, and covered with many small wart-like bumps, particularly on his face. Some were oozing little yellow drops of pus. He head was bare of hair, but had multiple scarred gashes running across it from what I assumed were healed wounds."

Ulqwizar: A magickal word used by the demon Hamerac to intercept and divert me to his domain when I tried to transit. *"As you are observing them, and you see them preparing to blink, you merely say their name once and the magickal word of power Ulqwizar three times. When they try to blink anytime during the next seven seconds, they will blink to you instead of to their intended destination."*

Vanquish: An action taken by a Taz upon a demon that sends them far away from the place they were. If they are inhabiting a human and are vanquished, they are removed from the human and propelled to a remote location thousands of miles away. Vanquishing is distinct from Banishing, which also gets rid of demons. However, Banishing sends them to Oblivion where they will remain alone in darkness and cold for several hundred years.

Varina: A demoness who was present with the demon Gilgore in chapters 2 and 3. *"Both he and the bare-chested voluptuous woman standing on the other side of the bed broke into uncontrolled fits of laughter after he spoke as if he had just told the funniest joke they had ever heard.*

"I spotted Gilgore in his red suspenders and green Speedo swimsuit and Varina with her luscious long red hair sitting on the opposite side of the fire. I assumed she was still wearing her tiny G-string but from my semi obscured vantage point I could not see it and she just looked ravishingly naked."

Vazaron: "From within the same small vest pocket that he had withdrawn his truth crystal, Qadir now pulled out a beautiful pendant. At its center was a deep green emerald, three concentric circles of silver or platinum supported at least twelve radiating rays of gold that each terminated in a different colored gemstone."

"Qadir noticed my look of admiration at the beautiful piece of jewelry. 'This is an enchanted beacon. It is called a **Vazaron** and is used to call Taz. It has other helpful magickal summoning powers as well."

Waral: A gold coin used as currency in the demon world. It has a picture of Lucifer on one side and a letter representing the 13 Sacred Blessings (for demons) on the other side.

"A few of the demons squatted down so they could be closer to me. One bald oaf held a broad-bladed knife up. 'I am going to cut off some souvenirs; a couple of toes, a couple of fingers, an ear and his penis. Three gold warals if anyone else wants one, except the penis will be twenty gold warals because there is only one.'"

Wazdon: A magickally created force field bubble that is virtually impenetrable by physical or magickal means. "My last act before I died was to encase in a Wazdon Bubble." There were a few gasps from the Taz at that revelation. I guess there were ramifications to a Wazdon Bubble that I was unaware of, whether good or bad I didn't know."

Xanadu: The refuge of the Taz on Sx. The Taz had called it differnt names over the previous centuries. We started calling it Xanadu after the movie by that name that came out in 1980. *"If any of us get too injured to continue the fight, transit to Xanadu. When the battle is concluded, whether we succeed or fail, let us all rendezvous at Xanadu to heal our wounds and plan our next action if necessary."*

Xeador: A planet in the 1st Dimension with many volcanoes where my Night Self often visited to go Volcano Hopping.

Yargon: *"Ugar reached over to open the hinged top of a simple cube-shaped wooden box on his desk, and withdrew a small, peculiar device about the size of a basketball. It had a smooth outer metal ring that appeared to be made of gold, with two successively smaller inner rings. The middle one was the color of silver and the smallest looked like it was copper. Ugar held the device by the outer ring with one hand before he set the base down on his desk. The strangest part was the rings just seemed to be floating in space. At least from my vantage point, I couldn't determine how they were attached to one another or to the flat base."*

Yzwerb: *"The fellow that came up to meet me was the largest of the bunch. He came up to about my chest height. He was bald on the top of his head with short gray hair on the sides. His face was wrinkled and gray-bearded from what I assumed was old age, but his bulging muscles were still evident, pushing tightly on the fabric of his plain brown* tunic. *Qadir pointed to the old man, 'I, this is Yzwerb. He is the chieftain of the Hollavoy clan of akara.'"*

Zakcon: A small pill-like object used by demons to create torturous pain. *"Ugar opened the palm of his hand and picked up a tiny object that was the size and shape of a small gelatin capsule, except it was black and had a dull metallic look. He held the pill up and there were audible gasps from several of the demons. Ugar looked around the circle. 'Oh yes, this is what you think it is, a Zakcon,' he said with ghoulish delight to the demons."*

Zargarz: In the book dragons are called by their Earth name. Their actual name on Sx is *Zargarz*. However, as all of the Taz in Demon Hunter were from Earth we preferred calling them by the name we were familiar with – dragons.

NOTE FROM EMBROSEWYN

Thank you for taking the time to read *Demon Hunter*. I hope you have been both entertained and enlightened. I would be grateful if you would take a moment to leave a review on Amazon. If you have questions or need help with what might be demons, aliens, ghosts, or other paranormal problems, please don't hesitate to contact me through my website: *www.embrosewyn.com*

Namaste,

Embrosewyn

Additional Services Offered by Embrosewyn

I am honored to be able to be of further service to you by offering multiple paranormal abilities for your enlightenment and life assistance. On a limited basis as my time allows I can:

- discover your Soul Name and the meaning and powers of the sounds

- custom craft and imbue enchantments upon a piece of your jewelry for a wide beneficial range of purposes

- discover the name of your Guardian Angel

- have an in-depth psychic consultation and Insight Card reading with you via a Skype video call.

My wife Sumara can also create a beautiful piece of collage art on 20" x 30" internally framed canvas, representing all of the meanings and powers of the sounds of your Soul Name.

If you are interested in learning more about any f these additional services please visit my website: *www.*

embrosewyn.com and click on the link at the top for SERVICES.

If you would like to purchase enchanted jewelry or gemstones for specific purposes such as love, health, good fortune, or psychic protection please visit my website: *www.magickalgems.com.*

For great info on a wide variety of psychic, paranormal and magick subjects, please visit my YouTube Channel, *Esoteric Mystery School with Embrosewyn Tazkuvel.*

"Unto this generation has my Father and Mother saved the greatest spirits of Heaven to come forth upon the world, and to them will be given the plentitude of truth, both that which was lost and that which is new."

Oracles of Celestine Light
Nexus 1:22